本书获

- 淮北师范大学学术著作出版基金资助
- 淮北师范大学附属实验中学"全国教育硕士专业学位研究生联合培养示范基地"项目资助

本书系

- 2018年度上海外语教育出版社外语类委托项目"高校、市名师工作室和中学三方联动下的基础教育英语教师发展研究"（SK2018A1169）和安徽省"信息技术与核心素养背景下中学英语课堂教学有效融合行动研究"（AH2018125）的实践成果

新课程理念下
英语教学设计研究

徐修安 著

上海三联书店

自 序

很幸运,2015 年我被淮北师范大学聘为校内硕士生导师,为外国语学院学科教学(英语)研究生开设《中学英语教学设计与实施》一门课,至今算来,已经整整五年了。在过去的五年里,我集自己的阅读和教学经验,为五届研究生们开设了这门课,受到学生们的好评。他们普遍感到收获很多,以至于毕业后仍有很多学生继续与我探讨英语教学设计理论和实践的问题。英语教学设计理论和实施的相关知识,不仅学科教学的研究生们需要,师范院校的本科师范生们更加需要。每年本科生实习、教师资格证和教师编制考试时,就会有不少学生来请教。关于这方面的书籍,市面上也有,要么理论性较强,学生读得吃力,要么大多数是案例,缺乏和理论的结合。鉴于此,我产生了自己编写一本《新课程理念下英语教学设计研究》的想法,让读者既能了解英语教学设计的理论知识,又能获得英语教学设计实施的策略,还能获得自己需要的教学设计范例。

本书分为上编和下编两部分,共 5 章。上编是理论篇,主

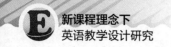

要介绍英语教学设计的理论内容，分为 4 章；下编是实践篇，推出了英语教学设计的案例，分为小学、初中和高中教学设计，共 1 章。本书既可以供在校研究生、本科生学习使用，也可以供在职中小学英语教师在教学中使用。读者既可以了解教学设计的相关知识，也可以读到自己需要的不同阶段的教学设计范例。既有理论指导，又有实际操作指导。

本书的编写在本人的教学内容基础上，选出淮北师范大学外国语学院 17、18、19 级全日制和非全日制部分研究生的优秀课程作业，作为案例。由于作者本人学识和经验有限，书中肯定有许多不足之处，真诚期待相关专家及广大一线英语教学工作者提出宝贵的意见和建议，以便进一步完善。

徐修安

2020 年 3 月完稿于疫情防护期间

Contents

目　录

上
编

理论篇

Chapter 01

第一章 · 教学设计概述

第一节　教学与教学设计概述

一　教学与设计

1. 教学。教学作为一种活动,贯穿于人类社会的产生和发展过程中。在我国,"教学"二字最早连用是在《尚书·商书·说命下》:"惟敩学半"(敩,音 xiào,指教)。宋朝蔡沈注释其词义为:教师先学后教,在教的过程中又在学的单向的活动,即强调"学"的活动。教学包含"教与学"双向活动的涵义是《学记》提出的:教学相长。真正将"教学"理解为教师的"教"的和学生的"学"是在胡瑗先生的墓表中"弟子来去常有数百人,各以其经传相传授,一起教学之法最备……"

在英语中,人们一般用 teaching 和 instruction 表示"教",用 learning 表示"学"。Teaching 和 instruction 在大多数情况下可以相互替换,但在具体的使用过程中,teaching 多与教师的行为相联系,指一种活动,而 instruction 多与教学的情景有关,指活动的过程。

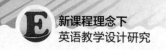
关于"教学"的定义，也存在不同的定义：

《英汉双解　现代汉语字典》给"教学"的定义是，教师把知识、技能传授给学生的过程，其英语翻译是 teaching 和 education。*Longman Dictionary of Contemporary English* 给 teaching 的定义是，work, or profession of a teacher，即"教书、教学"。百度百科给教学的定义是，教学指学生在教师引导下，在有计划的系统性的过程中，依据一定的内容，按照一定的目的，借助一定的方法和技术，主动学习和掌握知识、培养技能，同时全面发展的活动。贾冠杰认为教学包括三层含义：（1）"教学"（teaching）；（2）"教"和"学"（teaching and learning）；（3）教如何学习（teaching how to learn）。

按照贾冠杰的解释，在教学的过程中，不仅要强调教师的作用，也应该强调学习者的作用，只有这样才能达到教学相长的目的。然而，在我国现实的英语教学中，由于多种原因，不少教师真的把"教学"仅仅理解为 teaching。因此，在他们的教学里，强调教师和教学的作用，而忽略了学生和学习的作用。

2. 设计。所谓设计，是人类为改变现状、依据已有原理、方法和技术而制定计划方案的活动。设计是一种活动，一种技术，一种文化。很显然，实际教学活动中存在许多要改变的问题，教学需要设计，教学活动是一种设计活动。

二　教学设计的定义

教学设计作为一门学科是 20 世纪 60 年代末在美国兴起的。我国对教学设计的研究也是近几十年的事情。不同的研究者，对教学设计的定义有不同的理解。

1. 国外学者对教学设计的定义有不同的解释。

帕顿在其著作《什么是教学设计》中指出，教学设计是设计科学大家庭的一员，设计科学各成员的共同特征是用科学原理及应用来满足人的需要。因此，教学设计是对学业业绩问题的解决措施进行策划的过程。

加涅的《教学设计原理》则认为，教学设计是一个系统化规划教学系统的过程。教学系统本身是对资源和程序作出有利于学习的安排。任何组织机构,如果旨在开发人的才能均可以被包括在教学系统中。

赖格卢特的著作《教学设计是什么及为什么如是说》则把教学设计定义为一门涉及理解与改进教学过程的学科。任何设计活动的宗旨都是提出达到预期目的最优途径,因此,教学设计主要是关于提出最优教学方法的处方的一门学科,这些最优的教学方法能使学生的知识和技能发生预期的变化。他对教学设计的定义基本上同对教学科学的定义是一致的。因为在他看来,教学设计也可以被称为教学科学。

梅里尔的《教学设计新宣言》写到,教学是一门科学,而教学设计是建立在这一科学基础上的技术,因而教学设计也可以被认为是科学型的技术。

肯普是教学设计研究的著名学者,他认为教学设计是运用系统方法分析研究教学过程中相互联系的各部分的问题和需求。在连续模式中确立解决它们的方法步骤,然后评价教学成果的系统计划过程。

我国的研究者也对教学设计的定义进行了描述,具体可以体现在以下几种说法。第一,教学设计用系统的方法分析教学问题,研究解决问题途径,评价教学结果的计划过程或系统规划。第二,教学设计是运用系统方法分析教学问题和确定教学目的,建立解决方案、评价试行结果和对方案进行修改的过程。第三,教学设计是研究教学系统、教学过程和制定教学计划的系统方法。第四,教学设计是运用系统方法和步骤,并对教学结果作出评价的计划过程和操作程序。第五,教学设计是旨在促进教学活动程序化、精确化和合理化的现代教学技术。

2. 国内外学者对于教学设计的概念做了充分的研究,在这里不必一一列举,归纳起来主要有以下四类观点:

第一种观点认为教学设计是对教学进行规划的过程。如加涅认为教学设计是具体计划教学系统的过程。南国农、李运林(1998)认为教学设计是规划、安排教学活动的过程。

第二种观点把教学设计定义为一套方法。如狄克(W. Dick)与凯瑞(L.Carey)认为教学设计是一套帮助教师进行教学准备、决策的方法。钟志贤(2007)认为教学设计是设计、实施、评价教师教的过程和学生学的过程的方法。

第三种观点认为教学设计是一种教学技术。如鲍嵘(1998)将教学设计定义为一种使教学活动更加合理、精确的教学技术。盛群力、李志强(1998)认为教学设计是教师为学生提供学习经验、环境的一种技术。鲁子问教授认为，教学设计是一种基于现代学习理论的教育技术，它是教师基于学生的需求分析，来设计教学目标、教学策略、教学过程、教学技术，并进行评价和反馈，以进行教学准备的过程(鲁子问，2009)。

第四种观点，北京师范大学教授何克抗认为，教学设计主要是运用系统方法，将学习理论和教学理论的原理转化成对教学目标、教学内容、教学方法、教学策略、教学评价等环节进行具体计划、创设教与学的系统过程或程序，而创设教与学系统的根本目的是促进学习者的学习。

三 教学设计的内涵

不同学者对教学设计的理解不同，因此产生了不同的认识。教学设计是一项技术，代表学者是美国著名教学设计学者梅瑞尔(David Merill)；教学设计是一个过程，加涅和我国大多数教学设计者都持这种观点；教学设计是一种理念，因此，加涅说，"为什么我们用教学这个词而不是用教授这个词？原因是，我们希望描述对人们的学习有直接影响的所有事件，而不是只描述由教师个人发起的那些事件"。

四 教学设计与教案、备课

1. 教学设计与教案的区别。第一，教学设计是一个分析教学问题、设计解决方法、对解决方法进行试行、评价实行结果，并在评价基础上修改方法的过程。教案是实施教学设计的研究思路的具体操作(执行)方案。第二，教案是教学设计的一个组成部分。教学设计是教学研究层面的活动，教案是日常教学操作层面的活动。

2. 教学设计与一般意义上的备课的区别。教学设计不是一般意义上的备课。一般的备课只是教师自己根据惯例进行教学准备的活动，没有必须使用的工具；教学设计则是一种具有自身的工具系统的技术，是一个不断修正的过程，更体现了以学习者为中心的理念。

五　研究教学设计的目的

　　研究教学设计,可以引导教师转变教学思想、教学观念,探索新课程的教学途径和方法。尤其是当前,高中英语新课程改革要求教师推进教学设计与实践的改革探索,改变传统的教育者角色和任务,更要形成教学研究思路,形成科学化、系统化的教学过程,将教科书的所谓教学设计,转化为落实核心素养的教学设计,以核心素养为纲,以学业质量标准为要求,重构学科内容,设计大单元、具体情况、具体任务或项目,提出真实问题,围绕解决问题展开学习。教师要从以往的教案撰写转向有意识的教学设计研究,不断学习,掌握现代教学理论和学习理论,进一步提升专业水平。

第二节　教学设计的历史及其发展

　　关于教学设计的历史发展,不同的研究者提出了不同的发展阶段。相当多的研究者认为,教学设计的历史发展经历起源阶段、初步发展阶段、正式发展阶段、转型阶段这四阶段。

　　1.教学设计的起源阶段

　　通常认为,教学设计的正式发展起源于 20 世纪 30 年代,尤其在 20 世纪初期,众多的教育学家提出了重要的教学设计理论,促进了教学设计的正式发展。最早提出教学设计理论构想的是美国的教育家、哲学家杜威(J. Dewey)以及美国的心理学家桑代克。杜威在 1900 年发表的《我们怎么思维——经验与教育》中提出要发展一门连接学习理论和教育实践的"桥梁科学",这种学科把心理学研究同教学实践的结合,重点关注教学设计。杜威对教学设计的相关研究对教学设计学科的发展起到了奠定基础的作用。1912 年心理学家桑代克(E. Thorndike)通过动物实验提出"联接主义学习理论",建立起一套包括任务分析、教学方法、教学评价、教学测量的教学设计系统,为教学设计的初步发展奠定了研究基础,也为教育的标准化和高效率的发展发挥了重要的推动作用。但在此时期,教学设计的发展仅仅停留在初步形成阶段,并没有形成系统的科学理论体系。不同的教育者对教学设计有着不同的观点,如:夸美纽斯倡导直观教学,提倡用图片、实物模型等直观教具进行教学活动设计。教育家杜威则提倡"学校科目的相互联系的真正中心是儿童本身的社会活动",主张从"做中学"。他认为儿童应从实际生活和活动中获取知识,而不是单纯地依靠听课和读书来掌握知识。

2. 教学设计的初步发展阶段

在20世纪40年代～60年代时期,随着教育心理学和社会发展的需求,教学设计的理论体系在前人研究的基础上逐渐建立和发展起来。在20世纪40年代第二次世界大战时期,美国为了培训大量战时需要的外语人员和军事人员,让众多教育家进行教学相关研究。在第二次世界大战后,随着科学技术的发展、音频视频等新媒体技术的出现和使用,大量新的教学相关学术理论和教学方法开始出现并流行起来,出现了教育技术的大转型。在20世纪60年代初中期,任务分析、目标陈述和标准参照测试等概念兴起,促进了多种教学设计模式的出现。在此期间出现了大量的教育者进行教学设计研究,其中最为著名的是教育学家斯金纳(B.Skinner,1954)发表的《学习的科学与教育的艺术》,提出程序教学的构想并进行教育实践,在当时的教育学界引起了巨大的反响。程序教学认为教学材料应以小部分呈现给学生;学生必须对每个问题做出回答;教学材料要提供及时的反馈和允许学习者自己控制学习进度。斯金纳与其他教育学者经过多次实验不断深化理论,对今天的教学设计模式产生了深远影响。20世纪60年代初期,梅格(R.Mager)编写了《程序教学的学习目标编写》一书,对编写学习目标的方法以及所期望的学习行为、行为产生的条件和评价行为的标准进行了阐述,受到了当时教育界的广泛关注。在此期间格莱瑟(R.Glaser)标准参照测验的提出又一次推动了教学设计的发展,格莱瑟认为标准参照测验可以用来检测学习者在接受某一教学活动计划之前的实际水平,确定学习者在接受某一教学计划之后能达到的水平程度。标准参照测试成为了教学设计初步发展阶段中的另一大核心特征。

3. 教学设计的正式发展阶段

在 20 世纪 60 年代后期至 70 年代初期，教学设计在美国才真正的作为一门学科开始正式发展。系统工程学和行为主义理论成为当时教学设计的两大理论基础。教学设计在此期间将过去的十年中出现的不同的教学设计相关研究成果进行整合，创造出了"系统方法"，并对过去出现的大量的教学设计模式进行整理归纳，形成了相对稳定的教学设计模式结构。安德鲁斯和古德森(Andrews & Goodson)通过对以往兴起的 60 多种教学设计模式的分析和概括，提出了教学设计模式的六个基本组成部分：确定目标、学习者已有知识技能的评估、确定教学内容、确定教学策略、教学开发和测验评价。20 世纪 70 年代到 80 年代期间，教学设计学者受到认知心理学发展和信息技术发展的影响，开始逐渐关注认知心理学、微机和绩效技术在教学设计中的作用。20 世纪 80 年代后期，随着科学技术的发展以及计算机的普及，信息技术开始融入教学设计之中。同时，建构主义和交互媒体的发展，使得教学设计更加整体化、更具弹性，教学设计出现了系统化教学设计和整体化教学设计两种模式，其中整体教学设计是系统化教学设计的扩充、延伸，延续了系统教学设计在分析、设计、发展和评价等阶段的特点。教学设计自 20 世纪 60 年代起，历经了 30 年的发展，最终形成了集系统工程学、传播学、学习心理学与技术的传统教学设计理念。

4. 教学设计的转型发展阶段

自从 20 世纪 80 年代以来，教学设计的发展进入了低迷期，传统的教学设计的局限性开始暴露出来，传统教学设计的基本假设主义受到了建构主义的影响。随着建构主义理论、教学理念和教学模式的兴起，传统的教学设计受到了多种教育理论的冲击，教育学者开始寻求一条教学设计的发展新路。90 年代后，计算机的快速发展与普及为教学设计的发展带来新的启示。数字技术和互联网在教学领域的运用促进了学校教育模式的改变以及教学设计的发展。互联网教学应用的盛行，使学习者在多媒体的帮助下不受时间与地点的限制，按照自身学习需求进行学习活动。教育界关于教学设计理念争论不已，教学设计受到了绩效技术、原型开

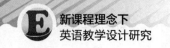
发技术、知识管理、混沌理论、阐释学、模糊逻辑等影响，进入了转型发展时期。

第三节 教学设计的理论基础

一 不同观点

每一门独立的学科都有支撑它生长的理论基础，教学设计也不例外。我国教学设计研究者对教学设计的理论基础进行了大量的研究，提出了许多观点，概括起来有如下一些论点：

第一种，"单基础"论。认为"教学设计的理论基础是认知学习理论。"并强调"主要是指加涅（Robert M. Gagne）的认识学习理论"。（李克东，1990）

第二种，"双基础"论。主张"教学设计是以传播理论和学习理论为基础"。

第三种，"三基础"论。认为"教学设计是以学习理论、教学理论和传播学为理论基础"。（乌美娜，1994）

第四种，"四基础"论。认为"教学设计理论基础包括四个组成部分，即系统论、学习理论、教学理论和传播理论"。并强调"学习理论应当是四种理论中最重要的理论基础"。（何可抗，1998）

第五种，"五基础"论。提出教学设计要"以学习心理理论、现代教学理论、设计科学理论、系统理论和教育传播学为理论基础"。（张筱兰，1998）

第六种，"六基础"论。主张"学习理论、传播理论、视听理论、系统科学理论、认识论和教育哲学共同构成了教学设计的理论基础"。（冯学斌，1998）

为分析方便起见，将上述论点列表如下：

	学习理论	传播理论	教学理论	系统理论	设计理论	视听理论	认识论	教育哲学
单基础	✓							
双基础	✓	✓						
三基础	✓	✓	✓					
四基础	✓	✓	✓	✓				
五基础	✓	✓	✓	✓	✓			
六基础	✓	✓		✓		✓	✓	✓

从表中可以清楚地看出，人们对哪些理论作为教学设计的理论基础是有争议的。那么，怎样选择与确定教学设计的理论基础呢？

我们认为，是否成为教学设计的理论基础，关键是由教学设计的研究对象来决定。造成上述情况的主要原因是人们对教学设计概念的理解和研究对象确立的视差所致。应该肯定地说，人们把学习理论、传播理论、系统理论和教学理论作为教学设计的理论基础的认识是相对集中的。其中，系统理论和传播理论构成的是教学设计的"形式"，而教学理论则是教学设计的"内嵌"。

对于学习理论，人们一致认为是教学设计的理论基础。表明教学设计的取向是以学生的学习为中心的，这是符合时代需求和特点的。

从实践角度看，解决教学问题必须研究教学理论，应用教学理论。可以这样说，巴班斯基把系统方法作为一般科学方法论引入教学理论研究领域，形成了教学过程最优化理论，为教学设计的产生和发展提供了理论依据。教学设计正是根据该理论，把教学理论研究的重要范畴，如教师、学生、目的、任务、内容、形式、方法等要素都置于系统形成之中，加以考察研究和应用；而斯金纳的程序教学理论、布鲁姆的目标分类理论、布鲁纳的引导——发现法、奥苏贝尔的"先行组织者"的程序教学、加涅的信息理论、赞可夫的"以最好的教学效果来促进学生最大发展"的理论、瓦根舍因的范例教学理论，都是促进教学设计发展的丰富而坚实的理论基础。可见，把教学理论作为教学设计的理论基础是毋庸置疑的。

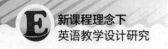

二 几种典型的基础理论

1. 学习理论。从教学设计的发展来看,截至目前,已经有三代教学设计模型相继问世,教学设计的更新换代跟社会人文、物质技术有关,尤其是学习理论研究的新成果,为教学设计的快速更新换代提供了科学的理论依据。学习理论在发展过程中,对教学设计影响最大的莫过于行为主义、联结——认知主义和建构主义三种。正是这种学习理论,成为划分三代教学设计并指导其发展的理论界标。

概括地说,行为主义观点在教学设计中最基本应用是把可观察行为作为教学基础,提出用可观察行为动词界定各类教学目标(包括价值观与态度教学)并依此进行教学传递与评价。认知理论探讨学习者内部的认知活动,其中主要是信息加工学习理论和认知建构学习理论。信息加工学习理论把人类的学习过程看成是由一系列信息加工的转换过程,例如,加涅的信息加工的学习与记忆的 8 个阶段的学习模型。认知建构学习理论是在皮亚杰和维果茨基的学说基础上发展起来的,认知建构学习理论对教学设计的指导意义是:建构过程要引导学生发现原有知识结构与新知识之间的不协调性,然后主动去改变它。学习的认知建构发生在具体的情景中,在具体的情景中,能够使学生感受到知识的意义。

当然,人本主义学习理论对教学设计的影响越来越受到重视。人本主义学习理论对教学设计的意义大都是在观念上,如何发挥人的潜能等问题。

2. 教学理论。当代最具有影响的两种教学理论:程序教学思想和结构主义教学思想。

教育学家斯金纳(B. Skinner, 1954)发表的《学习的科学与教育的艺术》,提出程序教学的构想并进行教育实践,在当时的教育学界引起了巨大的反响。程序教学认为教学材料应以小部分呈现给学生;学生必须对每个问题做出回答;教学材料要提供及时的反馈和允许学习者自己控制学习进度。20 世纪 60 年代初期,梅格(R. Mager)编写了《程序教学的学习目标编写》一书,对编写学习目标的方法以及所期望的学习行为、行为产生的条件和评价行为的标准进行了阐述,受到了当时教育界的广泛关注。

结构主义(Structuralism)教学理论以结构主义教育理论及皮亚杰结构主义心理学为理论基础。布鲁纳(J.S.Bruner)是一个结构主义者,他深受结构主义心理学家皮亚杰的影响。他的理论不仅提出了学(教)什么、什么时候学(教)、怎样学(教)等问题,而且在结构主义思想的指导下,对这些问题做了使人比较满意的回答,提出了基础学科早期学习,掌握学科的基本结构,广泛应用发现法等主张。要让学生掌握学科的基本结构。提倡早期学习(学习准备观念的转变)。

布鲁纳发现学习的理论"发现学习"是布鲁纳在《教育过程》一书中提出来的。这种方法要求学生在教师的认真指导下,能像科学家发现真理那样,通过自己的探索和学习"发现"事物变化的因果关系及其内在联系,形成概念,获得原理。发现学习以培养探究性思维的方法为目标,以基本教材为内容,使学生通过再发现的步骤来进行学习。发现学习是以布鲁纳的认知心理学学习理论为基础的。他认为学习就是建立一种认知结构,相当于我们所说的主观世界,头脑中经验系统的构成。建立认知结构是一种能动的主观活动,具有主观能动性。所以布鲁纳格外重视主动学习,强调学生自己思索、探究和发现事物。

3. 系统理论。系统理论是作为一种科学的方法论对教学设计产生举足轻重的影响。任何系统都包括五个要素:人、物、过程、外部限制因素和可用资源,这五个要素间有三种联系形式:①过程的时间顺序;②各因素间数据或信息流程;③从一个系统中输入或输出的原材料(人或物)。

4. 传播理论。信息传播是由信息源、信息内容、信息渠道与信息接收者为主要成分的系统。进行信息传播,必须对信息进行编码,考虑信息的结构与顺序是否符合信息接收者的思维与心理顺序。信息不能"超载",过于密集的信息直接影响传递效果,增加负担。而且不同信息的注意获得特性不同。有些材料宜以视觉方式呈现,有些则宜用听觉方式呈现。还可以运用多种暗示技巧来增强这种注意获得特性,更重要的是考虑信息接收者的特性(年龄、性别、偏好等),激发其内在学习动机等。很显然,教学是师生间的传播活动。

传播理论有两种常见模式:5W 模式和 SMCR 传播模式。5W 模式是指 who(传播者)，what(讯息)，which(媒体)，whom(接受者)和 what(效果)；SMCR 传播模式是指 source(信息源)，message(信息)，channel(通道)，receiver(接收者)。

本章参考文献：

[1] R.M.加涅、W.W.韦杰、K.C.克勒斯、J.M.凯勒著，王小明、庞维国、陈保华、汪亚李译，皮连生校审.教学设计原理[M].华东师范大学出版社，2005.

[2] 鲁子问、唐淑敏.英语教学设计[M].华东师范大学出版社，2016.

[3] 章兼中.英语课程与教学论[M].福州：福建教育出版社，2016：4.

[4] 贾冠杰.英语教学基础理论[M].上海：上海外语教育出版社，2010：2.

[5] 谢百治.多媒体教材制作与教学设计[M].北京：中央广播电视大学出版社，1999：7.

[6] 全国十二所重点师范大学联合编写.教育学基础[M].北京：教育科学出版社，2008：207—209.

[7] 石平秀.英语教学设计研究新进展文献综述[J].教育教学论坛，2015(27)：141—143.

[8] 陈琦，刘儒德.当代教育心理学[M].北京：北京师范大学出版社，2007.

[9] 何克抗，郑永柏，谢幼如.教学系统设计[M].北京：北京师范大学出版社，2002.

[10] 瞿葆奎.教育学文集.教育目的[M].北京：人民教育出版社，1989.

[11] 李定仁，徐继存.教学论研究二十年[M].北京：人民教育出版社，2001.

[12] 李龙.教学过程设计[M].呼和浩特：内蒙古人民出版社，2000.

[13] 邵瑞珍.教育心理学[M].上海：上海教育出版社，1988.

[14] 盛群力，李志强.现代教学设计论[M].杭州：浙江教育出版社，1998.

[15] 盛群力等.教学设计[M].北京：高等教育出版社，2005.

[16] 张华.教学设计研究：百年回顾与前瞻[J].教育科学，2000(04)：25—29.

[17] 其他网络文献(略)

Chapter 02

第二章 教学设计的模式

第一节 模式与教学模式定义

一 模式及教学模式概述

1. "模式"一词是英文"model"的译文,与"范式"、"模型"同义,模式即"再现现实的一种理论性的简约形式",在一个学科的理论进化过程中是非常重要的。

常有教师说,"教学为什么需要模式?""教学按照模式不会教条和僵化吗?"并且,教学上有个俗语叫"教无定法",我想怎么教就怎么教,为什么非得按照一个模式? 是的,从个人讲,每个人都有自己的知识背景、教学背景、教学风格、教学条件,每个人都不能完全按照别人的路子走。但是,从教学这门科学讲,不管老师怎么教,都必须遵循教学规律和青少年身心发展规律,遵循规律的过程就是要有法度。所以,"教无定法",前面还有一句"教学有法",有的还加上一句"贵在得法"。所以,完整的说,"教学有法,但无定法,贵在得法",才更为全面、科学。从实践讲,我们对理论的实践,先进理念的探究,都不是一下子就能做到位的,有的理论需要几代人探究,那更需要先找到一个路子、一个范式、一个抓手去探索，慢慢在这个范式基础上不断完善。因此，我们对教学模式的态度应该是始于模式，超越模式。

2. 对教学设计模式的理解和态度也应该如此。教学设计模式是在教学设计的实践中逐渐形成、再现教学设计现实的一种理论性的简化形式，具有概括性、可操作性、普遍适用性的特点和预见性、启发性、创造性的功能。教学设计模式的目的在于提供教学设计指南，而不是告诉教师他们应当教什么，应采用哪些特定的教学法。

二 教学设计的模式的划分

从"教学设计"作为一门正式的学科，已经经历了将近半个世纪的发展历程，教学设计理论与实践发展到今天，关于教学设计的模式也已有数百种之多，用一个标准划分是很难的。因此出现了对教学设计的多种分类方法。

1. 第一种划分。巴纳锡（Bela H.Banathy）区分出四代设计方式：

第一代设计是受系统工程学方法极大影响的"按指令设计"（designing by dictate）方式，它通常既通过立法实施又通过自上而下推行。第一代教学设计（ID1）的代表性模式受行为主义学习理论影响。第一代教学设计（ID1）的代表性模式主要有"肯普模式"和"迪克—凯里模式"。

第二代设计是"为（决策者等）的设计"（designing for），它引进顾问和专家，研究某个特定的系统问题，进行需求分析，向决策者提供他们的解决方案。一旦方案被采纳就将强制执行。第二代教学设计（ID2）的代表性模式是"史密斯—雷根模式"。

第三代设计是设计者与决策者一起通过具有实际意义的讨论而进行的。这或多或少是一种真正的参与式设计，是设计者与决策者"一起进行的设计"（designing with）或者"设计者指引的设计"（designer guided）。

第四代设计是"置身于其中的设计"（designing within），表明人的活动系统必须由那些处于其中的人、利用这些系统的人以及这些系统所服务的人共同来设计。第四代设计理念表明，该系统中每一个人都是设计的参与者，共同承担着设计的责任，即我们能对设计我们的系统负责，我们也必须学会如何设计这样的系统。基于这样一种理解，设计过程必然是与学习的过程整合在一起的。迪克—凯瑞的系统教学设计模式就属于第四代教学设计模式。

2. 第二种划分。①建立在系统理论基础上的教学设计模式。这类教学设计模式的代表主要有巴纳赛的教学设计模式和布里格斯的教学设计模式；建立在学习和教学理论基础上的教学设计模式。几种影响较大的教学设计模式：迪克和凯瑞的教学设计模式、加涅和布里格斯的教学设计模式、梅里尔的教学设计模式。②建立在传播理论基础上的教学设计模式。这类模式的代表有马什的一般传播模式、莱特和皮亚特的文本组织模式。

3. 第三种划分。以教为主的教学设计模式、以学为主的教学设计模式、主导—主体教学设计模式、信息化教学设计模式。

4. 第四种划分。第一，经验型教学设计。教师根据自身的教学经验、知识水平和教学条件等设计教学过程，是一种传统的教学设计方法。这种设计方法不但受到教师本身经验和知识水平的限制，而且要使之达到完善，需要有长期工作经验的积累。第二，程序型教学设计。自 19 世纪 40 年代以来，在斯金纳等人的推动下，根据刺激—反应学习理论把教学内容序列化，编制成一套教学程序，用程序教学书、程序教学机、电子计算机等来执行教师的功能，完成教学任务。第三，系统型教学设计。以传播理论和学习理论为基础，应用系统的观点和方法，分析教学中的问题和需要。根据教学目标和教学资源，探索和规划教学过程中诸因素的相互关系和合理组合，通过评价不断改进，以求得教学效果最优化。

5. 第五种划分。教学设计划分为以"教"为中心的教学设计和以"学"为中心的教学设计。如北京师范大学何克抗老师对教学设计的划分。

第二节 国内外教学设计模式

尽管模型的名目繁多，北京师范大学现代教育技术研究所教学设计研究专家何克抗总结多年来国外在教学设计领域的研究，认为教学设计从其理论基础看,不外乎向以"教"为中心的 ID 理论和以"学"为中心的 ID 理论这两个方向发展。其中,以"教"为中心的 ID 理论的发展又分为第一代和第二代教学设计,第一代代表性模型是肯普模型,第二代代表性模型是史密斯-雷根模型。以"学"为中心的教学设计方法与步骤应如下面所述:(1)教学目标分析,(2)情境创设,(3)信息资源设计,(4)自主学习设计,(5)协作学习环境设计,(6)学习效果评价设计,(7)教学模式设计。下面依次介绍:

1. 迪克-凯瑞模式

迪克与凯瑞(W. Dick & L.Carey)的系统取向模式于 1978 年提出,并于 2001 年修改了第五版。如图所示:

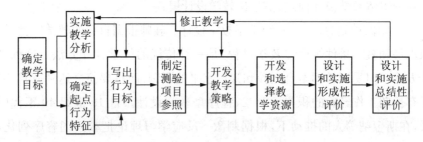

迪克-凯瑞教学设计模式(摘自于鲁子问、唐淑敏著的《英语教学设计》2016,p.26)

具体内容包括如下几个方面:(1)确定教学目标;(2)进行教学分析;(3)分析学习者和情境;(4)编写行为表现目标;(5)开发评价;(6)开发教学策略;(7)开发和选择教学材料;(8)设计和实施形成性教学评价;(9)修改教学;(10)设计和实施总结性评价。

2. 肯普模式

肯普模式采取的是一个椭圆形表征,他强调了随机进入、循环往复的有机性和融合性。如图所示:

肯普模式是从学习者、教学具体目标、教学方法和教学评价这四个最基本的成分出发形成的,正是这些组成部分的相互联系性质,构成了一个完整的教学设计。

该模式由肯普在 1977 年提出,在模式中,他列出了 10 个教学设计的"因素",而不是步骤,说明设计的整体性及其过程的弹性。该模式强调系统

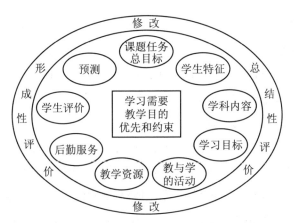

肯普模式(摘自于鲁子问、唐淑敏著的《英语教学设计》2016，p.34)

方法的分析→设计→评价→反馈修正的工作策略以及在教学设计过程中必须将"学习需要"、"教学目的"、"优先顺序"和"约束条件"等因素作为参考的依据(J.E.Kemp，1977)。肯普模式适应传统教学习惯,教学环节、步骤具体明确,因而有较强的实用性和可操作性。

3. **史密斯-瑞(雷)根模式**

史密斯-瑞(雷)根模式包括分析、策略开发和评价三个阶段。如图所示：

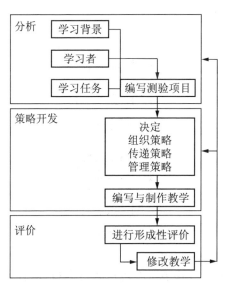

史密斯-雷根模式(摘自网络)

分析阶段也称为前期分析阶段,设计者主要分析三个要素:学习背景、学习者、学习任务。策略开发阶段主要阐明了组织策略、传递策略和管理策略的开发。评价阶段主要阐明了形成性评价和总结性评价。

"史密斯-雷根模式"是由 P. I. Smith 和 T. J. Ragan 于 1993 年发表的合著——《教学设计》一书中提出的。该模式是在"狄克-凯瑞"模型的基础上,吸收了加涅的"学习者特征分析"环节中关注学习者心理过程的思想,以及重视认知学习理论对教学内容安排的积极作用而逐步形成的(Smith, P. I. & Ragan, T. J., 1993)。该模式较好地结合了行为主义与认知主义的长处。该模式与 ID1 相比,具有三个明显优势:一是突出了策略设计的作用,认为应进行三类教学策略设计,且重点在教学组织策略的设计上;二是在教学分析中增加并突出了学习环境分析;三是深化了对学习者特征的分析。该模型突出学习环境和学习者特征的分析,充分考虑了学习发生的内、外部条件,包括学习者原有的认知因素和学习者现有的学习环境等因素。

4. ADDIE 模式

ADDIE 是指一套有系统地发展教学的方法。ADDIE 五个字母分别表示:Analysis—分析,Design—设计,Development—开发,Implement—实施,Evaluation—评估。

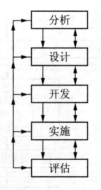

ADDIE 模式(摘自百度百科)

Analysis—分析。对教学所要达到的行为目标、任务、受众、环境、绩效目标等进行一系列的分析。

Design—设计。对将要进行的教学活动进行课程设计。

Development—开发。针对已经设计好的课程框架、评估手段等,进行相应的课程内容撰写、页面设计、测试等。

Implement—实施。对已经开发的课程进行教学实施,同时进行实施支持。

Evaluation—评估。对已经完成的教学课程及受众学习效果进行评估。

主要包含:要学什么?(学习目标的制定);如何去学?(学习策略的运用);以及如何判断学习者已到达学习成效?(学习评量的实施)。在ADDIE五个阶段中,分析与设计属前提,发展与执行是核心,评估为保证,三者互为联系,密不可分。

该模式中的各主要成分或子成分都会随模型所应用的情境而变化。如图所示:

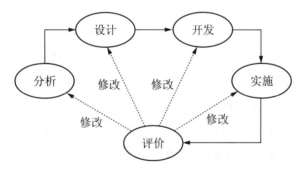

(摘自加涅等著、王小明等译的《教学设计原理》第五版 p.21)

5. 一般教学设计过程模式

在借鉴国内外各种教学设计过程模式的基础上,结合我国基础教育课程改革的背景和教学实践的需要,我国学者认为完整的教学设计过程可以包括以下组成部分:教学设计的前期分析,教学目标的阐明,教学过程的设计(包括教学顺序、教学组织形式、学习方式、教学模式、教学方法、学习环境和课堂管理等方面的设计),教学设计方案的编制与实施,教学设计的形成性评价与修改及教学设计的总结性评价。该系统可以称之为一般教学设计过程模式。

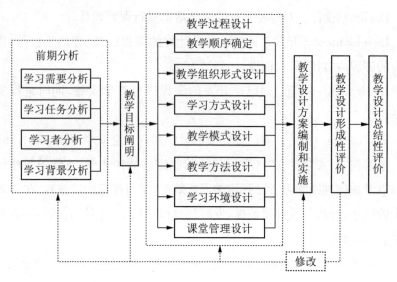

一般教学设计过程模式(摘自蔡铁权、王丽华.现代教育技术教程[M].[第2版])

　　该模式是"以教为主"的设计模式,具有较强的可操作性,目前在教学设计实践中仍是占有主导地位的模式。该模式有利于教师主导地位的作用的发挥,便于教师组织监控整个教学活动过程,便于师生间的情感交流,因而有利于科学知识的系统传授,并能充分发挥情感因素在学习过程中的重要作用。但是该模式完全由教师主宰课堂,忽视学生在学习过程中的主体地位,不利于有创新精神和创新能力的创造型人才的成长。

　　6."以学为主"的教学设计模式

　　"以学为主"的教学设计模式是进入20世纪90年代以后,随着多媒体和网络技术的日益普及(特别是基于Internet的教育网络的应用)以及建构主义的学习理论在国际上广为流行才逐渐发展起来。这种基于建构主义理论的、"以学为主"的教学系统设计,一般也称之为建构主义的教学设计,重视"情境"、"协作"在教学中的重要作用,强调发挥学习者在学习过程中的主动性和建构性,有利于创新型人才的培养,因此近年来备受人们重视。该模式如图所示:

　　建构主义教学设计强调学生是认知过程的主体,是意义的主动建构者,因而有利于学生的主动探索、主动发现、有利于创造型人才的培养,这是其

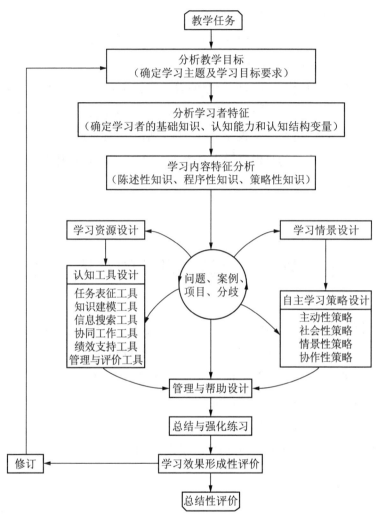

基于建构主义的教学系统设计模式（摘自于鲁子问、唐淑敏著的《英语教学设计》2016，p.41）

突出的优点。但是，由于强调学生的"学"，往往容易忽视教师主导作用的发挥，忽视师生之间的情感交流和情感因素在学习过程中的重要作用；而且，由于忽视教师主导作用，当学生自主学习的自由度过大时，还容易偏离教学目标的要求。所以受到一些学者的批评，这是我们在建构新型教学设计模式时所需要考虑和注意的。

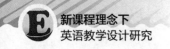
7. "学教并重"的教学设计模式

第六、七两种教学设计模式都有其优势与不足。我国教育专家把教师主导型教学结构和学生主体型教学结构有机结合,彼此取长补短,提出了主导—主体型教学结构。在这种新型的教学结构下,现代教学系统的四个要素的功能被充分挖掘并体现出来,如教师、学生,他们的积极性和主动性同时都得到了发挥,再如教学媒体不再单纯是辅助教师突破重点、难点的形象化教学工具,更重要的是促进学生自主探究的认知工具、协作交流工具与情感激励工具。

第三节　英语教学设计的具体形式

英语教学设计的具体形式是英语教学设计的外在表现,是英语教学设计结果的呈现,通俗地讲,就是英语教学设计的撰写形式。

一般来说,英语教学设计的具体形式有三种:文本式、表格式和流程图式。有时,还会出现三种形式的混合形式。

一、文本式。以下是苏教译林版小学英语(三年级起点)六年级下册 Unit 8 Our dreams(Story time)的教学设计,采用的就是文本式。

课　　题

苏教译林版小学英语 六年级下册 Unit 8 Our dreams(Story time)

教材简解

本单元的话题是"我的梦想",通过 Miss Li 与她的学生的对话启发学生对自己未来职业的思考,引导其树立正确的人生观。本单元的语用功能是使用问题"What do you want to be in the future?"及答句"I want to be ..."谈论自己的职业梦想。在五年级上册 Unit 5 What do they do? 一单元中,学生们已经学习过部分和职业相关的词汇,具有了在本单元中谈论和交流职业梦想的语言知识基础。对于即将离开小学校园的六年级学生们而言，在英语课堂中尝试揭开自己未来的职业之梦显得尤为可贵。编者在新版教材中将 Our dreams 列为一个单元，用心良苦。

目标预设

1. 借助"17 作业"或"纳米盒"等信息技术辅助教学手段，学生课前预学后能够会听、说、读单词及短语：dream, future, tooth, astronaut, care about, spaceship, World Cup, dancer, pianist, football player, come true, dentist。本课时教学完成后，学生能够会写上述单词及短语。

2. 在与教师和同学的交流中，学生能够逐步掌握问题"What do you want to be in the future?"及答句"I want to be ...", 会谈论自己的梦想。

3. 通过课中小组合作探究学习，学生能够在思维导图的帮助下理解 Story time 文本内容，能够梳理出不同人物的梦想，会读并能复述文本。

4. 通过教师的启发和自己的思考，学生能够树立较好的职业观。

重点、难点

1. 在与教师和同学的交流中，学生能够逐步掌握问题"What do you want to be in the future?"及答句"I want to be ...", 会谈论自己的梦想。

2. 通过课中小组合作探究学习，学生能够在思维导图的帮助下理解 Story time 文本内容，会读并能复述文本。

设计理念

学生在走进课堂之前并不是一张白纸，自己的生活经验和原有知识都将有助于其对新知识的理解和掌握。但既有的经验和知识具有不均衡性，课前有效预学有利于降低课堂学习的难度，缩短不同层次学生的差距。思维导图把主题关键词与图像、颜色等建立记忆链接，有利于学生调动左右脑的机能。在其帮助下，学生通过对文本内容的具象化梳理，在小组中讨论、交流和合作，学习和使用英语，在完成学习任务的同时，发散自己的思维，思考自己的职业梦想。

同时，小学阶段的学生好胜心强。课堂上教师可以将学生分为四个人一小组，利用分组竞赛，并在黑板记录小组得分的形式，充分调动学生的答题展示的主动性和学习积极性。

设计思路

在课前预习阶段,要求学生利用"17 作业"或者"纳米盒"预学 Story time;课上通过谈论《疯狂动物城》主角兔子的梦想引入课题;用头脑风暴的形式复习职业类单词,学生谈论并在小组内分享自己的职业梦想;未进文本前看配图,预测文本中人物的梦想;再通过看动画并将人物与梦想配对,求证猜测;读课文找梦想理由;小组合作完成思维导图。活动难度层层递进,符合学生的认知规律。最后学生调查他人的梦想,完成梦想树的制作,引导学生思考:如何才能实现自己的梦想,形成积极向上的职业观。

教学过程

Step 1 Warming-up(4 minutes)

1. Greetings

2. Free talk about *Zootopia*.

T：Yesterday I watched a film.(Show the film poster) What is the film's name?

S1：*Zootopia*.

T：Do you like the rabbit，Judy?

S2：Yes.

T：Why do you like her? You can say that in Chinese.

S3：...

T：Yes. She has a great dream. And she does a lot to make it come true. So today，let's talk about our dreams.(Write Unit 8 Our dream on the blackboard.)

3. Brainstorming：Write down the names of different jobs.

T：We know the rabbit wants to be a policeman. And I am a teacher.(PPT shows Picture 1，then Picture 2). Can you write the names of different jobs just like what I did just now?

d
r
teacher
a
policeman

Picture 1

d
r
e
a
m

Picture 2

设计意图 利用具有关联性的卡通人物,可以顺利揭示课题,既能激发学生学习兴趣,又能引起学生对为了梦想不懈努力的联想。头脑风暴中的填词游戏帮助学生回忆学习过的职业类的单词,也可检验学生预习效果,并为下一步骤谈论职业做好铺垫。

Step 2 Pre-reading (6 minutes)

1. Ask and answer. (Work in pairs)

T：We know a lot about different jobs. So what do you want to be in the future?

(Learn：in the future. Ask a student to read as a little teacher.) Let's work in pairs.

S1：What do you want to be in the future?

S2：I want to be a/an ...

······

2. Try to guess.

a. Show the pictures in the story time.(Pictures 3 and 4)

Picture 3

Picture 4

T：Who are they in the pictures?

Ss：They are Liu Tao，Su Hai，Wang Bing，Mike，Nancy and Yang Ling.

b. T：What do they want to be in the future? Can you guess?

设计意图 由词入句，同桌合作操练句型 What do you want to be in the future? I want to be a/an ...。猜测文本中人物的梦想，有利于激发学生的好奇心，同时也有助于学生从第一及第二人称的相互询问，转化为对第三人称的梦想的描述，训练学生的人称变换能力。

Step 3 While-reading (18 minutes)

1. Watch，match and say. (Picture 5)

Miss Li is writing about her students' dreams. Complete her notes.

My students' dreams

- Mike wants to be _____. He wants to take care of children's teeth.
- Su Hai wants to be _____.
- Yang Ling likes playing the piano. She wants to be _____.
- Nancy is good at writing. She wants to write stories for _____ _____.
- Liu Tao likes sport. He wants to be _____ and play in the World Cup.
- Wang Bing has a big dream. He wants to be _____ and fly to _____.

Picture 5

a. T：A good guess. Let's watch the cartoon and match to see whether you are right.

b. T：Can you tell us what Liu Tao wants to be?

S1：Liu Tao wants to be a football player.

T：What about the others?

S2：...

S3：...

设计意图 较有成效地预习有助于降低此任务的难度,通过看卡通求证自己的猜测,一方面帮助学生再次整体感知文本内容,形成文本内容的整体框架;另一方面通过说一说的形式,训练学生的口语表达。

2. Read and fill.

Miss Li is writing about her students' dreams. Complete her notes. (Picture 6)

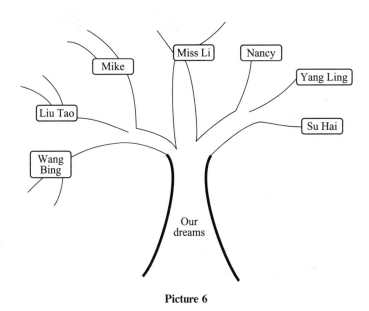

Picture 6

设计意图 略读文本,完成课文内容填空,内化语言结构,同时也注重学生思维品质的培养。

29

3. Read，find and say.

a. T：You have got what they want to be in the future. But what do they think of the different jobs? Underline their reasons and make up the mind maps in groups.（Picture 7）

b. Work in groups to tell about the dream trees according to the story time.

Picture 7

设计意图 精读文本，找出有关不同角色选择职业的原因，并通过小组合作完善思维导图梦想树的形式，进一步解读文本。随后小组说一说梦想树，锻炼学生小语篇输出的能力。

4. Listen and imitate.

Tip 1：Pay attention to the pronunciation and intonation.

Tip 2：Pay attention to the pauses in the long sentences.

设计意图 加强朗读的训练，注重语音、语调的模仿，并注意适当的停顿。

Step 4 Post-reading（9 minutes）

1. Let's read and act.

T：Let's read the story in different ways.

T：Let's have a role play. You can act out the story in groups.

2. Let's retell.

T：Please try to retell the story according to the mind maps on the blackboard.

3. Let's talk.

T：What do you want to be in the future? Talk in the group and do a survey.

4. Let's share.

T：What does your friend want to be? Share your friend's dream according to your survey.

设计意图 本文是一篇对话,所以通过小组你问我答,并做调查后组内汇报的形式,进一步锻炼学生口语输出的能力,做到学以致用。

Step 5 Sum up（2 minutes）

T：What do we learn today?

Yes. It's about our dreams.

T：How can we make our dream come true? Let's learn from Judy, the rabbit in the film *Zootopia*. Never give up, and work hard to make your dream come true.

设计意图 总结本课时所学内容,并进行情感教育。

Step 6 Homework（1 minute）

1. 17 zuoye：Read and recite story time.

2. Tell your parents about your dream and how to make your dream come true.

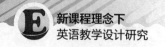

设计意图 借助17作业背诵评分功能,减轻教师后期检查作业完成情况的工作量,并将课堂所学语用功能延伸至课外。

板书设计

Unit 8 Our dreams

A:What do you want to be in the future?

B:I want to be ...

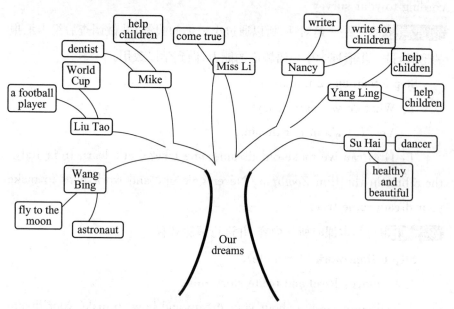

（制作者:淮北师范大学在读研究生张建祥,指导教师:徐修安）

二、表格式。以下是人教版高中英语必修五第一单元 Reading 的教学设计,采用的就是表格式。表格式是把教学设计各要素内容以表格的形式陈列出来。与文本式相比,表格式的教学设计,清晰条例,尤其方便使用电脑制作,也特别有利于教学过程中教师活动和学生活动的对照。

1）单元整体教学设计

基本信息			
省市区		学校	
姓名		联系电话	
学科		电子邮箱	
年级		教科书版本及章节	

单元（或主题）教学设计

单元（或主题）名称	

1. 单元（或主题）教学设计说明（依据学科课程标准的要求，简述本单元（或主题）学习对学生学科素养发展的价值；简要说明教学设计与实践的理论基础。学习单元可以按教材内容组织，也可以按学科学业发展和学科核心素养发展的进阶来组织，还可以按真实情境下的学习任务跨学科组织。）

2. 单元（或主题）学习目标与重点难点（根据国家课程标准和学生实际，指向学科核心内容、学科思想方法、学科核心素养的落实，设计单元学习目标，明确重点和难点。）

3. 单元（或主题）整体教学思路（教学结构图）（介绍单元整体教学实施的思路，包括课时安排、教与学活动规划，以结构图等形式整体呈现单元内的课时安排及课时之间的关联。）

第 1 课时教学设计（其他课时同）

课题	
课型	

1. 教学内容分析（分析本课时教学内容在单元中的位置，核心内容对发展学生核心素养的功能价值分析，蕴含的正确价值观念，已学内容与本课内容的关联。可用结构图示呈现。）

2. 学习者分析（学生与本课时学习相关的学习经验、知识储备、学科能力水平、学生兴趣与需求分析，学生发展需求、发展路径分析，学习本课时可能碰到的困难。）

3. 学习目标确定（根据国家课程标准和学生实际，指向学科核心内容、学科思想方法、学科核心素养的发展进阶，描述学生经历学习过程后应达成的目标和学生应能够做到的事情。可分条表述。）

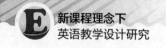
续表

4. 学习重点难点	
5. 学习评价设计(从知识获得、能力提升、学习态度、学习方法、思维发展、价值观念培育等方面设计过程性评价的内容、方式与工具等,通过评价持续促进课堂学习深入,突出诊断性、表现性、激励性。体现学科核心素养发展的进阶,课时的学习评价是单元学习过程性评价的细化,要适量、适度,评价不应中断学生学习活动,通过学生的行为表现判断学习目标的达成度。)	

6. 学习活动设计

教师活动	学生活动
环节一:(根据课堂教与学的程序安排)	
教师活动1 (教学环节中呈现的学习情境、提出驱动性问题、学习任务类型;对应学生活动,示范指导学科思想方法,关注课堂生成,纠正思维错漏,恰当运用评价方式与评价工具持续评价促进学习。下同。)	学生活动1 (学生在真实问题情境中开展学习活动;围绕完成学习任务开展系列活动与教的环节对应,学生分析任务—设计方案—解决问题—分享交流中学习并有实际收获。下同。)
活动意图说明:(简要说明教学环节、学习情境、学习活动等的组织与实施意图,预设学生可能出现的障碍,说明环节或活动对目标达成的意义和学生发展的意义。说出教与学活动的关联,如何在活动中达成目标,关注课堂互动的层次与深度。)	
环节二:	
教师活动2	学生活动2
活动意图说明	
环节三:	
教师的活动3	学生的活动3
活动意图说明	

7. 板书设计(板书完整呈现教与学活动的过程,最好能呈现建构知识结构与思维发展的路径与关键点。使用PPT应注意呈现学生学习过程的完整性。)

8. 作业与拓展学习设计(设计时关注作业的意图、功能、针对性、预计完成时间。发挥好作业复习巩固、引导学生深入学习的作用;面向全体,进行分层设计;检测类作业与探究类、实践类作业有机衔接;分析作业完成情况,作为教学改进和个性化指导与补偿的依据。)

9. 特色学习资源分析、技术手段应用说明(结合教学特色和实际撰写。)

10. 教学反思与改进(单节课教与学的经验性总结,基于学习者分析和目标达成度进行对比反思,教学自我评估与教学改进设想。课后及时撰写,突出单元整体实施的改进策略,后续课时教学如何运用本课学习成果,如何持续促进学生发展。)

(本教学设计表单摘自2019—2020年安徽省淮北市高中教师全员远程培训项目作业表单)

2) 课时教学设计

Teaching Design for Unit 1 Book 5

Title：Great scientists JOHN DEFEATS "KING CHOLERA"(Reading)

Teaching ideology
According to New Curriculum for English, English teaching focuses on comprehensive education, instead of simply using English as knowledge or skills. So in students' reading, I will follow the students-centered principle and act as a role of a guide, a helper and a facilitator of students.
Analysis of teaching material
This unit comes from book 5, which mainly talks about some great scientists in the world. There are some lexical barriers in the text, but the structure of it is clear. In order to train students independent thinking, on the surface of the text is the introduction of scientists, but the deep level is what we can learn from them.
Analysis of teaching condition
Grade：senior two   Number：55 1. 70% students can comprehend the text and 50% can express freely. But there are still 30% students who are weak in learning English, so they need more help. 2. Students are familiar with the topic but lack the specific information of some scientists. 3. Students in this period have lots of enthusiasm for the lesson, so they need a more vivid and interesting class.

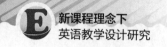
Teaching objectives
By the end of the class, students will be able to: 1. describe the procedures to make a research and express themselves in English.   2. use reading skills to find the information from the text and cooperate with others.   3. think creatively and critically about John Snow's quality.   4. have the awareness that no matter what occupation we want to have, we should learn from John Snow's spirits.

Teaching key and difficult points
Teaching key points: 1. Using reading skills to find the information of the procedures to make a research.   2. Getting John Snow's quality and learn from him.   **Teaching difficult point:**   Using adjectives to conclude John Snow's quality from his research.

Teaching methods
1. Interactive teaching   2. Comprehensive teaching   3. Situational teaching

Teaching aids
Multimedia devices, PPT document and blackboard

Teaching procedures			
Teaching procedures	**Teacher's activities**	**Students' activities**	**Design intention**
Step 1: Lead in (3 minutes)	1. Greeting. 2. Use electricity to let students guess the occupation of scientists.	1. Welcome. 2. Guess the occupation of scientists.	To help them connect the topic with our life and arouse their attention.
Step 2: Learning and understanding (20 minutes)	**1. To be a clever reader.** Let students guess the procedures of making a research. **2. To be a fast reader.** Ask students to check the procedures of making a research. **3. To be a careful reader.** Ask students to find the specific information of each procedure.	1. Guess the procedures of finding a problem, making up the assumption, testing the assumption, getting the conclusion, and finding the solution. 2. Check the procedures and find the specific information.	To train students' reading ability and help them learn to get the procedures by themselves.

Teaching procedures	Teacher's activities	Students' activities	Design intention
Step 3: Applying and practicing (10 minutes)	Role play: Tell students they are the hosts of a program and let them introduce the procedures of making a research.	Make the role play based on our learning.	To help them master the knowledge and use it freely.
Step 4: Transferring and creating (8 minutes)	Discussion: Conclude the quality of John Snow from his research.	Have a discussion with their classmates and share their ideas in the class.	To make them have a creative thinking about the good quality of a scientist and learn from them.
Step 5: Summary (3 minutes)	Tell students that no matter what occupation we want to have, we should learn from John Snow's spirits.	Get the summary from our learning and their discussion.	To help them make our learning clearly and have a correct awareness.
Step 6: Homework (1 minute)	**Compulsory homework:** Write a composition to make a research about the idea you find in your life. **Optional homework:** Find the difference between a scientist and a star. Try to make a speech about them.	Ask something about our learning and the task.	To deepen their impression about our learning and give different levels of students more chances to improve themselves.

Teaching reflection

1. The teacher should give students more kinds of activities in class in order to attract their attention and help them take part in the class actively.
2. Some students are lack of ability in finding information, so the teacher should give them more guide and encouragement.

Blackboard design

Unit 1 Great scientists

Making a research
$\begin{cases} \text{Finding a problem} \\ \text{Making up the assumption} \\ \text{Testing the assumption} \\ \text{Getting the conclusion} \\ \text{Finding the solution} \end{cases}$

（本教学设计制作者王璐，淮北师范大学外国语学院 2020 届本科毕业生，指导教师徐修安）

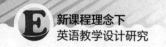
三、流程图式。英语教学设计完全使用流程图式的不多,较多的是按照教学流程,把教学过程的各个环节放在不同的图形内。如下图:

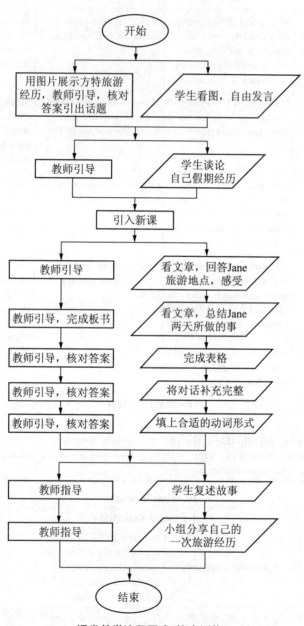

课堂教学流程图式(摘自网络)

使用流程图,必需掌握一些专门的图示和符号,而不是随心所欲,教学设计制作者本人一目了然,而读者却一片茫然。

图形(Symbol)	意义说明
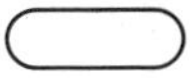 ⬭	开始,结束
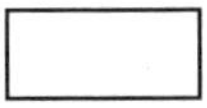 ▭	教师活动
 ▱	学生活动
 ◇	决策,判断
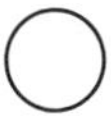 ◯	重要教学内容
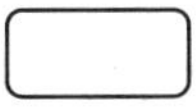 ▢	一般教学内容
 ◖▭	教学媒体
 ⟶	流程线

课堂教学流程图图例(摘自网络)

四、混合式。混合式的教学设计,顾名思义就是文本、图表、甚至流程图结合在一起使用。这种教学设计内容和形式丰富,但制作需要花费很多时间,不建议在限制时间的比赛和考试时采用。

Teaching Design for Unit 7

1. 整体设计思路、指导依据说明

《义务教育课程标准 2017 版》倡导学生在一定的社会文化背景下,借助于教师的帮助,利用必要的教学资料,通过亲身的经历和图示不断建构自己的知识、能力和价值观,并丰富自己的情感体验。这样一来,就必然要求学生在真实而富有实际意义的任务活动中去学习,体验和运用语言知识,而且要求学生学会与他人合作学习。

基于这一基本要求,根据九年级学生的特点,结合第七单元的教学内容,我在课堂的教学实践中,通过展示一小段关于介绍赫本的英语视频,让学生对于今天要讲的内容有一定初步了解。结合"合作探究"的学习途径,通过视频的展示、小组讨论、辩论使学生积极地参与教学活动,把握本篇文章的主要内容,所以我要设置两个活动:一是通过展示纪录片和赫本所演的电影让学生了解赫本传奇而丰富多彩的一生;二是通过小组讨论、辩论等方式让学生理解到内涵美、心灵美远比一张美丽而空洞的脸庞重要。从而帮助学生完成知识目标,能力目标和情感目标的实现。

2. 教材分析

本节课的教学内容源于牛津版教材初三年级(上)Unit 7,本单元的话题是电影以及对于赫本的介绍。通过视频的欣赏、听说练习、辩论,学生能够了解赫本传奇的一生,并且能够理解优雅的气质和高尚的内涵远比漂亮的外表重要。

3. 学情分析

九年级的学生有良好的英语听说能力和阅读能力,拥有强烈的好奇心和求知欲,课堂上他们善于表现自我并且能够积极参与到课堂的讨论和辩论。但是这一阶段的学生正处于青春期,开始越来越关注自己的外表,还没有形成全面的对美的理解。通过这一篇课文的学习,学生将会意识到内涵美、心灵美比漂亮的外表重要。

4. 教学目标分析

本节课结束时,学生将能够:

(1) 了解赫本传奇的一生,能够说出她演过的电影,以及她对于联合国教科文组织的贡献。

(2) 掌握并能够正确拼读重要词汇,比如:humanitarian, charm, catch one's attention, play the lead role of, nomination, achievement。

(3) 理解并掌握关键句型,并能够仿写句子。

(4) 用时间轴画出赫本的生平功绩。

(5) 能够感悟理解什么才是真正的美,从而端正自己的人生观。

5. 重难点分析

Key points：

（1）了解赫本的传奇一生和生平功绩。

（2）掌握关键词汇，关键句型，并且能够根据要求仿写句子。

Difficult points：

（1）能够欣赏美，树立正确的人生观。

（2）根据时间轴复述全文。

教学方法分析：

Direct approach，audio-lingual approach，situational approach

Step 1(5 mins)

T：Greeting.

I will present 2 remarkably different pictures about the role Hepburn played in the film *My Fair Lady*.

T：If you can choose one of the two ladies to be your friend, which one do you like?

S：The right one.

T：Why?

S：The left one looks poor, vulgar, and uncivilized, while the right one is a princess, who is the embodiment of great beauty, charm and elegance.

T: You made a great description, especially the use of the noun "charm", which means a quality sb owns to tremendously attract one's attention.

T: The two ladies are the same person played by.

S: Hepburn.

[Design intention]

1. To attract my students' attention by presenting 2 distinctively different people by the same person.

2. Offer opportunities to express themselves to stir their interest in English learning.

Step 2: Pre-reading(6 mins)

In the step, I will show a piece of video on a documentary about Hepburn to my students.

T: Which part of the video impresses you most?

S: She played the movie *Roman Holiday*.

S: She used to be a ballet dancer.

S: She is the greatest beauty that the world has ever seen.

S: She made great contribution to the African poor children.

T: You all did a great job, and I really appreciate it.

[Design intention]

1. Students can get a brief understanding about the text, which help them to clear obstacles.

2. Students can practice their listening, comprehending and speaking competence.

Step 3: While-reading(20 mins)

Section 1 Read extensively about the passage and make a time table about the event about Hepburn.

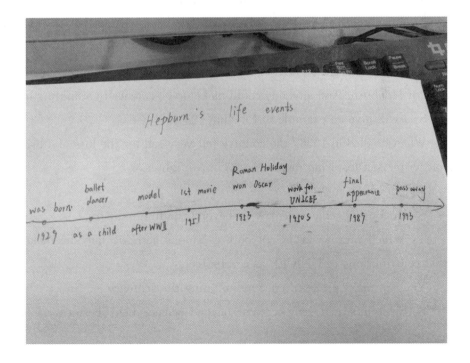

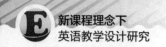
Section 2

T：What are the words and collocation you don't understand?.

S：Humanitarian.

(Illustrate the picture of Nightingale（南丁格尔）and Bethune（白求恩），and then make 2 sentences)

T：Nightingale is a humanitarian, and also Bethune a humanitarian.

S：Charm.

T：Charm is a noun, its adj is charming.

(illustrate the picture of a famous actor Chen Daoming（陈道明）)

T：Actor Chen Daoming is a man of great charm, we can also say that he is charming.

（Then I will teach these words and collocation in the same way by illustrating and making up sentences）

Section 3

T：Are there any sentences you don't understand?

S：When she died in 1993, the world felt very sad for the loss of a great beauty, a great actress, and a great humanitarian.

T：Here we use 3 parallel collocation in order to underline the importance of Hepburn. And anybody could make up a sentence by imitating it?

S：I will give an example of Lu Xun（鲁迅）.

When he died in 1936, the country felt very sad for the loss of a brilliant writer, an inspiring mentor and a brave fighter.

T：Are there any?

S：Hepburn's achievement went beyond the film industry.

T：Which means she is not only a famous actress, but she makes great contributions to UNICEF as a volunteer.

You can make up a sentence by imitating the sentence.

S：Einstein's achievement went beyond science field（besides, he is talented violin player）

[Design intention]

1. Ss can get a brief understanding about the text.

2. Ss can read and understand the new words and important sentences.

Step 4: post reading

Section 1

I will ask my students to retell the passage according to the timetable.

Ss: Hepburn was born in 1929, and she aspired to be a ballet dancer when she was a child.

Ss: After World War II, she worked as a model, then she emerged in her first movie in 1951 by the appreciation of a writer.

Ss: The gold time of her career is in the 1950s, during which she acted in the most famous movie Roman Holiday, which helped her win Oscar, and her achievement went beyond the film industry.

Ss: She made her final appearance in 1989, and then passed away in 1993, when the world felt very sad for the loss of a great beauty, a great actress, and a great humanitarian.

Section 2

Debate

T: Which one do you think is more important, a charming appearance or a kind soul?

Ss: (For the ones who support appearance is more important, their ideas are as follows)

1. The first priority is to make a good first impression.

2. People are not ready to know about you through a plain face.

3. A charming appearance plays an important role in the interview, promotion, especially in a relationship.

Ss: 1. We can't judge a man by his/her appearance just like we can't judge a book by its cover, because time will tell, sooner or later.

2. A beautiful face can't last long, while a great soul can.

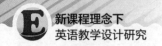

3. It can make a much more fulfilling, satisfying, worthwhile life for yourselves, not an empty face can.

Summary:

I will invite 2 students to talk about what have they learned in today's class, and make up for their opinions.

Homework:

I will ask my students to search more information about Hepburn, then make a PPT to share with us.

Step 5: Blackboard design

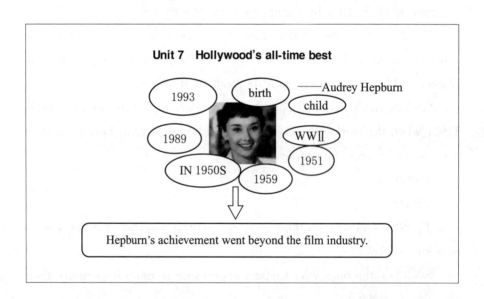

Step 6:教学过程结构图

Step 7: After-class evaluation & reflection

I will ask my students to grade themselves (A, B, C). If their evaluation is A, please write down their advantages; if B or C, please write down what they can do to improve it, and the suggestions on my teaching.

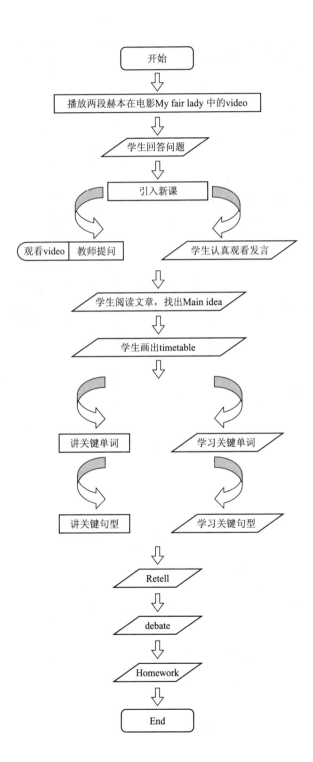

The things I can do	A	B	C
I can take part in the lessons activity			
I can understand the reading passage			
I can understand the oral question			
I can answer the question			
I can write out the time table			
I have known some background info of the text			
I can talk something about Hepburn			
Total			

As for after-class, I will reflect from the following aspects.

	Yes/no	How to improve
Whether I have achieved my teaching goal		
Whether it is well organised		
Whether ss take an active part in my class		
Whether the class is efficient		

（本教学设计制作者，李景妮，淮北师范大学在读研究生，指导教师，徐修安）

本章参考文献：

[1] 何克抗.运用"新三论"的系统方法促进教学设计理论与应用的深入发展[J].中国电化教育,2010(1):7—18.

[2] 任友群.教学设计发展的新趋势[J].全球教育展望,2005(5):27—30.

[3] 钟志贤.论教学设计的发展走势[J].外国教育研究,2005(5):66—71.

[4] 高文.教学系统设计研究的历史回顾——教学设计研究的昨天、今天与明天(之三)[J].中国电化教育,2005(3):24—28.

[5] 施良方.教学理论:课堂教学的原理、策略与研究[M].上海:华东师范大学出版社,1999.

[6] 乌美娜.教学设计[M].北京:高等教育出版社,1994.

[7] 李龙.教学过程设计[M].呼和浩特:内蒙古人民出版社,2002.

[8] 孙立仁.教学设计:实践基础教育课程改革的理论与方法[M].北京:电子工业出版社,2004:229.

[9] 何克抗.建构主义的教学模式、教学方法与教学设计[J].北京师范大学学报:社科版,1997(5):9—11.

[10] 盛群力,褚献华.现代教学设计应用模式[M].杭州:浙江教育出版社,2002.

[11] 何克抗,郑永柏,谢幼如.教学系统设计[M].北京:北京师范大学出版社,2004:132.

[12] 鲁子问、唐淑敏.英语教学设计[M].华东师范大学出版社,2016.

[13] 蔡铁权、王丽华.现代教育技术教程[M](第 2 版).北京:科学出版社.2005:209—211.

Chapter 03

第三章·教学设计模式的要素

　　发展到今天,英语教学设计并无固定统一的模式。教学设计公认的一般模式是 ADDIE 模式,它的要素包括:Analysis——分析,对教学所要达到的行为目标、任务、受众、环境、绩效目标等进行一系列的分析;Design——设计,对将要进行的教学活动进行课程设计;Development——开发,针对已经设计好的课程框架、评估手段等,进行相应的课程内容撰写、页面设计、测试等;Implement——实施,对已经开发的课程进行教学实施,同时进行实施支持;Evaluation——评估,对已经完成的教学课程及受众学习效果进行评估。

　　还有一种常见模式,它的要素包括设计原因分析(理论依据、呈现方式)、设计内容分析(教学内容、教学对象〈学习者分析〉、教学目标)、设计过程分析(教学步骤及课堂流程图)、设计效果分析(课堂设计的评价或检测)。

　　还有一种模式,包括这样一些要素:整体设计思路、指导依据说明,教学背景分析(教学内容分析(含本课时在本单元的教学定位分析),学生情况分析),教学目标分析,教学重点、难点分析,教学过程设计(注意:每一教学步骤后要说明设计意图),教学评价设计(评价内容、评价方法)。

　　美国教育学家哥莱斯(R.Glasser)认为,所有的教学活动都包括四个部分,即教学目标、起点行为、教学活动和教学评价。在此基础上对应的教学设计包括教学目标设计、达成教学目标的诸要素分析与设计、教学效果的评价。其中,达成教学目标的诸要素的分析与设计中又包括:教学对象的分析、教学内容的分析、选择教学策略、确定教学媒体。这与前面提到的教学设计四个最基本的环节(分析教学对象、制定教学目标、选择教学策略、开展教学评价)也是一致的。

我国学者(盛群力等,2001)编译的《现代教学设计应用模式》中,对教学设计的组成有更细致的分类,即教学设计过程的九要素说:(1)明确教学问题,详细说明设计教学方案的目标。(2)在整个规划过程中都要注意考察学习者的特征。(3)明确学科内容,并对描述目标和目的的相关任务成分进行分析。(4)向学习者交代教学目标。(5)在每一个教学单元内按序排定教学内容,以体现学习的逻辑性。(6)实施教学策略使得每个学习者都能掌握教学目标。(7)规划教学信息和传递方法。(8)开发评价工具以评估目标。(9)选择支持教学活动的资源。

国外学者对教学设计的模式的研究数以百计,从教学设计实践角度而

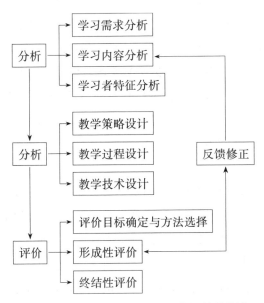

教学设计的一般模式(摘自鲁子问、康淑敏著《英语教学设计》,2016,p.43)

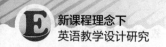

言,我国教育学者提炼概括出教学设计的一般模式,该模式的基本构成要素有:学习需求分析、学习内容分析、学习者特征分析、教学策略设计、教学过程设计、教学技术设计、评价目标确定与方法选择、形成性评价和总结性评价。

不管教学设计模式包含哪些要素,和世界上其他事情一样,教学设计也一定有最基本的要素。例如,我们想做一件事,首先会思考这样几个问题:想干什么(教学目标),怎么干(教学过程),干得怎么样(教学评价)。教学设计也应该如此,最基本的要素也应该包括教学目标、教学过程、教学评价三个部分。其他的要素都是在这些基本要素基础上扩展开的。目标确定前,教学理念肯定会产生影响,也一定要分析教学材料和研究对象;同时目标确定后,必然要选取教学方法和教学手段。在教学过程中,前面的要素一定会体现出来。教学过程中和结束后,我们肯定需要进行评价,看看教学效果,也一定会进行反思。基予这样的分析,我们认为,较完整的教学设计应该包括教学理念、教材分析、学生分析、教学目标(含教学重难点)、教学方法、教学手段、教学过程和教学反思八个方面。

《普通高中英语课程标准》(2017)明确强调发展学生的核心素养。发展核心素养是落实立德树人根本任务的一项重要举措,也是适应世界教育改革发展趋势,提升我国教育国际竞争力的迫切需要。以新课程理念为指导,是新课程大背景下进行教学设计的必然要求。因此,我们的教学设计,在吸收新的教学理论、学习理论,融合现代信息技术手段的同时,也一定体现新一轮课程改革的基本理念。但是值得注意的是,教学设计的要素也不是固定的,一成不变的,教师需要根据一定的范式设计出适合学生且具有创造性的教学设计。

实际上,大多数学科教学设计的基本思路都是类似的,它是经典教学设计组成的细化,将每一个操作步骤罗列出来,可以帮助经验不是很丰富的教师将工作做全面。就如上述的九要素说中,九要素构成了一个逻辑的、顺时针的序列,但在操作每一个要素时不一定非要按此顺序。每个人可以按照自己的意愿实施这一教学设计过程,不管从哪里切入,都可以根据他们认为合适的顺序进行设计。这就需要教师自己下功夫了。

第一节　教学设计的理念分析

一　教学理念分析概述

教学理念是教师对教学活动的基本看法和持有的基本的态度和观念，是教师从事教学活动的信念。教学理念有理论层面、操作层面之分。我们常说，这位教师教学理念较陈旧，另一位教师的教学理念较为先进，一要看他（或她）受什么样的教学理论和学习理论所指导，二要看他（或她）的教学实践中表现出了什么样的教学行为。

明确表达的教学理念对教学活动有着极其重要的指导意义。因此，完整教学设计的第一个要素，应该是教学理念分析。把教学理念分析作为教学设计的第一要素，这是由教学理念的重要性决定的。

那么在教学设计过程中，如何进行教学理念分析呢？

首先，要分析真正指导我们的教学理论。例如，我们认为教学不是由教师把知识简单地传递给学生的过程，而是由学生凭借自己已有的经验和认知结构对知识进行建构的过程。那么我们就是以建构主义理论作为我们的理论做指导。

其次，分析英语课程标准。课程标准是体现国家或地方教育行政部门意志，指导我们教学的纲领性文件。例如，2017年版《普通高中英语课程标准》指出，英语课程是全面贯彻党的教育方针，落实立德树人根本任务，发展英语学科核心素养，培养社会主义建设者和接班人的基础文化课程。英语学科由于其学科特点兼具工具性和人文性融合统一的特点，英语课程的育人功能是其人文性的突出表现。英语课程强调发展学生的语言能力、文化意识、思维品质和学习能力的综合素养，落实立德树人根本任务。普通高中英语课程倡导面向全体学生；倡导指向学科核心素养发展的学习活动观，鼓励自主、合作和探究等学习方式；倡导建立多元评价方式，聚焦并促进学生英语学科核心素养的形成和发展;提倡在课程教学中应用现代信息技术不断丰富英语课程学习资源。很显然,英语课程标准可以作为我们教学设计的理论指导。

当然,由于 2017 年版《高中英语课程标准》体现的是最先进的教学理论和学习理论的最新成果,我们在进行教学理念分析时,也可以只依据课程标准进行分析。

现实中,很多老师对于课程标准的学习是不够的,多数只依赖各级部门安排的培训,而不愿埋下头去亲自阅读,原因之一是,课程标准的内容较为枯燥。鉴于此,我们推出数字记忆法"一、一、四、六、三、八",来学习课程标准。第一个"一",指的是课程改革的目的是落实立德树人的根本任务;第二个"一",即提出了一个"核心素养"概念;"四"是指核心素养的四个方面,语言能力、学习能力、思维品质和文化意识;"六"指的是英语课程内容的六要素,"三"指的是英语学习活动可分为三类,即学习理解类、应用实践类和迁移创新类;"八"指的是课程标准实施的八条建议。

另外,为了帮助大家更好学习《普通高中英语课程标准》(2017 版),我们还可以从以下问题入手。1)如何整体把握课程标准? 2)英语核心素养四个方面的具体内涵是什么? 3)如何理解普通高中英语课程的具体目标? 4)如何理解英语课程内容的六要素? 5)如何理解六要素整合的英语学习活动观? 6)英语学习活动可分为几类? 7)如何理解六要素整合的英语学习活动观? 8)英语学习活动可分为几类? 9)如何理解英语学习活动观中的活动? 10)英语学习活动的设计应注意什么问题? 11)在以主题意义为引领的课堂上,教师该怎么做? 12)教师如何研读语篇? 13)教师如何进行语音教学? 14)新课程标准提倡如何进行词汇教学? 15)怎么理解新课程标准的语法知识教学? 16)如何进行语篇知识和语篇教学? 17)语用知识及语用教学是怎样的? 18)如何理解课程标准提出的学业质量标准? 等等。

在撰写英语教学设计时,常会用到课程标准英语专业词汇,也是我们必需具备的。如:"立德树人"可翻译为 foster integrity and promote the rounded development of people.英语学科核心素养可以翻译为 core competence, language competence, culture awareness, thinking quality, learning capacity.

二 教学理念分析案例

1. 中文撰写的案例。本教学设计是以《普通高中英语课程标准(2017年版)》中的基本理念为依据,旨在构建多元的英语课程结构,以满足高中学生个性发展的需求。要实现英语学科核心素养的课程目标,必须构建与其一致的课程内容和教学方式。具体而言,指向学生学科核心素养发展的英语教学应以主题意义为引领,以语篇为依托,整合语言知识、文化知识、语言技能和学习策略等学习内容,创设具有综合性,关联性和实践性的英语学习活动,引导学生采用自主、合作的学习方式,参与主题意义的探究活动,并从中学习语言知识,发展语言技能,汲取文化营养,促进多元思维,塑造良好品格,优化学习策略,提高学习效率,确保语言能力、文化意识、思维品质和学习能力的同步上升。高中阶段英语语法知识的学习是义务教育阶段语法学习的延伸和继续,应在更加丰富的语境中通过学会在语境中理解和运用新的语法知识,进一步发展英语语法意识。(第十二届全国高中英语教师教学基本功大赛暨教学观摩研讨会 Book 2 Unit 2 Grammar Future in the Past & Future continuous tense 采用各种英语学习和实践活动进一步巩固和恰当运用义务教育阶段所学的语法知识。)

2. 英语撰写的案例:New English Curriculum Standards(2017) carries out the fundamental task of fostering integrity and promoting rounded development of students, develops the core competence of English learning, puts into practice the activity viewpoint of English learning and stresses the promotion of students' learning and applying abilities, learning strategies and cultural awareness.

In this intensive reading class, I will focus on content by repeatedly and carefully reading and analyzing discourse. For the propose of developing the core competence of English learning I will integrate the knowledge of language learning, the development of language skills, The formation of cultural awareness and the application of writing methods in the process of guiding students to explore deep meaning of this topic.

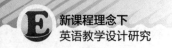
第二节　教材分析

一　教材分析概述

教材是课程目标的载体,是课程实施的重要凭借,因此,英语教材分析是教学设计的要素之一,也是课堂教学目标设计的重要依据之一。教材分析是英语课堂教学的基础,只有全面分析教材,教师才能根据实际情况因材施教,才能更好地构建更加高效的课堂教学。

那么,如何进行教材分析?

第一,单元整体分析。教师拿到教材之后,在对教材进行一个整体了解的基础上,要进行单元整体分析。认真梳理单元教学内容,梳理并概括与主题相关的语言知识、文化知识、语言技能和学习策略。在学科理论和新课标要求的背景下,吃透教材的内容。

第二,研读语篇。研读语篇就是对语篇主题、内容、文体结构、语言特点、作者观点等进行深入的解读。建议教师首先尝试回答三个基本问题;第一,语篇的主题和内容是什么? 即 What 的问题;第二,语篇的深度含义是什么? 也就是作者或说话人的意图、情感态度或价值取向是什么? 即 why 的问题。第三,语篇具有什么样的文体特征、内容结构和语言特点? 也就是作者为了恰当表达主题意义选择了什么样的文本形式、语篇结构和修辞手法? 即 how 的问题。

第三,教材调整。研读语篇后,在明确教材的地位以及其与前后知识联系的基础上,需要再次审视教材,明确"在教什么"、"教什么更好"、"教什么才能更好地让学生有所发展"这三个问题,对教材进行删减、增补、重组、置换、整合等,从而形成适合学生发展的教学内容。

第四,开发课程资源。如何积极开发课程资源以及对其进行合理利用是英语课程实施主要考虑的部分。英语课程资源不仅仅局限于英语教材。

总之,新课程理念下,课堂教学不再仅仅是传授知识,教学的一切活动都是着眼于学生的发展。在教学过程中如何促进学生的发展,培养学生的核心素养,是课程标准的要求。因此,教学应由教教材向用教材教转变。

二 教材分析案例

1. 中文撰写的案例:本课是牛津译林(2013年版)九年级上册第一单元第二课时阅读部分(Reading),介绍阳光镇里四位在不同领域取得杰出成就的人物。整个文本由四篇介绍艺术家、经理、工程师、医生的短记叙文组成。意在帮助学生探讨自己的性格特征,确立未来人生奋斗方向,进行合理的人生规划。

2. 英文撰写案例:Analysis of teaching material(Reading in Book 2 Unit 2 the Olympic Games)

This Unit mainly talks about the basic knowledge of the Olympic Games. The structure of the text is clear and the lexical barrier is less. In order to train students' independent thinking, on the surface of the text is the comparison and contrast between the ancient and modern Olympic Games，but the deep level is the correct attitude towards holding it，which needs students to explore.

第三节　学情分析

一 学习者分析概述

建构主义指出,学生是学习的主体,积极主动地进行知识的建构,是学生有意识地去学习。分析学习者的目的是了解学习者的学习状况,促进学生的意义建构,分析学习风格和学习能力,为教学设计提供依据。对学习者进行分析,了解学习者的长处和短处,有利于培养学习者的自主学习能力,提高学生的自我效能感,尤其是在英语教学设计中,激发学生的兴趣,对知识的渴望,培养学生学习英语的能力。分析学习者是教学设计的基础。

1. 学习者分析内容。对学习者分析,可以从智力因素和非智力因素两方面进行。其中智力因素包括学习者的起始能力、学习能力等;非智力因素包括学习动机、兴趣爱好以及认知风格等变量。

(1)初始能力水平。依据克拉申语言输入假设理论,教师在进行英语教学设计时必须把握学生的起点水平,即学生原有的学习基础,包括学生与本课或本单元相关的语言及文化基础知识、技能水平,为教学目标设定提供依据。具体来说,就是掌握学生"现有水平"的详细情况,并以此为基础来设定合理的教学目标。

(2)认知结构特征。根据皮亚杰对儿童认知发展阶段的划分,学生在特定年龄阶段具有特定的认知心理情感特点以及智能发展特点。因此,在教学设计前,教师不应忽略所教对象的年龄、性别以及个人生活经验等情况。只有根据儿童智能和情感发展阶段的特征来进行教学设计将使教学更符合学生的发展特点,对于不同学段的学生选择与其认知特点相适应的教学内容、教学方法、教学策略,才有助于得到最好的教学效果。

(3)学习动机。根据奥苏伯尔的解释,学习动机包括认知内驱力、自我内驱力以及附属内驱力。教师只有在了解了学生学习动机状态之后才能在教学设计中有效地启动学生的学习动机,甚至在教学活动进行中及时维持和调节,帮助学生保持一个正确、积极的学习动机,使得教学效果最大化。

(4)学习态度。学习态度是学生对学习及其学习情境所表现出来的一种比较稳定的心理倾向,它包括学生对待学习材料以及对待教师、学校等的态度。它直接影响学生课上的注意、情绪以及意志状况,对教学效果起着非常重要的作用。因此,教师在进行教学时需要了解学生对于自己、本学科或者本节课主题等的态度倾向,以助于后期进行教学时及时调节教学行为与策略。

(5)学习风格。学习风格也称为认知方式,是学生在学习时所偏爱的方式。它包括学习者在进行信息加工方面的不同思维方式、对学习环境和学习同伴的不同需求、在认知结构方面的差异、某些个性意识的倾向、生理差异等。它一般分为场独立与场依存型认知方式,冲动型和沉思型认知方式,甚至从感知通道偏爱的角度进行划分为视觉型、听觉型以及触觉型的认知方式等。了解学习者的学习风格对教学效果至关重要。例如在呈示教学内容时,可以针对不同认知风格学生使用不同正面强化手段来提高学习效果,如通过动态视觉刺激(如电视、电影),或是听觉刺激(如听讲或录音),亦或学生喜欢安静的学习环境还是热烈的互动讨论等。

2. 学习者分析方法。在日常进行教学设计时,很多教师靠经验获得学情,这是教师常用的方法,并且在学情分析中的确扮演了重要角色。但是仅靠经验是不够的,还需要其他一些方法进行补充和完善。例如作业分析、试卷反馈、课堂观察、课后交流(访谈)、学生学习档案、教师日志等等。有经验的老师还会定期通过开放式或封闭式问题对学生进行问卷调查。因此,问卷调查,也是教师进行学习者分析的可行性方法。

二 学习者分析案例

1. 中文撰写的案例:课题:How to do cloze tests

参与上课的是我校高三(1)班 43 名学生。高三(1)班是我校的理科好班,学生的整体学习素质和能力相对较好,但英语偏科的现象还是很相当突出,学生英语水平参差不齐。课堂上如果老师采用传统的讲授法,好的学生会吃不饱,弱点的学生会听不懂,效果会很不理想。采用兵教兵,通过讨论、感悟、发现等小步子教学比较适合学生的情况。

2. 英语撰写的案例:Teaching Design for Unit 1 Book 5

Title:Great scientists JOHN SNOW DEFEATS "KING CHOLERA" (Reading)

Grade:senior two　　　Number:55

70% students can comprehend the text and 50% can express freely. But there are still 30% students who are weak in learning English, so they need more help.

Students are familiar with the topic but lack the specific information of some scientists.

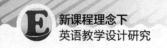
Students in this period have lots of enthusiasm for the lesson，so they need a more vivid and interesting class.

第四节　教学目标分析

一　教学目标分析概述

美国教育学家布鲁姆说过："有效的教学，始于期望达到的目标。"教学目标不仅制约着英语教学的过程、教学方法和教学手段的选择，而且对英语课堂的活动方式也具有限制作用。

教学目标的设计依据，应该从三个方面考虑，即课程标准、教材分析和学情分析。《普通高中英语课程标准》(2017)是高中英语课堂教学目标设计的依据之一，以核心素养为教学目标的支撑，根据一定的策略对各个级别的教学目标的总体描述进行分解，为不同的学生、教材内容制定出不同的课堂教学目标。教材是课程目标的载体，是课程实施的重要凭借，因此，英语教材分析也是课堂教学目标设计的重要依据之一。《普通高中英语课程标准》(2017)建议关注主题意义，制定指向核心素养的单元整体目标。每个课时目标的设定都要为达成单元整体目标服务，有机整合课程内容六要素，并根据教学实际有所侧重，避免脱离主题或碎片化的呈现方式。有效教学的理念关注的是学生的发展和教学效益。学生的基本情况也是制定高中英语课堂教学目标的依据。根据最近发展区的原则，在课堂教学目标的设计时要注意学生在学习本节课之前的基础水平、兴趣爱好和学习习惯。从新课标中的核心素养对学生的学情进行分析，为学生设计适合他们的课堂教学目标。教学目标既要体现对全体学生的基本要求，又要兼顾学生的个体差异，既要确保共同进步，又要满足个性发展。

教学目标的设计策略。《普通高中英语课程标准》(2017)指出，教学目标的设定应该可达成、可操作、可检测。在目标表述上应尽量使用能反映外部行为变化的词语,避免目标的"模糊、笼统、抽象和不可预测性"。同时要体现新课程的理念,注重学生的参与和体验,教师通过创设良好的语言环境并提供大量的语言实践机会,使学生通过自身的感知、体验、实践,逐步提高分析问题、解决问题以及合作交流的能力。始终把"以学生为中心"的教学理念贯彻到教学实践中。还要注意预设和生成关系。教学目标的设计是教师预先确定的,并在具体的教学活动中付诸实践的一种预期设计。但课堂教学是一个具备一定的情境且较为复杂的过程,受诸多外界因素的制约,存在着许多不可预知的突发事件,预设的教学目标在教学实践中不一定得以完美实现。因此,教师还应注意处理目标的预设与生成之间的关系,给教学目标设计和生成留出一定的空间,为教学过程的动态生成创造条件。教师还要重视目标评价与分析,对课堂教学目标的评价指的是教师自身在课堂教学目标设计实施前后的对比性评价,即教师在实施前的预期和实施后的效果是否达到一致。这种评价不仅停留在关注学生语言能力、学习能力和思维品质的变化上,更应重点关注教师自身在教学目标的制定与实施过程当中所取得的经验和认识。这是一种直接指向教师进行自我反思的过程。它让教师既注重学生学习能力的发展,又注重自身教学实践的改善,对推动教师的专业化发展有着积极的意义。

教学目标的撰写还需要注意一些事项。目标的主体应是学生,而不是教师,这是"以学生为主体"教学理念的真正体现。目标的表述应遵循英语学科的特点,核心素养的四个方面根据具体内容体现出来。体现核心素养目标,一定也根据具体内容,有的课时目标可以体现四个方面,有的可能只体现两三个,不能设置千篇一律的四条目标。

教学目标的表示可以采用 ABCD 形式。A 即 Audience,意指"学习者",它是目标陈述句中的主语。教学目标描述的是学生的行为,而不是教师的行为。规范的行为目标开头应是"学生";B 即 Behavior,意为"行为",要说明通过学习后,学习者应能做什么,是目标陈述句中的谓语和宾语。这是目标陈述句中的最基本的成分,不能缺少。在新课程改革中,特别强调用具体的行为动词来陈述课堂教学目标,以增强教学目标的可观察性和可测性,如可采用 to list...(能列举出……), to distinguish...(能区分出……), to state...（能陈述出……），to recognize...（能辨认出……）等一些可测量、可评价、具体而明确的行为动词，也可采用"说出"、"绘制"等能直接反映学生活动的动词；C 即 Condition，意为"条件"，要说明学生的行为是在什么条件下产生的，是目标陈述句中的状语。条件是指影响学生学习结果的特定的限制或范围，如"借助工具书"，"在老师的帮助下"等；D 即 Degree，意为"程度"，即明确上述行为的标准，是指学生对目标达到的最低表现水平，用来评价学习表现或学习结果所达到的程度，如"能流畅地背诵全诗"，"每分钟能阅读多少字英语短文"等。

二 教学目标分析案例

1. 中文撰写的案例。高三复习课："如何做完形填空"教学目标分析

基于教学内容和学生情况的分析，本节课的教学目标设定为：

1）学生能够通读整篇文章，掌握大意；

2）学生能够通过自己思考、小组讨论解决错误的题目，并知道错误原因；

3）学生能够把经过讨论后不懂的问题提交课堂，向老师求助；

4）学生能够更进一步掌握完型填空的特点，进一步熟悉完型填空的解题方法；

5）学生基于完型填空题型的掌握，逐步减少对这类题目的畏难情绪，增加英语学习的兴趣。

教学难点分析。在教学目标的引领下，本节课教学重点弄懂本篇完型填空，难点为通过本篇完型填空，举一反三，进一步把握完型填空的特点。

2. 英语撰写的案例

Teaching Design for Unit 1 Book 5 教学目标分析

Title：Great scientists JOHN DEFEATS "KING CHOLERA"（Reading）

Teaching objectives

By the end of the class, students will be able to：

1）describe the procedures to make a research and express themselves in English.

2）use reading skills to find the information from the text and cooperate with others.

3）think creatively and critically about John Snow's quality.

4）have the awareness that no matter what occupation we want to have，we should learn from John Snow's spirits.

Teaching key and difficult points

Teaching key points：

1）Using reading skills to find the information of the procedures to make a research.

2）Getting John Snow's quality and learn from him.

Teaching difficult point：

Using adjectives to conclude John Snow's quality from his research.

第五节 教学方法概述

一 教学方法概述

本节简单总结了常见的英语教学方法，简述每种教学法的优缺点。这些常见的教学方法包括语法翻译法、直接教学法、听说教学法、情景教学法、交际教学法、任务型教学法。另外，我们还要重点介绍其他一些教学法。

1. 语法翻译法（The Grammar-Translation Method）。又称翻译法（Translation Method）、传统法（Traditional Method）、阅读法（Reading Method）或古典法（Classical Method）。是用母语翻译教授外语书面语的一种方法，即用语法讲解加翻译练习的方式来教学外语的方法。语法翻译法的典型教学流程：复习—新授单词—教授语法—讲解课文—巩固练习—布置作业。优点是帮助学生深刻理解抽象复杂的语法，学生可以掌握大量语法和词汇、有利于写作，课堂教学简洁方便，易于教师管理，也易于检验学习成果,对教师要求降低。不足是重书面,轻口语,教师权威性不利于课堂教学开展,不利于培养学生的积极性,过分强调语法,与现实生活脱离,使学生过分依赖翻译,语言无法自动生成。

2. 直接教学法(The Direct Method)。直接教学法是一种不借助母语,直接用要教授的语言进行教学的方法。简单地说,就是用外语教外语。主要特点是直接用外语思维,初级阶段不进行系统的语法教学,教学中完全不使用或大部分时间不用母语进行语言与翻译练习,以避免母语的干扰,重视语音和口语教学,语言学习中注重文化知识的灌输。优点是1)重视语音、语调和口语教学,有利于增强听与说的能力。2)重视模仿、朗读和熟记等语言实践,有利于培养学生正确的语音、语调、外语语感及语言习惯。3)重视使用实物、图画、手势、动作等各种直观教具进行外语教学,加速了外语和客观事物的直接联系,有利于学生理解、掌握语言材料和组织思维,活跃课堂气氛,激发学习积极性。不足是1)忽视母语的作用。当讲解一些抽象的概念的词或语法规则时,极容易造成误解,又浪费时间。2)忽视学生或成年人学习外语的特点,完全照搬幼儿习得母语的方法,给外语教学带来不必要的困难。3)忽视语法和读写能力的培养。4)对教师的口语水平要求过高,过于依赖教师的教学技能。

3. 听说教学法(The Audio-lingual Method)。听说教学法(The Audio-lingual Method)是一种以对话模仿和句型操练为主要教学活动,以"刺激—反应—强化"为主要教学程序,采用准确定向的教学方式。

听说教学法的教学理念是1)听说领先,在口语的基础上培养书面语;2)围绕句型学习语言,把教学过程看成是刺激—反应—强化过程;3)语言是一套习惯。要反复模仿、记忆和操练;采用准确定向的教学方式;要求学生的表达准确,有错必纠;4)提倡用直观的手段,尽量不使用母语。5)对比结构,确定难点。6)讲语法知识,主张通过归纳法掌握语法。优点是强调外语教学的实践性,要求熟练地掌握句型。句型操练体系的运用既避免了语法翻译法繁琐的语法分析、抽象推理,又不像直接法那样对教师的外语水平和组织教学的能力有很高的要求,有利于外语语言习惯的养成。

重视听说训练,使学生在外语学习的初级阶段,根据有限的材料就能流利地听说外语。不足是句型操练脱离语言内容和社会环境,过于注重机械操练,不利于学生对外语的真正掌握;过于注重训练的语言形式,忽视语言训练的内容和意义,学的语言很不自然;教学方法机械、单调,使学生容易产生厌倦情绪。

4. 情境教学法(Situational Teaching Method)。情境教学法是指在教学过程中,教师有目的地引入或创设具有一定情绪色彩的、以形象为主体的生动具体的场景,以引起学生一定的态度体验,从而帮助学生理解教材,并使学生的心理机能能得到发展的教学方法。情境教学法的核心在于激发学生的情感。基本途径表现在 1)生活展现情境,2)实物演示情境,3)图画再现情境,4)音乐渲染情境,5)表演体会情境,6)语言描述情境。优点是符合新课程标准的基本理念,具体表现在符合以学生发展为中心,注重学生的主体地位,符合激发学生学习兴趣,符合培养学生核心素养的意识,符合关注个体差异与不同需求,确保每个学生发展。不足在于不易把握教学的进程和效率。

5. 交际教学法(The Communicative Approach)与 3P 教学法。交际教学法是以培养学生的语言交际能力为目的、以意义为主的交际性活动为主要教学活动的教学方式。其特点是教学过程交际化,突出学生主体;语言教学以流畅为主,而不是以准确为主,交际的最终评判标准是意义倾向的真实转达,对学生的语言错误采取容忍的态度;不排斥讲解语法;以学生为中心,教师作用体现在主导作用。

"3P"教学法是在 20 世纪 70 年代形成的交际语言教学(Communicative Language Teaching,即 CLT)模式下的产物。"3P"教学法把语言教学分为以下三个阶段:演示(presentation)→操练(practice)→成果(production)。在教学过程中教师通过对语言知识的呈现和操练让学生掌握,然后再让学生在控制或半控制状态之下进行假设交际,从而达到语言的输出,形成学习成果。

6. 任务(型)教学法(Task-based Teaching)。任务型教学法是从 20 世纪 80 年代逐渐发展起来,是教育部制定的中学英语课程标准所推荐和提倡的外语教学法。它是指教师通过引导语言学习者在课堂上完成任务来进行的教学。在教学活动中,教师应当围绕特定的交际和语言项目,设计出具体的、可操作的任务,学生通过表达、沟通、交涉、解释、询问等各种语言活动形式来完成任务,以达到学习和掌握语言的目的。

其优点是 1)完成多种多样的任务活动,有助于激发学生的学习兴趣。2)在完成任务的过程中,将语言知识和语言技能结合起来,有助于培养学生综合的语言运用能力。3)促进学生积极参与语言交流活动,启发想象力和创造性思维,有利于发挥学生的主体性作用。4)在任务型教学活动中,在教师的启发下,每个学生都有独立思考、积极参与的机会,易于保持学习的积极性,养成良好的学习习惯。应该说任务型教学法对教师的影响较大,教师的教学过程环节深深留下了任务型教学法的印痕,如 pre-, while-, post-等,但是实际上大多数教师并没有真正实施任务型教学法。

7. 全身反应法(Total Physical Response)。全身反应法倡导把语言和行为联系在一起,通过身体动作教授外语。主要特点是 1)听力理解领先,首先培养学生的听力理解能力,然后再要求学生用口语表达。2)学生应通过身体对语言的反应动作来提高理解力。这种身体反应应该由教师用计划的指令来控制。学生根据教师的指令做出相应的动作,从而感知并理解掌握语言。3)允许学生在预先做好准备的情况下发言。教师不强迫学生发言。4)教学应强调教学的意义而不是形式,这样可以降低学生的紧张情绪。

优点是 1)它能够一下子就抓住学生的注意力,吸引学生参加活动,让他们在身临其境的实验体验中学习英语。教学的重点在于帮助学生理解英语、用英语交流,不在于纠正学生在学习过程中所犯的错误。这样做有利于帮助学生消除紧张心理,让学生在一个不用害怕挫败的环境中学习。2)它能够提供一个与实际生活紧密相连的学习环境,使学生在多种多样的活动中、在循环反复的练习中学会英语。3)协调学生的左、右脑,有助于学生的左脑发展以及语言学习的成效。学生通过听觉来吸收信息,是由左脑来完成的,而将这些信息用肢体动作表达出来是通过右脑来完成的。4)全身反应法这一教学方法,验证了"快乐"是人类的基本需求。人们喜欢活动给他们提供生理的、认知的、心理的快乐。5)主张以句子为教学单位,整句学、整句用,重视语言内容和意义,有利于培养学生实际运用语言进行交际的能力。6)采用大量挂图、小纸条等教具,创设语言情境。

不足体现在 1)该教学法只适用于语言学习的初级阶段,其动作及言语大都是简单的动作,不可能单靠它学习较深的内容,必须同别的方法结合在一起使用。2)TPR 教学中包含了大量的游戏活动、角色表演、小组竞赛等,而孩子一开心就手舞足蹈,没有好的课堂教学管理模式,再好的教学方法,再丰富的教学活动,也难以取得预期的效果。

8. 沉默法(The Silent Way)。沉默教学法认为,在课堂上,教师应尽量少说话,而鼓励学生多说话。沉默教学法理论设定了三条基本假设:其一,让学习者自己去发现或创造,而不是去背诵和复述那些指定他们学习的东西,这样会有利于他的学习。其二,如有一些物体的帮助,学习也会变得容易些。其三,通过利用解决问题的方法来学习语言,会使学习变得容易些。

沉默教学法遵循一个原则,那就是成功的学习需要学习者对语言学习的投入。首先是有沉思的意识,然后是积极主动地试用。沉思可以给大脑最多的机会去从语言中获得信息;沉思可以允许并强迫学习者对所学材料付出最多的注意力和进行最佳的加工处理。

优点在于 1)使学生积极参与课堂活动。2)激发学生潜能,培养学生自主性。教师在课堂中鼓励学生各抒己见,积极主动思考。3)使教师充分了解学生的学习需求,便于因材施教。不足在于 1)浪费学生学习时间。在课堂中老师很少说话,即使学生出现错误也不能及时指出。2)适合学习自主性高的学生,不适合学困生。4)在应对较难知识点时无法达到预期效果,学生无法全面系统的理解语法知识。

9. 五步教学法。中英合编的初中英语教材(1993 年正式版)课堂教学采用五步教学法 Revision, Presentation, Drills, Practice, Consolidation。课堂一般采用以下五个步骤,即五步教学法:步骤 1(Step 1):复习(Revision)、步骤 2(Step 2):介绍(Presentation)、步骤 3(Step 3):操练(Drill)、步骤 4(Step 4):练习(Practice)、步骤 5(Step 5):巩固(Consolidation)。这个教学方法因其思路清晰、操作性强、加强了学生的活动和操练受到了教师的欢迎。与此配合的全国和各省市英语优质课大赛又更好地推广和丰富完善了这种教学方法。当时从全国和省市走出的一批优质课获奖选

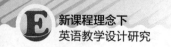
手都成了此种教学法的推广者、传播者、实践者和完善者。

10. 产出导向法（Production-oriented Approach）。产出导向法是文秋芳等外语教育专家在尝试探寻中国特色的外语教学方法过程中提出的教学方法。教学流程包括驱动—促成—评价。驱动要求教师创造并给出交际场景并促使学生尝试完成任务；促成部分要求教师提供输入材料供学生进行选择并尝试产出；评价部分要求教师进行即时和延时评价方式。文秋芳教授在 2016 年对评价部分进行了完善，提出了"师生合作评价"，这是对传统评价方式的完善，认为师生合作评价方式对教师应用产出导向理论具有极大的益处。

产出导向法挑战了"课文中心"的精读教学模式，主张"学用结合"。但由于该教学法理论的提出时间较近，对此理论的尝试和实践研究还不够充分，关于其有效性有待于在以后的实践和研究加以证实。

二 任务型教学本土化研究

1. 任务型教学本土化研究。近几年来，任务型教学这个术语在中学英语教学被使用的频率有所减少，但其对中学英语教学的影响却留下了深深的痕迹。Task（任务）的使用，几乎是中学英语教学设计中必不可少的环节。并且，任务型教学法之后还没有更好的教学法可以替代它，足见其对中学英语教学的影响。鉴于此，继续研究任务型教学法，对它加以改造和重构，使之成为本土化的教学法，扎根于中国英语教学的土壤，就显得尤为必要。

本土化任务型教学模式应具有的主要特征在于 1）针对性。本土化任务型教学模式就是为了适应新课程标准的要求，将任务型教学引进我国的英语教学课堂，结合我国的教学实际而建构的一种教学模式。2）实用性。本土化的任务型教学模式的实用性应体现在它的理论和实际内容非常具体，有较为完整而清晰简明的教学程序，可操作性非常强。3）灵活性。虽然本土化的任务型教学模式有较为完整的教学程序供广大一线教师加以使用，但这个程序不是一成不变的。对于有的步骤，教师在使用时可以根据自己的实际情况，省略或保留。4）发展性。本土化的任务型教学模式作为在一定的理论基础上构建的教学模式，仅仅是这种理论或理念在我国高中英语教学中的一个探索,并不成熟,需要进一步的完善,有较大的发展空间。

5)融合性。在整个本土化的任务型教学模式的建构中,既立足于语言学的理论,也吸收了教育学和心理学的观点,既体现了国外任务型教学模式的精神,又吸收了我国传统英语教学法的精华。特别是在 Jane Williis 任务型教学的教学程序中融入了语法翻译法、听说法、交际法及 RPDPC(复习——呈现——操练——实践——巩固)模式中好的经验和做法,体现了该模式融合性的特点。

本土化任务型教学模式的基本要素"教学模式"表述各异,但有几点是核心的。首先,教学模式与教学理论密切相关。在某种教学理论指导下建立某种相应的教学模式。其次,教学模式与教学目标密切相关。教学模式为达成教学目标服务。第三,教学模式与教学方法相关。某些教学方法适用于某些教学模式,或者某些教学模式要求使用某些教学方法。第四,教学模式与教学结构相关。教学结构从宏观上把握教学活动整体及各教学要素之间内部关系的功能。第五,教学模式与教学程序相关。一种教学模式的建构必须具备下列的基本构成要素:教学理论、教学目标、操作程序、实施条件(对师生的要求、策略、方式、方法、手段等)和评价标准与方法。根据以上分析,本土化任务型教学模式的基本要素为:理论依据、教学目标、操作程序、实施条件、教学原则和评价。

2. Jane Willis 任务学习法的实践与重构

1) Jane Willis 任务学习法三阶段概述。Jane Willis 的经典著作《任务型学习法概览》对任务型教学进行了详尽地叙述。她的任务型学习的三阶段理论是其任务型教学理论的核心。第一阶段,任务前。在这个阶段,教师介绍和定义主题,使用各种活动帮助学生回忆和学习有用的词和词组,确保学生明白指示语;也可以播放别人完成相同或相似任务的录像。学生记下从任务前的活动或录像中获得的有用词或词组;也可以用几分钟时间单个人为完成任务做些准备。第二阶段,任务环。在这个阶段,同伴或小组执行任务。执行任务可以借助于阅读和听力课文。教师则充当监控者,并对学生进行鼓励。之后,小组准备向全班同学汇报完成任务的过程以及他们的发现或决定。可采用草稿或腹稿形式。教师则是为了确保汇报的目的明确,充当语言顾问,帮助学生演练口头。最后同伴或小组向全班同学做口头汇报,或向全班同学呈现书面报告。第三阶段,语言聚焦。学生利用意识强化活动,辨别和分析;如果有必要,教师则可以分析处理课文或记录中得到的特殊语言的特点,也可以询问学生注意到的语言的特点,也可以与学生一起复习每一个分析活动,让学生注意其他有用的词、词组和句型,也可以从汇报环节挑选语言知识。之后进行练习活动,以培养学生的信心。学生可以练习分析活动中的词、词组和句型;练习出现在课文或汇报阶段的语言现象,把有用的语言知识记在笔记本上。如下图所示:

任务前(包括主题和任务)

老师:介绍和定义主题,使用各种活动帮助学生回忆和学习有用的词和词组,确保学生明白指示语;也可以播放别人完成相同或相似任务的录像。

学生:记下从任务前的活动或录像中获得的有用词或词组;也可以用几分钟时间单个人为完成任务做些准备。

任务环

任务	计划	汇报
学生:同伴或小组执行任务。执行任务可以借助于阅读和听力课文。 老师:充当监控者,并对学生进行鼓励。	学生:准备向全班同学汇报完成任务的过程以及他们的发现或决定。可采用草稿或腹稿形式。 老师:确保汇报的目的明确;充当语言顾问;帮助学生演练口头报告或组织书面报告。	学生:向全班同学做口头汇报,或向全班同学呈现书面报告。

语言聚焦

分析	练习
学生:利用意识强化活动,辨别和处理课文或记录中得到的特殊语言的特点,也可以询问学生注意到的语言的特点。 老师:与学生一起复习每一个分析活动,让学生注意其他有用的词、词组和句型,也可以从汇报环节挑选语言知识。	老师:如果有必要,在分析活动后进行练习活动,以培养学生的信心。 学生:练习分析活动中的词、词组和句型;练习出现在课文或汇报阶段的语言现象。把有用的语言知识记在笔记本上。

(摘译自 Jane Willis 的《任务学习法概览》)

　　从以上概述我们可以看出,在 Jane Willis 任务型教学中,任务始终处于中心地位,学生每个阶段都在为任务而做事。它侧重于对学生完成任务的能力和策略的培养,重视学生在完成任务中的参与和交流活动中所获得的经验。学生为完成任务进行合作交流,并且以交流为目的真实地使用语言。学生是学习的中心,教师充当帮助者、监控者和语言顾问。总之,Jane Willis 的任务型学习活动强调"意义至上、使用至上"的原则。

　　2) Jane Willis 任务学习法在我国英语教学实践中的局限性。第一、由于国外的英语教学大多是小班教学,在每次介绍主题、组织学生执行任务前,教师不需要花费太多的时间对学生进行分组,学生在活动中有较多的机会可以互相合作、互相交流。而在我国目前的英语课堂中,即使比较标准的班级,学生人数也有 50 多人,相当多的班级有 60 人左右,甚至更多。如果教师不采用多种形式进行分组,学生间的交流将会非常有限。因此,Jane Willis 任务学习法缺少对学生分组的步骤。第二、对第二语言环境下的学生来说,完成任务所需要的知识远比在外语环境下的中国学生多得多,因此,增加一个复习环节,专门作为一个操作步骤,以激活学生的旧知识,是十分必要的。在语言聚焦阶段,让学生根据上下文进行翻译练习,对巩固新知识也将非常有益。第三、任务型教学要求多层次、多角度、多形式地评价学生的学习过程和结果,重视过程性评价,这在国外的语言教学中十分常见。而我国传统教学中经常采用的却是单一性的终结性评价,这种评价方式根本无法适应任务型教学的需要。因此,应增加"任务评价"的内容,以体现对学生完成任务的过程和结果的评价。第四、在 Jane Willis 任务型学习三个阶段中,教师基本上充当了帮助者、监控者和组织者的角色。而在我们的长期教学中,我们认为听说法中的教师讲述教学内容、交际法中的教师呈现新课等好的作法,更好地发挥教师的主导作用。第五、在第二语言环境下,学生在任务完成过程中习得和学得的语言,课后可以立即应用于实际的生活。但对中国学生来说,学生离开英语课堂,面临的是汉语环境,无法应用所学知识。因此,流行于我国中学英语教学多年的 RPDPC 模式(即"复习——呈现——操练——实践——巩固"模式,简称 RPDPC 模式)中的实践步骤,让任务重演,可以弥补语言环境缺乏的不足。

3）Jane Willis 任务学习法的实践与重构。基于教学实践和上述评析，我们将 Jane Willis 的任务型学习三阶段改造为四个阶段、八个步骤，如下图所示：

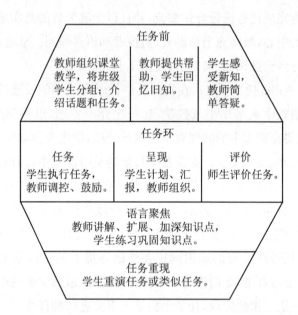

按照这个阶段模式图，重构后的任务型教学分为：任务前、任务环、语言聚焦和任务重现四个阶段，并从以下八个步骤进行操作：第一步，组织课堂教学、导入话题和任务要点。组织课堂教学主要指教师按任务将学生分组。分组方法要灵活多样，多提供学生间交流的机会。在此基础上，教师可采用问题导入法、话题导入法、谜语导入法、游戏导入法、简笔画导入法、实物导入法、体态语导入法等，引导学生进入话题，并借助话题展示任务。第二步，回忆旧知识要点。教师充分发挥自己的主导作用，调动学生的积极性，用比赛、列表等形式帮助学生激活记忆中与话题和任务有关的语言知识。此环节也可以穿插第一步中进行。第三步，感受新知识要点。当学生原有的知识远远不足以完成任务时，教师可以让学生阅读新课（对话、课文或教师特制的电脑课件），提示学生从中找出自己认为与话题和任务有关的知识。这些工作可以放在课堂上进行，如果学生有预习的好习惯，也可以放在课前进行。在阅读新课，查找与话题和任务相关的知识时，学生肯定会遇到一些问题和困难,此时教师对学生提出问题只须加以简单提示,让学生对这些新知识略加感受,能尝试使用就行了。有些话题和任务相对简单,学生原有的知识可以用来完成任务,此步骤可省略。第四步,执行任务要点。在前三步的基础上,学生就可以执行任务了。在执行任务的过程中,教师在学生中来回走动,充当调控者、激励者,还要起到记录员的作用,及时记录学生为执行任务进行语言交际时出现的问题,以及超出他们能力不能表达的语言。教师要鼓励学生采用换说法,手势体态语等形式,必要时也可以使用母语,继续完成任务。第五步,呈现任务。学生在任务完成后,各小组由小组长组织,计划向全班汇报,汇报既要包括任务的结果,也要包括他们在完成任务中遇到的语言困难,在汇报语言困难时,学生可适当运用母语,最后根据小组的计划,教师依次安排各小组汇报任务。第六步,评价任务要点。任务汇报结束后,教师组织全班同学和部分学生代表对各小组完成任务的情况进行评价,教师要做好指导者,也可以参与评价。第七步,扩展加深、练习巩固新知识要点。教师可用投影片将第三步和学生执行任务过程中出现的语言困难展示出来,教师先讲解这些语言知识的基本用法,让学生对它们有一个感性认识,然后扩展和加深这些知识,使学生以后能灵活运用这些知识,同时也为高考服务。此步骤的巩固练习要求教师精选词语或句型来练,要放在上下文语境中有针对性地练,要精练。第八步,重演任务要点。此步骤是本土化的任务型教学特有的步骤。任务型教学根本目的就在于要求学生在课堂上通过完成真实生活的任务而达到以后用英语进行实际交际的目的,既然我们缺乏语言环境,就可以采用此环节进行弥补。同时学生经过前面几个步骤的练习和巩固,已具备了完成此任务的语言能力,重演任务会让学生更好地体验成功的喜悦,另外,根据笔者的体会,即使重演同一任务,有些学生也会创造性地加以改变,这样就能更好地培养学生灵活运用语言的能力。因此,教师可以要求学生创造性地重演任务,也可以略将任务改动,让学生来完成。这些任务可以留作课后作业,作为课上任务的延续,还可以让学生在下节课的前几分钟时间内展示,作为对上节课知识的复习和巩固。第一步、第二步和第三步为任务前阶段,第四步、第五步和第六步为任务环阶段,第七步为语言聚焦阶段,第八步为任务重现

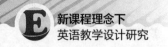

阶段。

4) 任务型教学本土化的典型课例

现以全日制普通高级中学教科书(必修)英语第一册下(Senior English for China Student's Book 1B)第 14 单元 Festivals 第二课时为例：

教学目的：创建班级节日(create a class festival)；培养学生运用英语进行真实交际的能力；通过学生完成任务，培养学生的合作能力；学生掌握一些与创建节日有关的语言知识。

教学重点：创建一个真实的班级及节日

教学难点：学生完成任务的过程

教学过程：

Step 1 Organizing class and Leading in(组织课堂教学、导入话题和任务)

T：Good morning, class.

Ss：Good morning, teacher.

T：How many students are there in your class?

Ss：Sixty-four.

T：Oh, a very big class. Would you like me to divide it into seven groups?

Ss：Ok.

T：You nine, would you like to form a group?

You ten, group 2, ok?

And you nine, group 7.

教师将学生分成 7 个小组后，就可以导入话题和任务了。

T：Now, we have seven groups. Would you like to a play a game?

Ss：Of course, what game?

T：A guessing game. Can you guess what's in my hand?

教师边说边举起握着的一只手。

S1：Money!

T：No.

S2：Air!

T：Of course not.

S3：……

T：Look，what is it?

Ss：Oh! Firecrackers!

T：What are firecrackers used for?

Ss：to celebrate festivals.

用猜东西的游戏，教师导入了今天的话题——节日。

T：Yes，then how much do you know about festivals?

S4：the Spring Festival

S5：the Mid-autumn Festival

…

教师此时可组织男生、女生间的比赛，看哪一组学生说出的节日名称多。教师还可采用头脑风暴法复习旧知、激活学生的记忆。

S6：Celebrate the festival.

S7：create a festival.

S8：Let out firecrackers.

T：Do you have your class festival?

Ss：Our class festival?

T：Yes，I know your class is a good class in your school，and you've done everything very well. I think such a good class should have its own class festival. Do you think so?

Ss：Yes.

T：Why not create our class festival?

此时，教师布置本次的任务——创建班级节日。

Step 2 Reading for language points for festivals.（阅读探究与节日有关的语言知识）

（1）Reading the passage "The Birth of a Festival" on page 10.

（2）Talk about what Ss learn from the passage about the festival （General ideas）。

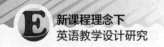
（3）Exchange the ideas about the language points that can be used to create a new festival. Let Ss work in groups. The group leader writes down what they have discussed and then reports the difficulties to the teacher.

For example：

（a）a seven-day festival celebrating the culture and history of ...

（b）get together to greet ...

（c）get together to think about ...

（d）have a long history and a rich culture

（e）have ... in common

（f）celebrate the harvest

（g）give thanks for life

（h）honour sb.

（i）build unity of ...

（j）build our lives，think for ourselves and speak for ourselves

（k）remember our past and build our future

（l）enjoy the spirit of ...

（m）enjoy a large meal

（n）keep our culture alive

（o）share our hopes for a happy future

对学生来说，以上语言知识虽然是新知识，但教师在此只需用英语稍加解释，让学生明白意思就行了。

例如：

a seven-day festival celebrating the culture and history of ...：a seven-day festival which celebrates the culture and history of ...

Step 3 Performing the task（执行任务）

T：Now it is your turn to create a festival. The following questions and the form may help you.

（1）When would you celebrate it?

Why would you celebrate it?

How would you celebrate it?

What principles would you use?

（2）Name of the festival：

Date：

Meaning：

Principles：

How is the festival celebrated?

What is the symbol of the festival?

学生以小组为单位,讨论确定班级节日的名字、日期、意义、原因、庆祝节日的过程、以及班级节日的标志。

各小组成员畅所欲言,发表自己的看法,小组长负责协调不同的意见,达到小组内统一的意见,并记下在交谈中遇到的语言困难。

教师四处走动,促进小组的活动,同时把听到的不正确的表达记录下来。

例:教师听到学生说"We are too tired, so I want to celebrate a festival, which we can rest."教师就可以记录下来,在后面步骤中指出 which 应改为 where,并对定语从句的知识加以巩固;还可以把学生使用的"rest"的用法,扩展到"relax oneself"。

Step 4 Reporting the task（呈现任务）

（1）Planning,小组讨论确定向全班同学汇报的形式。例如:选择一位口语好的同学向全班同学介绍自己的班级节日;采用一问一答的形式介绍自己小组的班级节日;采用实物投影仪展示自己的班级节日的描述;采用活动的形式像演小品一样展示自己的班级节日等。

（2）Reporting,计划确定以后,各个小组按自己的计划向全班同学汇报自己创建的班级节日。

Step 5 Evaluating the task（任务的评价）

教师可以把完成任务情况分为 A.出色,B.尚好,C.一般,D.需努力四个等级,从个人、小组和教师的角度对任务进行评价。

评价方式	评价等级	简单评语
个人评价		
小组评价		
教师评价		

Step 6 Expanding, intensifying and consolidating the language points(扩展加深、练习巩固新知识)

在这个步骤中,教师把学生在步骤 2、3、4 所遇到的一些语言问题加以讲解、扩展,并可采用语法翻译法、交际法等模式的一些环节进行巩固练习。

例如 get together to do sth,教师可以扩展为 gather to do sth, meet to do sth, assemble to do sth,之后让同学编几个对话。例如:

——I hear we are going to visit the Youth Palace at 3 tomorrow afternoon.

——Really? That's great. Where shall we gather(to go there).

再如:教师让学生将下列汉语翻译成英语。

(1) Mrs. Robinson,我想请你召集所有工作人员。We'll have an important meeting in the meeting room right now.

(2) I have some close friends.我们朋友每年聚会一次。It's really a time when we talk freely and enjoy ourselves.

(3) 好久没有和汤姆见面了。I miss him very much. Do you know if everything is going well with him?

Step 7 performing the task again(重演任务)

教师选择一组,或选取一些口语好的学生组成一个新小组,在步骤 6 的基础上,重演任务。

S1(group leader):Hi, everyone, would you please get together to listen to me? What do you think of our class?

S2:Good, of course. We are always doing very well in everything in our school? Everyone knows our class, I think.

S3:Yes, I think so.

S4：We are all proud of our class.

S1：(group leader)：But do you think it a pity that we haven't a class festival?

S4：Why should we have a class festival?

S5：Do it matter much that we have a class festival?

S1(group leader)：Yes, it matters much to us. It is a symbol for our class. It will show our unity.

S2：Show the characteristics of our class.

S5：I didn't think of that. Why not create a class festival right now?

S3：What does a class festival contain?

S1：A name.

S2：Its name should be Class 6 festival, of course.

S5：When is it celebrated?

S4：You mean we should fix a date for our class festival.

S5：Yes.

S1：What about April 7th? The day before the School Spring Sports Meeting.

S2：Good idea.

S3：Why is it that?

S2：That day, everyone will meet to discuss our sports events.

S1：So that is how we will celebrate our class festival.

We can hold a class meeting and call every one in our class to do something for our class. Competitors can relax themselves, while others can prepare some slogans.

S5：What kind of slogan?

S4：Faster, stronger and higher, which can help us enjoy the spirit of the Olympic Games.

S5：But that's not ours.

S2：Class 6, number 1.

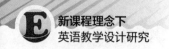
S1：Good，it can be used as the symbol of our class festival. Tom，would you please to write down what we discussed just now，and we should plan to report to the class next.

S3：With pleasure.

三　自主型课堂研究——六步教学

1. 自主课堂的内涵。自主有效的课堂应该是一种灵动的课堂。学生自我决定课堂目标和自我发展目标，自选学习方法，自主探究，并且独立对教学和学习效果进行评价、总结和补救。教师的作用则是引导和帮助学生在自主课堂中的活动，为学生的学习提供方法和策略指导，对学生学习结果的不足进行补充和提示。

2. 高中英语自主课堂教学原则结合英语学科特点，高中英语自主课堂教学原则可以归纳如下：(1)以促进语言实际运用能力和自主学习能力的提高为课堂教学目标。(2)教师与学生角色的精准定位。(3)教学组织形式多样化。(4)教学内容丰富多样。(5)教学评价方式多样化。

3. 高中英语自主课堂教学模式的理论依据。(1)英语课程标准。英语课程标准认为语言运用能力的培养、有效的学习策略、积极的情感态度和正确价值观的形成都必须通过学生主动参与大量语言实践活动才能得以实现。(2)人本主义教学理论。罗杰斯的人本主义教学理论主张教师要认真组织好教材以便于学生自己学习，要用咨询、辅导等方式启发学生自己去发现、去创造；要采用学生自我评价的办法，以代替外来的学习评价。(3)建构主义学习理论。建构主义学习和教学理论把学生自主学习的教学环节以一种明确的线性关系排列了出来：创设问题情境—学生自主学习—小组讨论—结果评价。这为构建高中英语自主学习课堂教学模式提供了框架。

4. 高中英语自主课堂教学模式的操作程序。借鉴现有的自主学习课堂教学研究成果，我们提出的英语自主课堂模式操作程序主要包括六步：1)定任务、2)读材料、3)议问题、4)解疑惑、5)讲规律、6)测所学。下面就各环节进行详细的说明：(1)定任务：学生确立学习任务。这一阶段，学生的主要任务是确定和明确自己的学习目标,清楚地认识到自己在本节课中需要学什么,应该达到什么标准,以及如何达到这些标准。教师不仅要为学生分析教材的教学活动和认知层次,根据活动要求明确教学目标,还要将目标具体为行为表现,以便学生更好的达成。(2)读材料:学生自主学习相关材料。本环节是学生自主学习相关教学内容的过程。在这一过程中教师应保证给予学生充足的自主学习时间,要根据不同阶段的教学目标选取相应的教学内容和教学方式,在学生自主学习过程中,要随时监控学生的表现,并给予肯定和拨正,以保证学生的自主学习质量,要根据科学的教育理念指导和培养学生自学能力与技巧。(3)议问题:学生合作讨论问题。在合作讨论环节,学生会在自己所属的小组中就自主学习环节中所产生的问题进行交流与探究,并对同伴的表现通过肯定和质疑的方式给予评价与反馈。当然,教师也会巡场监控小组讨论进度,并随时给予必要的协助。(4)解疑惑:学生分享讨论结果,初步解决问题。这一环节中,充当汇报员角色的小组成员要分享所在小组的讨论结果,其他成员则要随时准备解答来自其他小组的问题和质疑。而教师要思考的就是如何组织好大家畅所欲言,如何协调好小组间的你来我往。(5)讲规律:教师讲授相关知识与规律。教师的讲解不必从头开始,而是要根据在监控小组内部活动和小组间交流所获得的反馈信息,针对学生的难点讲解,并对该课堂的教学重点给予强调。教师的讲解应该侧重于知识的结构和逻辑关系以及要注重学习创新和发散思维的培养。(6)测所学:学生对自身学习情况进行检测。学生进行自我检测的最终目的仍然是促进教学目标的实现。教师要引导学生认识到自我检测对其自身发展的重要作用,同时要给学生提供明确的自我检测内容和采取的方式。学生自我检测的内容和方式需灵活多样,以适应不同层次,不同个性的学生的需求。

这六个环节还需要两点保障。第一、学生自我评价。如果学生的自我评价为否,那学生有两种处理方式选择,一是直接寻找老师帮助,二是回到所在小组中与同伴进行探讨后,再跟教师确认结果。第二、教师进行教学评价。在自主课堂中,教师的教学评估和总结是教学活动必不可少的一个组成部分。教师充分利用评价的导向作用,可对教学产生积极的作用。

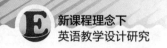
5. 六步教学案例

高中英语自主型课堂语法课教学设计
——以只能用 V-ING 形式做宾语的动词归纳为例

教学背景分析

教学内容分析

高中英语人教版选修七的前三单元的语法学习任务是非谓语动词。第一单元学习动词不定式作主语、表语、宾语、宾语补足语、定语和状语；第二单元学习动词不定式的被动语态；第三单元学习 V-ing 形式。本节课是在前三单元的基础上，对 V-ing 形式作宾语的细化，重点梳理只能用V-ing形式的动词，并加以强化。

学生情况分析

参与上课的是我校 2015 级高二（一）班 43 名学生。2015 级高二（一）班是我校的理科好班，学生的整体学习素质和能力相对较好，但英语偏科的现象还是很相当突出，大部分学生对语法的学习相当吃力。课堂上如果老师通过讲解语法并配以大量练习，效果会很不理想。选取一个或两个语法点，通过讨论、感悟、发现等小步子教学比较适合学生的情况。

教学目标分析

基于教学内容和学生情况的分析，本节课的教学目标设定为：

1）学生能够知道中学阶段只能用 V-ing 形式的动词；

2）学生能够通过一定方法记忆这些动词；

3）学生能够自己思考、小组讨论、巩固练习熟练掌握这些动词；

4）学生通过这些动词的掌握，逐步减少对语法学习的畏难情绪，增加英语学习的兴趣。

教学重难点分析

在教学目标的引领下，本节课教学重点为掌握只能用 V-ing 形式的动词，难点为记忆、领会、应用这些动词。

教学方法　六步教学法，归纳法

教学过程

教学环节	时间分配	教 师 活 动	学生活动	设计意图
Step 1 定任务	2—3 分钟	1. 教师展示高中英语人教版必修七一段课文(P20),请一学生找出其中的 V-ing 形式。 Without pausing we jumped into the boat with the other whalers and headed out into the bay. I looked down into the water and could see Old Tom swimming by the boat, showing us the way. A few minutes later, there was no Tom, so George started beating the water with his oar and there was Tom, circling back to the boat, leading us to the hunt again. From James's face, I could see he was terrified of being abandoned by us. 2. 教师请一学生说出其中做宾语的 V-ing 形式。 3. 教师板书课题:只能用 V-ing 形式做宾语的动词	1. 学生找出 V-ing 形式。 2. 学生说出 V-ing 形式。	激活学生已有 V-ing 形式的知识,导入本节课的任务。
Step 2 读材料	(7—8 分钟)	教师分发填空练习,让学生根据所给词的正确形式填空。 1) It seemed the sea lion didn't mind ____ ____ (photograph) with the tourists after all. 2) In fact, the chances of anybody _____ (swallow) by a whale are rather low, said the researcher. 3) The is tired of _____ (shout at) by his boss. 4) We're considering _____ (pay) a visit to the Science Museum. 5) Tom pretended _____ (not hear) about it, but in fact, he knew it very well. (速度慢的同学,只做前六题) 6) She insisted on _____ (give) the hardest work. 7) He couldn't bear _____ (make fun of) like that. 8) They only allow _____ (smoke) in restricted areas. (速度快的同学做 8 个小题)	1. 学生思考、填出正确形式。 2. 不同层次的同学选择不同的任务。	在承认学生不同层次的基础上,促使学生思考、判断,并完成材料要求。
Step 3 议问题	(5分钟左右)	教师请学生以小组为单位讨论所填形式并说出在句子中所做成分。	学生以小组为单位讨论所填形式并说出在句子中所做成分。	促使学生通过讨论产生问题并就问题互教互学。

续表

教学环节	时间分配	教 师 活 动	学生活动	设计意图
Step 4 解困惑	(10—12分钟)	教师分小组提问,并请同学再次尝试解答。	1.学生以小组为单位提问经过讨论仍然没有解决的问题。 2.其他同学或老师解答。	解决学生讨论后仍然不懂的问题。
Step 5 讲规律	(5—8分钟)	1.教师用 PPT 对只能用 V-ing 形式做宾语的动词进行归纳。 M：mind, miss, mention E：enjoy, escape, excuse I：imagine, insist on, involve P：practice, pardon U：understand C：consider H： A：admit, allow, avoid, advise, appreciate R：risk, require, resist F：finish, fancy 2.教师用一句"妹妹不吃咖啡"给出记忆规律。 即：mei mei pu chi car fi,它是由单词的首字母组成的,且每个单词只能用 V-ing 形式做宾语。	学生边听边看,记下老师归纳的规律。	帮助学生找出规律。
Step 6 测所学	(5—8分钟)	1.教师让学生同伴活动,根据"妹妹不吃咖啡"这句话说出只能用 V-ing 形式做宾语的动词。 2.教师用 PPT 给出五个选择题,让学生判断。 1) Do you feel like ____ for dinner with me tonight? A. to go out B. go out C. going out D. gone out 2) —How can I improve my spoken English? —You have to practice ____ as much as possible. A. speak B. speaking C. spoken D. to speak 3) He put off ____ a decision till he had more information. A. make B. to make C. making D. made	1.学生同伴活动,记忆只能用 V-ing 形式做宾语的动词。 2.学生做选择题、改错题和语法填空题。 3.学生记下课后作业。	通过各种形式巩固学生所掌握的规律,并帮助学生灵活运用。

教学环节	时间分配	教 师 活 动	学生活动	设计意图
		4）They couldn't help when hearing the good news. A. jumping　　　　B. to jump C. jumped　　　　D. jump 5）Before he came，I'd finished _____ the whole book. A. to read　　　　B. to have read C. reading　　　　D. read 3. 教师用 PPT 给出五个改错题，让学生改正。 1）Doctors recommended being taken a walk after supper.（　　） 2）Government has to prevent the tourism areas from polluted.（　　） 3）The doctor advised take more exercise.（　　） 4）I prefer swim to playing basketball.（　　） 5）With no evidence，he refused to acknowledge to steal the lady's purse.（　　） 4. 教师给出一段含有 5 个空的段落，让学生用所给词的正确形式填空。 Jack was born in 1982 in a poor family. When he was only 11，his father became mentally ill and one day he _____ （come）back with an abandoned（被遗弃的）baby girl. A year later，his mother left home with his younger brother because she couldn't stand _____ （live）the hard life and the pressure from her mad husband. The 12-year-old boy began to _____ （support）his whole family：he took care of not only his sick father，but also the little girl. At the same time，he didn't give up _____ （study）. Later he went to college. _____ （care）for the little girl，he rented a room near his college and afforded her education by _____ （do）part-time jobs. After the young man's story went public，he was regarded as a hero in people's eyes. 5. 教师布置作业，用 V-ing 形式做宾语写出 10 个句子。		

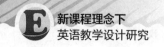
板书设计

> 只能用 V-ing 形式做宾语的动词归纳
>
> 1. without pausing(做介词的宾语)
>
> Started beating the water(做动词的宾语)
>
> …was terrified of being abandoned by us

教学评价或反思

下课以后教师将从以下几个方面进行评价和反思:教学目标达成情况,学生课堂参与情况,教师的讲解和课堂掌控情况,小组活动情况,课堂生成情况,对"六步教学"的思考。

四 英语学习方法概述

本节论述了在英语中重要的几种学习方法。包括合作学习法,发现学习法,自主学习法和探究学习法。

1. 合作学习

合作学习法是提高教学质量的重要方法,它对于提高学生运用知识的能力起着极其重要的作用。所有的合作学习方法都具有合作激励结构和合作任务结构两个重要成分。在合作激励结构中,两个或更多的个人相互依赖,共享小组活动成功的果实。合作任务结构允许鼓励或要求两个或更多的个人一起工作,群策群力,以完成某个学习目标或任务。合作学习法具有以下特点:第一,学生以小组为单位,共同完成学术任务。第二,奖励机制是以小组为导向而不是以个人为导向。第三,小组内部的交往由小组成员自己控制。第四,小组按其成员能力高、中、低水平和不同性别进行组织。

2. 发现学习

发现学习这一概念由布鲁纳于 20 世纪 50 年代末提出,它意指要学习的内容不是以定论的形式存在,而是只存在有关线索或例证,学习者必须经历一个发现过程,自己得出结论或找到答案。

3. 接受学习

接受学习这一概念由奥苏贝尔加以明确化,所指的是要学习的内容是以定论的方式呈现,学习者可以直接获取,不需要经历发现过程。接受学习的特征是学习的主要内容是由教材或教师以定论的方式呈现,学习者不需要发现,只需要接受或理解。在这种接受或理解中,贯穿着教师系统的有计划地指导。

4. 自主学习

"自主学习"(autonomous learning)有时又称"学习者自主"(learner autonomy)。对自主学习概念的理解也不尽相同,其观点大致有下列三种:第一种观点认为自主学习是一种学习模式或学习方式。程晓堂认为自主学习有以下三方面的含义:一是学习者的态度、能力和学习策略等因素综合而成的一种主导学习的内在机制,就是学习者指导和控制自己学习的能力;二是学习者对自己的学习目标、学习内容、学习方法以及使用学习材料的控制权,也就是学习者对这些方面的自由选择的程度;三是一种模式,即学习者在总体教育目标的宏观调控下,在教师的指导下,根据自身条件和需要制订并完成具体学习目标的学习模式。

5. 基于问题的学习和探究性学习

基于问题的学习起源于医学教育,它是指通过理解或解决问题所进行的学习。在这种学习过程中,个体首先面临的是问题,然后以问题为中心或诱因来选用问题解决策略、推理技能,最终获取解决这一问题所需要的知识和技能。探究性学习起源于科学探究实践,它特别强调提出问题、收集和分析证据、形成基于证据的结论。探究式学习具有问题性、参与性、实践性、开放性等基本特点。语言探究式学习是指将探究式学习方式应用到语言学习及教学中去的行为。探究式学习与语言学习相结合,重视语言情境的创设,立足学习任务的解决,强调知识的自主建构,鼓励师生之间的协作与交流。这些探究活动的特点能够促进英语语言基本知识的巩固;促进英语语言听说读写译等基本技能的提高;促进学习者实际运用语言能力的进步。《英语课程标准》(2017)中一条实施建议为:"要为学生提供自主学习和相互交流的机会以及充分表现和自我发展的空间"。英语语言的探究式学习就是通

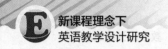
过师生之间、生生之间的互动交流,从而形成掌握英语技能、学会运用英语的能力。另外,英语语言探究式学习具有情境性。英语的探究式学习首先要通过创设情境,促使学生主动参与其中,学生们围绕一定的情境问题开展活动,在真实的语言情境中学会运用语言,实现语言知识的正迁移,最终圆满完成任务,预设问题得到顺利解决。

6. 创新性学习

创新性学习是以学生的自主性、探索性学习为基础,引导学生从自己的生活实际和社会生活中选择和确立研究专题,通过个人或小组合作等形式进行学习,并在学习中善于发现问题、思考问题、探索研究问题以及运用知识来解决问题,具有开创性、自觉性、坚韧性、进取性等意志品质。它包括学生自主学习的意识、强烈的学习愿望、对知识的探究意识、学习积极性和创造力、科学精神和实践能力、收集信息和处理信息的能力以及学生自我进行课题研究和撰写小论文的能力等。

第六节　教学过程

教学过程设计在教学设计中具有十分重要的地位,教学过程包括课程教学程序的安排,还包括具体活动的布置、组织与反馈。

一　教学过程的内涵

这里的教学过程可分为宏观的教学过程和微观的教学过程。宏观的教学过程设计包括分析总教学目标、教学内容、教学对象、编写目标体系、制定教学策略、选择教学媒体、组织教学实践、进行教学评价等环节;而微观的教学过程所指的就是不同的教学环节组成的教学程序。

二　影响教学过程的因素

教学过程设计是否合理操作、是否得当,将直接影响教学目标的达成和教学质量。

而要保证教学的有效进行,就必须了解影响其过程操作的因素。一般说来,影响教学过程的因素有:

1. 教学理念

教师的教学理念是影响其过程设计与具体操作的第一因素。教师对教学过程的认识,对教学模式或教学方法的倾向会直接影响其教学过程的设计。教师对学生在教学过程中所应该扮演的角色的认识将影响其组织活动,影响课堂上教师与学生、学生与学生的互动,也因此影响学习模式的构建及学生学习能力的发展。

2. 活动的组织形式

活动的组织形式同样是影响教学过程的因素之一。小组活动和个体活动,同伴活动和全班活动,活动的组织形式不同,学生之间的交互也就不同。

3. 情感过程

情感过程同样影响教学过程。如果课堂教学引起了焦虑、不安、势必影响学生的文本解码、信息提取及认知加工。当然,引起焦虑不安的可能是文本本身,但是活动的设计、环节的安排、活动的组织以及教师的反馈方式、态度等都可能对实际的课堂操作带来影响。如果文本很难,教师却没有设置准备活动;或者活动很难,教师却没有搭建支架,教学很难以顺利开展。对于学生的成功教师不表扬,对学生的欠佳表现不鼓励,而是斥责等,师生的互动就难以开展。

三 英语教学过程设计的策略

1. 课堂教学过程设计要以学生为主体,充分发挥学生主观能动性

结合学生的英语实际水平,旨在帮助学生打下扎实的语言基础,全面提升其英语水平,进而培养学生的核心素养,与此同时发展自主学习能力,提高综合文化素养,满足国家、社会和个人发展的需要。

2. 融合多媒体等现代信息技术教学方式和手段,提高学生英语语言输出能力

英语不仅仅是一门知识,更是一种技能。技能主要是靠反复训练才能

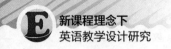

获得。以往的英语教学模式基本上是"老师讲，学生听"，教师是英语教学过程的主体。随着多媒体等现代信息技术教学方式和手段发展和丰富，学生积极主动地参与各种活动的渠道和环境将更加丰富。

四　常见的教学过程程序

常见的英语教学过程主要包括以下几个阶段：激发学习动机阶段、领会知识阶段、巩固知识阶段、运用知识阶段以及检查知识阶段。

1. 激发学习动机阶段

学习兴趣和求知欲是直接推动学生学习的动力，具有浓厚的学习兴趣和学习愿望则是进行学习的基本条件和心理起点。在学习过程中充分激发学生的学习兴趣、调动学生学习的积极性，对于英语学习将会起到至关重要的作用。因此教师应该想方设法培养学生的学习兴趣，激发学生的学习动机和求知欲望。在英语教学过程中，教师所教授的内容以及知识本身对学生要有吸引力，要强调学生的活动，让学生积极主动地参与到教学活动中，同时，教师要引导学生把所学的内容与学生的实际生活联系起来。

2. 领会知识阶段

在英语教学过程中，领会知识是教学过程的中心环节，包括学生感知和理解教材。教师引导学生通过感知形成清晰表象和鲜明观点，为理解抽象的概念提供感性知识的基础并发展学生相应的能力。此外，教师还应该引导学生在感知的基础上，通过分析、比较、抽象概括以及归纳演绎等思维方法的加工，形成概念原理，使学生掌握英语学习的规律。

理解所感知的英语意义是学生学习英语的主要目的之一，在感知英语的基础上理解英语的意义是学生掌握英语的重要环节。言语理解指懂得言语所表述的意思，语言理解是指理解语音、词汇、语法和句型的所表述的概念，结构和用法。理解是以原有的英语知识经验为基础，并通过积极思考实现的。积累丰富的英语感性认识材料并鼓励学生进行积极思维活动能提高理解的效果。理解与思维紧密联系是为了正确理解和使用语言，做到语言得体，必须学习英语语言国家的生活习惯、社会文化、词语概念、禁忌习俗、风土人情、体态语言。此外，教师要有目的地、全面地、创造性地进行思维活动来发展学生的思维能力。

3. 巩固知识阶段

巩固知识是指把所学的英语知识在大脑中记忆和保持,是英语教学过程的一个重要阶段。巩固知识对学生学习英语十分重要。学生在课堂上所获得的英语知识是间接的,容易遗忘,必须通过复习加以巩固。学生只有掌握与记住所学的英语知识,才能为下一步的学习奠定基础,才能顺利地学习新知识、新材料。

学生学习英语必须运用有效的方法及时巩固所学的英语知识,这样才能不断积累扩大和完善英语知识的结构。巩固英语知识是通过识记、保持、再认和回忆的记忆过程实现的。识记、保持是再认和回忆的基础,再认和回忆是识记和保持的结果和发展。巩固知识首先要充分利用无意识记和有意识记、意义识记和机械识记相结合的方法,合理安排识记语言材料和组织复习,以及利用多感官、多渠道、多样化的方法提高记忆英语知识的效果。

4. 运用知识的阶段

英语教学目的是培养学生为交际运用英语的能力,英语知识不用于实践则难以记忆巩固,运用英语知识是加深知识理解、巩固丰富知识、使知识进一步系统化、结构化的根本途径。教师应充分发挥主导作用,随时根据各种反馈信息,对课堂教学进行调控。运用知识是英语教学过程中一个重要阶段,只有加强英语知识的运用,才能完成英语教学任务,提高学生的英语综合运用能力。

5. 检查知识阶段

检查知识是指教师通过作业、提问、测试等对学生的学习效果进行考查的过程。检查学习效果的目的在于教师及时获得关于教学效果的反馈信息,以调整教学进程与要求;帮助学生了解自己掌握知识技能的情况,发现学习上的问题,及时调节自己的学习方式,改进学习方法,提高学习效率。

五 英语教学过程中常采用的教学模式

1. 传统教学模式

我们现在经常把满堂灌的教学称之为传统教学,毫无疑问,语法翻译法

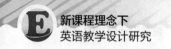
就是传统教学的鼻祖,语法翻译法的教学模式一直是满堂灌的主要形式。语法翻译法的典型教学流程:复习—新授单词—教授语法—讲解课文—巩固练习—布置作业。尽管语法翻译法过分以教师为中心而在新的课程改革背景下遭到批判,但由于它的课堂的可操作、可掌控性而仍有市场。

2.3P 教学模式

3P 教学模式由 presentation,practice,production 三个阶段组成。Presentation 阶段指呈现新知识和语言规则;Practice 阶段是通过各种活动反复操练帮助学生掌握规则;Production 阶段则要求学生能够根据具体要求在交际中应用所学知识,掌握语言技能。3P 教学法多用于语音、词汇、语法教学,有些英语素养好的老师在阅读和写作教学中也有较好的探索。

3.五步教学模式

五步教学即 Revision,Presentation,Drill,Practice,Consolidation。课堂一般采用以下五个步骤(即五步教学法):步骤 1(Step 1):复习(Revision)、步骤 2(Step 2):介绍(Presentation)、步骤 3(Step 3):操练(Drill)、步骤 4(Step 4):练习(Practice)、步骤 5(Step 5):巩固(Consolidation)。这个教学模式因其思路清晰、操作性强、加强了学生的活动和操练受到了许多教师的欢迎。

4.PWP 教学模式

PWP 教学模式主要由学习前(Pre-learning),学习中(While-learning),学习后(Post-learning)三个阶段组成。PWP 教学模式常用于以听、读、写语言技能训练为主的教学中。学习前阶段是教师进行教学准备,学生自我准备,教师激活学生已有知识和能力的阶段,其目的是为了新语言内容的学习进行准备。学习中阶段是学习新语言的阶段,一般是在课堂上进行的,但也可以在课堂之外进行的自我学习活动。在这一阶段教师进行知识呈现、讲解,引导学生进行训练,学生通过学习掌握语言内容,形成运用能力。学习后阶段是学习新语言之后的评价、运用阶段。

5.任务型教学模式

任务型教学可追溯至 20 世纪 80 年代初,这种教学模式是以具体的任务为学习动力或动机,以完成任务的过程为学习过程,以展示任务成果的方式来体现教学效果的教学过程。在我国外语教学中,对于处于基础阶段的学习者来说任务型教学的课堂教学程序包括任务的设计、任务的准备、任务的呈现、任务的展开和任务的评价等五个阶段。

6. 三类活动模式

《普通高中英语课程标准》(2017)倡导英语学习活动观,明确活动是英语学习的基本形式,是学习者学习和尝试运用语言理解与表达意义,发展多元思维,培养文化意识,形成学习能力的主要途径。它包括学习理解、应用实践和创新迁移三类。学习理解类活动主要包括感知与注意、获取与梳理、概括与整合等基于语篇的学习活动;应用实际类活动主要包括概述与阐释、分析与判断、内化与运用等深入语篇的学习活动;迁移创新类活动主要包括推理与论证、批判与评价、想象与创造等超越语篇的学习活动。根据这个理念,我们可以把它转化成我们的课堂教学过程模式,我们姑且称之为三类活动模式。

六　教学过程案例

1. 中文撰写的案例:高三复习课"如何做完形填空"的教学过程

教学环节	时间分配	教 师 活 动	学生活动	设计意图
Step 1:定任务	(2—3分钟)	1. 教师展示班级学生做试卷的一些照片,尤其是一些学生苦苦思索的照片。教师请学生英语试卷中最为困难的题型。教师板书课题:How to do cloze tests	看照片学生列举试卷中最困难的部分。	激发学生兴趣,导入本节课的任务。
Step 2:读材料	(10—15分钟)	教师分发一篇完形填空练习,让学生完成。	学生完成完形填空。做得快的同学可单独提前向老师要答案。	在承认学生不同层次的基础上,促使学生思考、判断,并完成材料要求。
Step 3:议问题	(10分钟左右)	教师展示答案。请学生以小组为单位讨论错误的选项。教师在教室内巡视,帮助小组并记录班级共同的问题。	1. 学生核对答案。2. 以小组为单位讨论错误的选项。	促使学生通过讨论尝试解决问题,并就问题互教互学。

续表

教学环节	时间分配	教 师 活 动	学生活动	设计意图
Step 4：解困惑	（5分钟）	教师请各小组依次提出没有解决的问题，并简明扼要回答。	学生以小组为单位提问经过讨论仍然没有解决的问题。其他同学或老师解答。	解决学生讨论后仍然不懂的问题。
Step 5：讲规律	（5分钟）	2. 教师用PPT对本篇完形填空的特点简明扼要列举。尤其标示题目特点和结题规律。	学生边听边看，记下老师归纳的规律。	帮助学生找出规律。
Step 6：测所学	（5—8分钟）	教师用PPT以单项选择形式给出相关的巩固练习，例如： 1.（2015 全国卷 I）Then my 17-year-old suggested giving him a ＿＿＿47＿＿＿ . I thought about it. We were ＿＿＿＿ 48 (low) ＿＿＿＿ on cash ourselves，but … … When I handed him the gift card，saying he could use it for ＿＿＿＿ 54（whatever） ＿＿＿＿ his family might need，he burst into tears. A. dollar B. job C. hot meal D. gift card	学生做选择题，进一步巩固完形填空的规律。	通过练习巩固学生所掌握的规律，并帮助学生灵活运用。

2. 英文撰写的案例　Teaching Design for Unit 1 Book 5

Title：Great scientists JOHN SNOW DEFEATS "KING CHOLERA" (Reading)

Teaching procedures			
Teaching procedures	**Teacher's activities**	**Students' activities**	**Design intention**
Step 1：Lead in（3 minutes）	3. Greeting. 4. Use electricity to let students guess the occupation of scientists.	3. Welcome. 4. Guess the occupation of scientists.	To help them connect the topic with our life and arouse their attention.

续表

Teaching procedures	Teacher's activities	Students' activities	Design intention
Step 2: Learning and understanding (20 minutes)	4. To be a clever reader. Let students guess the procedures of making a research. 5. To be a fast reader. Ask students to check the procedures of making a research. 6. To be a careful reader. Ask students to find the specific information of each procedures.	3. Guess the procedures of finding a problem, making up the assumption, testing the assumption, getting the conclusion, and finding the solution. 4. Check the procedures and find the specific information.	To train students' reading ability and help them learn to get the procedures by themselves.
Step 3: Applying and practicing (10 minutes)	Role play: Tell students they are the hosts of a program and let them introduce the procedures of making a research.	Make the role play based on our learning.	To help them master the knowledge and use it freely.
Step 4: Transferring and creating (8 minutes)	Discussion: Conclude the quality of John Snow from his research.	Have a discussion with their classmates and share their ideas in the class.	To make them have a creative thinking about the good quality of a scientists and learn from them.
Step 5: Summary (3 minutes)	Tell students that no matter what occupation we want to have, we should learn from John Snow's spirits.	Get the summary from our learning and their discussion.	To help them make our learning clearly and have a correct awareness.
Step 6: Homework (1 minute)	Compulsory homework: Write a composition to make a research about the idea you find in your life. Optional homework: Find the difference between a scientist and a star. Try to make a speech about them.	Ask something about our learning and the task.	To deepen their impression about our learning and give different levels of students more chances to improve themselves.

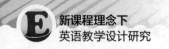

第七节 教学反思与评价

一 教学反思

反思性教学是 20 世纪 80 年代以来在欧美教育界兴起的一种促进教师专业发展的教师培养理论,它主要探讨教师如何在各种教学活动中通过不断反思来提高教学质量、促进专业的发展。

所谓教学反思,是指教师对教育教学实践的再认识、再思考,并以此来总结经验教训,进一步提高教育教学水平。

1. 教学反思的内容

教学反思包括教学前反思、教学中反思、教学后反思。

教学前反思的内容包含反思确定内容、阶段及具体实施方法对学生的需要和满足这些需要的具体目标,以及达到这些目标所需要的动机、教学模式和教学策略。还要对对本学科、本册教材、本单元、本课时进行教学计划时列出反思的关键项目。如:第一,需要教给学生哪些关键概念、结论和事实;第二,教学重点难点的确定是否准确;第三,教学内容的深度和范围对学生是否适度;第四,所设计的活动哪些有助于达到教学目标;第五,教学内容的呈现方式是否符合学生的年龄和心理特征;第六,哪些学生需要特别关注;第七,哪些条件会影响课的效果……

教学中反思是教师在教学过程中,对不可预料情况发生进行的反思以及教师在和学生互动作用中,根据学生的学习效果反馈,对教学计划进行的调整。不可预料情况发生时,教师要善于抓住有利于教学计划实施的因素,因势利导,不可让学生牵着鼻子走。根据学生反馈对教学计划的修改和调整要适当,不可大修大改。

教学中反思要求教师全身心地投入到教学活动中,调动各种感官捕捉反馈信息,快速、灵活地做出调整和反应。教学中反思教师可运用录音和录像技术,与观察手段一起为以后的教学后反思提供信息。

教学后反思围绕教学内容、教学过程、教学策略进行。具体为:

第一,教学内容方面:1.确定教学目标的适用性。2.对目标所采取的教学策略做出判断。

第二,教学过程方面:1.回忆教学是怎样进行的。2.对教学目标的反思:是否达到预期的教学效果。3.对教学理论的反思:是否符合教与学的基本规律。4.对学生的评价与反思:各类学生是否达到了预定目标。5.对执行教学计划情况的反思:改变计划的原因和方法是否有效,采用别的活动和方法是否更有效。6.对改进措施的反思:教学计划怎样修改会更有效……

第三,教学策略方面:1.感知环节,教师要意识到教学中存在问题与自己密切相关;2.理解环节,教师要对自己的教学活动与倡导的理论,行为结果与期望进行比较,明确问题根源;3.重组环节,教师要重审教学思想,寻求新策略;4.验证环节,检验新思想、新策略、新方案是否更有效,形成新感知,发现新问题,开始新循环。

教师教学反思的过程,是教师借助行动研究,不断探讨与解决教学目的、教学工具和自身方面的问题,不断提升教学实践的合理性,不断提高教学效益和教科研能力,促进教师专业化的过程。也是教师直接探究和解决教学中的实际问题,不断追求教学实践合理性,全面发展的过程。

2. 反思类型

反思类型可有纵向反思、横向反思、个体反思和集体反思等。

3. 反思方法

反思方法可有行动研究法、比较法、总结法、对话法、录像法、档案袋法等等。

二 教学评价

教学评价指课堂教学过程中对学生的学习行为、学习效果、目标达成等方面进行评价。评价的过程是复杂的,包括评价理念的了解,评价主体及评价方式的选择,评价计划的制定,评价标准的确立,评价过程的实施,评价结果的反馈等。具体说来,英语教学评价应包括以下部分。

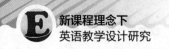

1. 英语教学评价的主体

英语课程的评价体系要体现评价主体的多元化。为了建立开放和宽松的评价氛围，需要学生、同伴、教师、家长共同关注，并参与评价，实现评价主体的多元化。

学生自我评价需要学生进行自我反思，客观地认识自己的学习变化。同伴互评需要同学之间、同伴之间根据课堂或平时的表现写评语，可以是表扬抑或是建议。同伴之间的评价更加具有真实性和可接受性，可以加强同学之间的相互了解，关心和帮助，也更加客观的评价同学、反省自己。教师评价，教师是最为传统的评价主体，主要表现为学生作业的评语。学生接触较多的就是教师，因此教师的评价更具有代表性。教师可采用日常记录、日志、评价表、座谈等，丰富评价的方式。家长评价，家长综合同伴评价和教师评价的结果，和学生一块学习、进步，定会加强家长和子女之间的亲密关系，促进学生的发展。

2. 英语评价的分类

根据评价在教学活动中发挥作用的不同，可把教学评价分为诊断性评价、形成性评价和总结性评价三种类型。

1）诊断性评价是指在教学活动开始前，对学生的学习准备程度做出鉴定，以便采取相应措施使教学计划顺利、有效实施而进行的测定性评价。诊断性评价的实施时间，一般在课程、学期、学年开始或教学过程中需要的时候。

2）形成性评价，也被称为过程性评价。在评价过程中进行，是能够指导教学过程、完善学习成果和教学效果的一种评价。形成性评价的目的是要激发学生的能力，加快学生的学习进度，从而为教师提供有质量的反馈意见、信息，可以有目的地改进学生的学习策略，使学习得到进步。

3）总结性评价

总结性评价是指将教学活动的成果作为判断教学活动价值的唯一标准。也就是说，将教育目标设定为标准，达到目标定为目的，只关注目的是否达成的一种评价方式，被称为总结性评价。它一般是在教学活动告一段落后，为了教学活动的最终效果而进行的评价。由于总结性评价的重要作用,它被广泛接受,通常用于教学工作、学生评价和学校工作评价。

3. 形成性评价与总结性评价的区别

二者既相互联系,又相互补充,并不存在绝对的区别,它们并不是互相矛盾的两种评价方式。见下表:

表1　形成性评价与总结性评价的区别

	形成性评价	总结性评价
评价主体	教师、学生、家长	教师
评价目的	发现学生潜质、强化学生学习,为教师提供反馈	给学生学习质量做出结论性评价,分等级
评价方法	课堂观察、档案袋、学生自评、家长评价等	纸笔测试
评价内容	知识技能、学习策略、情感态度等	知识技能
评价重点	学习过程	学习结果
评价时机	教学过程中	教学过程后
评价反馈	文字定性描写	分数

4. 分析形成性评价存在的问题以及解决方法

1) 存在的主要问题

第一,教师与学生对形成性评价的认知比较匮乏。

第二,评价方法缺乏多样性与针对性。

第三,评价内容不全面,缺乏导向性。

第四,评价反馈信息缺乏充分性与公平性。如果教师不能及时使用其他弥补手段就会导致评价的不公平。学生无法被激发学习的动力,只关心自己的分数。教师对这一部分的学生的评价将会产生偏差,无法使用形成性评价方法来提高他们的发展水平。

2) 对实施形成性评价的建议

形成性评价强调评价的人性化,注重评价学生的综合发展的各项能力,以此促进培养学生多方面的发展。形成性评价在一定程度上减轻了传统教育评价中以成绩判定学生优劣而产生的消极作用,提升学生在英语学习过

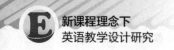
程中的兴趣与自信,这对教师的教学和学生的学习等方面都具有显著作用。

第一,构建科学的评价理念体系

教学评价得以能够顺利、有效运用的首位因素是科学的评价理念。因此,教师更应该积极更新评价理念。科学的评价理念,清晰、细致、可操作性强,对教学具有激励、诊断和促进作用。提倡评价主体的多元化,教师、学生和家长都可以融入到学生的评价过程中去,作为评价的主体。评价主体的多元化可以提升学生的学习成绩,还能充分调动各方面的积极性。并且评价主体的多元化将极大地增强评价的可信度,得到更加完善的评价效果。

第二,拓展形成性评价的内容

教师应该拓展评价情境,在多种情境下衡量学生对英语的了解与掌握,将评价内容与语言的使用情境进行高度结合。譬如,在对学生进行语法教学造句时,教师应该将语法创设在真实、有用的情境中让学生领会、使用,并不是为了造句而造句。

第三,综合使用多种评价方法

评价学生的英语学习过程应该在注意动态性与过程性的前提下使用,诸如课堂观察表、学习档案袋等多种多样的评价方法。多种评价方法的采用,会十分有利于学生调节学习行为。

第四,提高评价反馈信息的质量

形成性评价中的评价反馈功能作为弥补学生英语学习的不足的一个重要组成部分,对于英语教学中形成性评价的运用有着不可忽视的作用。评价反馈信息的利用要遵守以描述性语言为主,注重客观性、针对性、详细性等原则。

5.高中英语教学评价设计的过程

第一,确立评价标准。在确定评价标准之前,需要先确定何种评价理论,不同的评价理论根据其自身的特点,有着不同的评价标准。如形成性评价强调的是过程评价,其评价标准就需要根据学习阶段的实际情况确定,评价标准会更加具体;总结性评价是结果性评价,大到高中英语课程标准的要求,小到单元检测,均为总结性评价。因此评价标准的确定要具体理论具体分析。

第二,评价过程设计。评价可以出现在学习的不同阶段,不同阶段的评价有着不同的作用。学习之前的评价为诊断性评价,学习之中的评价为过程性评价,学习之后的评价为目标达成评价。评价阶段的选择要以评价目的为依据。

第三,评价内容及活动的选择。根据认知发展规律,学习经历了知识—理解—(分析和综合)—应用—评价的过程。根据评价目的和阶段的不同,评价内容也有不同的要求,如学习之前可考察背景知识的掌握、策略的掌握;学习之中可以是信息的辨认、筛选、转述及应用。不同的评价内容会有不同的评价活动,如理解能力的评价可采用选择、正误判断、匹配、排序等方式;应用能力的评价可采用设置新的语境。

6. 英语教学评价结果的反馈

英语教学评价最主要的目的是为了促进学生的发展、进步。在整个评价过程中最为重要的是让学生收到评价结果的反馈并做出相应的改变。中小学英语教学评价结果的反馈中常见的反馈为 good、excellent、need more practice 等,此种反馈太过宽泛,学生不能清楚的识别出现的问题。反馈应与评价标准相联系,既要清晰明了地指出问题,又要提出相应的建议。

三 教学反思或评价案例

1. 教学反思案例:Teaching Design for Unit 1 Book 5

Title:Great scientists JOHN SNOW DEFEATS "KING CHOLERA" (Reading)

Teaching reflection

The teacher should give students more kinds of activities in class in order to attract their attention and help them take part in the class actively.

Some students are lack of ability in finding information,so the teacher should give them more guide and encouragement.

---

2. 教学评价和反思:高三复习课"如何做完形填空"教学评价或反思

下课以后教师将从以下几个方面进行评价和反思,并将反思手写表格之后。

反思和评价项目	分　　值
教学目标达成情况	1　2　3　4　5
学生课堂参与情况	1　2　3　4　5
教师的讲解和课堂掌控情况	1　2　3　4　5
小组活动情况	1　2　3　4　5
课堂生成情况	1　2　3　4　5
对"六步教学"的思考	1　2　3　4　5

本章参考文献

[1] 中华人民共和国教育部.普通高中英语课程标准[M].北京：人民教育出版社,2017.

[2] 顾明远.教育大辞典,第三卷[M].上海：上海教育出版社.1990：211.

[3] 吴杰.教学论[M].长春：吉林教育出版社.1986：173.

[4] 施良方,崔允.教学理论：课堂教学的原理、策略与研究[M].上海：华东师范大学出版社.1999；15.

[5] 王映学.教学目标陈述中两个理论问题的探讨[J].教育科学论坛.2000(1)：52—53.

[6] 张明雪.浅谈英语课堂教学设计[J].教育界,2012(34)：344—344.

[7] 张舍茹.研究性学习理念下的英语教学设计[J].北京邮电大学学报(社会科学版),2009,11(2)：101—105.

[8] 盛群力.现代教学设计应用模式[M].浙江教育出版社,2002.

[9] 姚旺.教学设计中如何进行学习者分析[J].长春教育学院学报,2015(19)：148—149.

[10] 张航.英语教学学情分析的内涵、原则与方法[J].教学与管理：理论版,2017(8)：86—89.

[11] 马文杰,鲍建生."学情分析"：功能、内容和方法[J].教育科学研究,2013(9)：52—57.

[12] 陈智敏,刘美凤.近五年关于学习者分析要素的现状研究——基于中国知网2008—2013年相关数据[J].软件导刊(教育技术),2013(10)：57—60.

[13] 王蔷.从综合语言运用能力到英语学科核心素养[J].英语教师,2015(16).

[14] 加涅.教学设计原理.[M].上海华东师范大学出版社,2004.

[15] 蒙坤.高中英语课堂教学目标设计的现状及建议[J].名师论教,2013(8).

[16] 闫艳.课堂教学目标研究[D].华东师范大学,2010.

[17] 郑红苹,杨旭.语法翻译法再认识[J].乐山师范学院学报,2006(3),131—134.

[18] 章兼中.国外外语教学法主要流派[M].华东师范大学出版社,1983:41.

[19] 刘润清.西方语言学流派[M].外语教学与研究出版社,2002:128—132.

[20] 袁春燕.当代国际教学法研究[D].南京:南京师范大学,2006.

[21] Peter Skehan.语言学习认知法[M].上海外语教育出版社,2000.

[22] 董晓红.关于交际法的几点思考[J].外语界,1994(2).

[23] 丰玉芳,唐晓岩.任务型语言教学法在英语教学中的运用[J].外语与外语教学,2004.

[24] 龚亚夫,罗少茜.任务型语言教学[M].人民教育出版社,2003:39.

[25] 陈艳君,基于本土视角中国英语教学法研究[D].长沙:湖南师范大学,2015.

[26] 文秋芳,构建"产出导向法"理论体系[J].外语教学与研究,2015,(4):547—558.

[27] 文秋芳,"师生合作评价":"产出导向法"创设的新评价形式[J].外语界,2016,(5):37—43.

[28] 路海东.教育心理学[M].长春:东北师范大学出版社,2002.4.

[29] 何莲珍.自主学习及其能力的培养[J].外语教学与研究,2003(4):287—289

[30] 程晓堂.论自主学习[J].学科教育.1999(9):32—39.

[31] 庞维国.自主学习理论的新进展[J].《华东师大学报》(教科版).1999.

[32] 庞维国.自主学习研究中应该注意的几个问题[J].《中华教育》1999.

[33] 李吉林.情境教学理论与实践[M].北京:人民口报出版社,1996.

[34] 孔企平.论学习方式的转变[J].全球教育展望,2001,(8).

[35] 牛其刚.曲耀华.李文君.论自主学习和他主学习[J].基础教育研究,2016(21):31—36.

[36] 张笛梅.什么是创新性学习[N].中国教育报,2008-07-09(9).

[37] 樊玉国.基于学习风格的高中英语教学媒体选择与运用研究[D].华中师范大学,2009(5).

[38] 何克抗,郑永柏,谢幼如.教学系统设计[M].北京:北京师范大学出版社,2002.

[39] 彭梅,东水.基础英语教学设计与教学媒体的选择和运用[J].牡丹江教育学院学报,2014(2).

[40] 蔡婷.高中生英语学习兴趣的现状调查与培养策略研究[D].华中师范大学,2013.

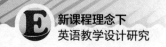
[41] 王秋月.论"3P"教学法在高职高专英语课堂教学中的运用[J].常州信息职业技术学院学报,2012,11(3):87—92.

[42] 束定芳、庄智像.现代外语教学 理论、实践与方法[M].上海外语教育出版社,2015.

[43] 高文.教学系统设计(ISD)研究的历史回顾——教学设计研究的昨天、今天和明天(之一)[J].中国电化教育,2005(1):17—22.

[44] 李斌.案例教学过程的设计与评价[J].教育与职业,2007(3):119—121.

[45] 李龙.教学过程设计的理论与实践[J].电化教育研究,1999(4):20—26.

[46] 王嘉艺.对英语教学方法和教学手段的研究与探讨[J].新课程研究,2009(1):41—42.

[47] 杨心德.教学过程设计的认知心理学原理[J].宁波大学学报,2001(5):1—5.

[48] 张典中,魏绍红.教师角色变化及教育科研定位浅析[J].中国教育科学探究,2005(1):28—30.

[49] 袁锦芬,浅谈英语课堂教学中多媒体辅助教学的应用[J].教学研究,2011(3).

[50] 王以宁.教学媒体理论与实践[M].北京:高等教育出版社,2007.

[51] 杨九民,梁林梅.教学系统设计理论与实践[M].北京:北京大学出版社,2008.

[52] 网络资源(略).

Chapter 04

第四章 课堂教学技能与策略

教学设计最终要到课堂中去实施,课堂教学是教学设计的检验,课堂教学实施,需要一定的技能和策略。目前比较一致的观点,课堂教学应该从教学组织、信息传递、管理和教学媒体的优化选择等四个方面去考虑。那么,就英语课堂教学而言,课堂教学究竟要组织哪些方面呢?

首先,组织教学内容。课堂是教学的主要场所,好的教学内容有助于课程的顺利完成,保证教学活动的有条不紊。

其次,组织教学方法。虽说不同的教师擅长的教学方法不同,但因学生个体具有差异性,不同的课堂也是具有显著的差异性的,教师应根据不同的课堂采取不同的教学方法,灵活运用。

再次,组织课堂时间。课堂时间的组织,有助于教学任务按时有效地完成。

最后,组织课堂活动。营造英语课堂学习的语言氛围,创造良好的英语课堂语言氛围。这是调动学生学习积极性,进行有效教学的必要手段。

优化英语教学信息传递策略,则包括信息输出策略、促进信息吸收策略和反馈信息策略等。英语课堂教学管理策略则从课堂教学纪律管理和课堂教学的时间管理角度进行研究。至于英语课堂教学媒体的优化选择与设

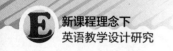
计,我们首先要认清媒体本质,使媒体设计与功能相匹配,然后把握媒体要求,使媒体设计与教学因素相整合,同时,应该注意,教学媒体选择与设计,应与学生认知水平相适应。

一位优秀的教师,不仅要掌握课堂教学策略,更需要掌握一定的课程教学技能。一般来说,英语课程教学技能分为三个部分:第一,英语课程的准备技能。第二,英语课堂教学的实施技能。第三,英语课程的研究技能。其中,英语课程的准备技能包括课程标准研修技能、课堂教学设计与撰写技能和教材分析技能;英语课程教学的实施技能包括导入技能与课堂呈现方法、课堂提问与反馈技能、课堂教学与管理技能、课堂活动开展与评价技能、板书设计与简笔画运用、多媒体的运用、教学语言与教态运用、结课技能和作业设计技能等九个方面;英语课程教学的研究技能则包括教学设计研究、公开课研究、说课、空堂讲课、评课、教学反思、教学效能与评价研究、课例研究、案例研究和课题研究等十个方面。在本节,我们只重点研究课程教学的实施技能。

第一节　导入技能与课堂呈现方法

一　导入技能

英语课堂教学的导入环节(the introductory procedures)是英语课堂教学中非常重要的一步,如果使用得当且新颖巧妙,就会如名曲的"引子",很容易吸引学生的注意力,激发学生学习的兴趣,增强学生的参与意识,自然而然将课堂内容导入下一环节,且有助于学生获得良好的学习成果。鉴此,笔者认为,英语教师很有必要了解一定的导入知识,掌握一定的导入技巧和方法。在高中英语教学中常用的导入方法有如下几种:

1. 问题导入法

这是比较常见的一种导入方法。教师通过提问,有时是追问,引导学生进入下一环节。

例如：T：What do you usually do in your spare time?

S1：Read books.

T：What about you?

S2：I often have sports.

T：Can you say something about sports?

S2：Yes，of course. Sports can make us strong and healthy. Sports can also...

T：Good. Today we are going to learn Unit 10 Sports.

2. 话题导入法

话题导入法是师生一起谈论一个话题，然后由该话题进入下一环节。例如：学习统编教材高三英语上学期第 12 单元第 46 课时，教师就可以由天气这个话题导入。

T：What's the weather like today?

S：It's cold.

T：Oh，winter is coming. It is getting colder and colder. I don't want to get up in the morning. I want to lie in bed. I want to sleep all the morning. I want to sleep all day. I even want to sleep all the winter. That is，I want to have a winter sleep.边说边在黑板上板书，Lesson 46 Winter Sleep.

3. 游戏导入法

猜谜语，应该是每个学生都喜爱的活动。教师应抓住这一点，根据课的内容，或摘选，或自编，会达到新颖巧妙的效果。例如教师在复习环节结束后，就可以拍拍口袋说："What's in my pocket?"学生就会猜测："Money"，"Chocolate"，"Stamp"等等。但猜到报纸是很难的。此时老师就可以说"I'll give you a hint. It is a piece of paper，but not an ordinary paper，it is very useful. In it，you can read news，ads and so on. What is it?"我想学生会异口同声回答"Newspaper"这时教师顺势发问"How newspapers are produced?"，此句正是该课课题。游戏在初中英语教学中处处可见，学反义词，学介词等都可采用游戏导入法。高中英语教学中同样也可采用游戏形式，因为，高中生同样对游戏感兴趣，只是要求教师课前做好适当的准备。

例如统编教材高三英语第 37 课，是着重练习猜测句型的对话，教师就可以用游戏的形式导入。教师课前悄悄安排学生 A 站在教室门时，不被其他学生看到，组织上课后，问班上同学："Where is A"？学生会说"I don't know."这样教师引导学生猜测，"Can you guess?"同时展示句型 I guess …, I'm sure …, she must have …, she might …, she must have …, It seems that …。

4. 简笔画导入法

较以上三种方法，简笔画导入更为直观形象，简洁明了。例如：教师在黑板上画一棵大树，从上到下指着问学生："What is it?"学生依次回答：a tree top, branches, leaves, trunk, roots.最后教师说："Every tree has its roots. Without roots, trees couldn't live. Human beings also have roots. Does anybody know his root? If he doesn't, maybe he will try to find his root. Today we are going to learn Unit 14 Roots"。

5. 实物导入法

实物是真实的东西，用实物导入，可以给学生以直观的感觉，留下深刻的印象。例如讲高二 smoking 一课时，教师就可以带上一包烟，引导学生谈论"Is smoking good or bad?"在学习统编教材高三下册 Bees 一课时，教师也可带一只蜜蜂进入教室，问学生：How much do you know about bees? Do bees have a language like that of human beings? How do bees communicate with each other? What are they able to tell each other? 自然而然就开始了高三下册第 22 单元的学习。

6. 视频导入法

随着信息技术发展，视频导入法越来越被广泛使用，年轻教师更是这方面的高手，他们信息化技术娴熟，驾驭电脑的手段较强。例如，在学习极限运动一课时，有的老师这样导入：

T：Talk about Huangshan with students and then ask students whether they like climbing mountains. Tell students that today we will talk about a completely different way to climb mountains. Then, show a video about rock climbing and some pictures and then tell students the focus today is extreme sports.

S：Take a look at a video and talk about different ways to climb Huangshan actively. And then，discuss other forms of sports.

需要强调的是，不管哪种好的导入方法，都要与课堂内容紧密联系，不可生拉硬扯；都要简洁明了，不可冗长空泛；都要生动有趣，不可枯燥乏味。

二 课堂呈现方法

实事求是地说，在教学过程中，尤其是公开课和优质课活动中，年轻教师们的导入环节做得是非常好的，导入的激趣（激发学生兴趣）、激智（激活学生已有知识）作用也充分发挥。但是，一个常见现象是，导入过后，好多教师的课慢慢趋于平淡，并且越来越乏味，学生的激情也像撒气的气球，慢慢瘪下去。究其原因，是缺乏课堂呈现方法和技巧。因此，课堂的呈现方法就显得尤为重要。

1. 先复习，后新课

课堂的教学内容，大多都不是孤立的，要么是单元的一课时，要么是课题的一部分，这样，我们平常开始一节课，从开始就要考虑对上节课内容的复习或梳理，以便于在此基础上进一步学习新的知识。

2. 先教授，后巩固，就是俗语说的"讲练结合"

在组织课堂教学时，教师不能只安排新知识传授或学习，还要考虑学生能不能掌握。要了解学生能否掌握，在新知学习后，就应该安排练习巩固，这是从课堂内容角度考虑的。如果从课堂活动的组织形式考虑，先教授，多是教师的活动，练习巩固则是学生的活动，这样两个活动的结合，也可以避免教师整节课满堂灌。

3. 先讨论，后总结

目前，自主型课堂的探索逐渐增多。自主型课堂，必需有学生的自主学习，同伴讨论或小组合作，可以是 pair work，也可以是 group work。但是，学生讨论之后，教师必须安排总结。可以是归纳，可以是点评，也可以是展示评价。只有讨论和总结结合在一起，才能提高合作学习的效果。否则，热热闹闹讨论一阵子，而不管效果和结果，就变成了作秀和表演。

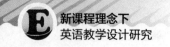

4. 先易后难

不论学习知识,还是安排活动,先易后难都是必须遵守的原则。前面容易一些,学生很容易进入角色,然后慢慢增加难度,"跳一跳,摘桃子",内容越学越有挑战,学生就会越学越有劲。否则,一上来就把学生难在那里,学生的积极性一下子被打消了,后面教师怎么发挥都很难调动学生。好多公开课,越上气氛越压抑,学生越沉默,这是原因之一。

5. 动静交错

好的课堂,永远是形式多样,单一的形式容易让人疲惫。所以,动静结合也是必须要给予重视的。上面一个环节是 Reading silently,下一个环节就应该安排 ask-and-answer,或 discussing in pairs/groups。

6. 学习理解、应用实践、迁移创新三类活动层层递进

《普通高中英语课程标准》(2017 版)提出了指向学科核心素养的英语学习活动观,明确活动是英语学习的基本形式。英语学习活动分为学习理解、应用实践、迁移创新三类活动。通过这三类层层递进的语言、思维、文化相融合的活动,引导学生加深对主题的理解;帮助学生在活动中培养核心素养。因此教师要善于提出和设计从理解到应用,从分析到评价等有层次的问题或活动,引导学生的思维从低阶向高阶稳步发展,鼓励学生由浅入深地发表自己的观点、表达自己的情感。

7. 环节与环节的过渡

课堂流程虽然被认为划分成几个环节,但在实施过程中,并不是界限分明的,绝对不应该变成"So much for the first step, let's move to the second step"或"OK, this is Step 2, let's look at Step 3"这样机械的操作。有经验的教师的课堂永远是浑然一体的,环节与环节之间,活动与活动之间,都没有明显的区分痕迹。做到这一点,功夫体现在过渡语的使用上。巧妙的过渡语,很好地弥补了环节与环节间的痕迹,学生不知不觉从课堂的开始走到了结尾。我们在很多省市级优质课上看到,教师过渡语的使用也是区分高分选手和低分选手的一个标准之一。另外,我们在平时课堂观察中也注意到,由于 PPT 课件的广泛使用,教师按照课件的设计一步一步讲,学生跟着课件的内容一步一步听,老师学生都被课件牵着鼻子走,成了课件的奴隶,环节

与环节之间,都体现在了 PPT 屏幕的转换上,课堂毫无生成和创造可言。

第二节　课堂提问与反馈技能

一　课堂提问技能

1. 课堂提问概念

传统意义的课堂提问往往是指课堂上教师对学生的提问,是单向的,但是新课程理念下的课堂提问则是双向的,即教师对学生的提问和学生对教师的提问,甚至是多向的,即教师对学生、学生对教师、学生对学生之间的提问。

2. 课堂提问原则

关于课堂提问的原则有很多,但总结起来,应该有以下几点:

1) 有效性原则。提问的目的不是为了提问而提问,而是为了发现问题、解决问题而提问,也不是为了体现课堂互动和自主课堂而提问,要因疑设问,因人设问,因内容设问。特别要避免没有 information gap 的假交际式的提问。

2) 层次性原则。内容不同、学生水平不同、课堂情景不同、回答质量不同,因此问题的设计要有层次性,层层递进、步步深入,一层层剥洋葱。

3) 多样性原则。课堂提问的多样性不仅体现在提问主体的多样性,即教师对学生、学生对教师、学生对学生之间的提问;还体现在问题的表现形式上,不能只是一般疑问句式的提问,还要有选择疑问句式的提问,更要有特殊疑问句式的提问;还体现在问题的开放形式上,可以是封闭式问题,还可以是开放式问题,等等。

3. 课堂提问策略

1) 掌握提问的问题的难易度。太容易的问题,很难吸引学生的兴趣,也难调动学生的积极性;太难的问题,可以回答的学生较少,会将大批学生拒之门外,变成少数学生的"个人秀",大部分学生就会变成课堂的看客,慢慢地不再参与提问活动。为了让提问难易适当,可以设置连环问题,几个问题连续,前面的问题容易,后面的问题逐渐变难,学生不知不觉进入问题的思考和讨论中。

2)掌握提问的频度。为了体现学生为中心,有的老师认为可以增加提问次数,认为提问越多越好。其实这是一种误区。提问次数设置,应该根据教学内容的难易、学生的反应等因素。提问次数过多,容易打断学生的思维,增加学生的紧张程度,也会给教学时间带来压力。

3)掌握提问的效度。英语课堂中,无效提问的例子举不胜举。就拿教师提问学生为例,教师举着铅笔,问学生"What's this?",还有,教师让一男生站起来,问"Are you a boy?"等。这类提问的效度可想而知。为了提高提问的效度,教师除了注意 information gap 外,还要结合课文内容,注意问题对学生考查的程度,是浅层理解问题,还是深层理解问题;是结论性问题,还是拓展性问题,教师设置和组织提问前都要注意。

4)等待回答的耐心度。英语课堂上,由于过多考虑课堂时间,无论师生,还是生生,教师特别希望提问后,学生能立刻顺利地回答出问题。这种想法,很显然是过于理想,也显然是不科学的。引发学生思考的问题,学生一次回答不全面的问题,甚至难住学生的问题,往往是好问题,有利于暴露学生的弱点,或培养学生的思维能力。这种情况下,需要教师要有等待的耐心,还要有循循善诱、点拨启发的耐心和能力。

5)提问方式的多样性。课堂提问单一,往往无法激发学生的思考积极性,很难培养学生的思维能力。多样性的提问,从内容上讲,可以采用叙述形式,也可以采用判断形式,还可以拓展形式,必要时还可以采用刨根问底式提问。从提问主体上讲,可以教师提问学生,也可以学生提问教师,更可以学生之间互相提问。

6)对回答的评价。英语课堂的评价语言,往往特别单一,有的老师评价学生只用"Good","Very good"。而实际上,当学生回答较好时,我们既可以用语言表扬评价,也可以用"竖起大拇指"等体态语对回答进行评价。即使用语言对问题评价,除去"Good"和"Very good",教师还可以用"perfect job","well done","excellent","amazing","unbelievable","You are so clever","You are so smart!","Perfect!","You did a good job!"等等。对回答的评价,除了语言评价外,教师还可以用简笔画进行评价,时不时奖给学生一个笑脸或给学生一个哭脸、一个足球、一台电脑,甚至一辆车(自然是画在黑板上),既节约时间,又具幽默感,可以活跃课堂气氛。当然,如果条件允许,也可以以实物奖励进行肯定的评价。教师还应注意评价的及时性。年级越低的学生,回答完问题后,越渴望教师及时给予评价,及时的评价会让学生随后的学习更加积极和专注。

二 反馈信息策略

1. 反馈是师生之间的一种重要信息交流活动。一般情况下,教师输出的信息会因各种原因不能完全传递给学生,这就需要教师迅速了解学生情况,抓住最好的教学时机调整教学,及时从学生中获得反馈信息,再及时地针对问题予以反馈、评价,保障教学信息的传输质量,优化教学效果。

2. 教师在课堂中可采取的反馈信息策略包括:1)语言反馈策略。与语言输出策略类似,语言反馈策略也具有简单直接的特点,是课堂上常用的一种反馈形式。语言反馈常指在学生回答相应问题后,教师利用语言对学生进行评价,其中包括简单认可、指示引导、明示纠错等形式。如,教师认可,除去"Good"和"Very good",教师还可以用"perfect job","well done","excellent","amazing","unbelievable","You are so clever","You are so smart!","Perfect!","You did a good job!"等等。教师使用语言反馈策略应注意反馈语言的准确性和恰当性。2)肢体反馈策略。教师除进行语言反馈外,还可通过动作反馈或神情反馈对学生进行相应的评价。所谓动作反馈,主要是指教师利用身体动作取代言语对学生进行评价,通常采用鼓掌、竖起大拇指或者摇头的形式。而神情反馈是教师运用丰富的表情来评价,在进行明示纠错时通常运用此种方式。肢体反馈策略在运用过程中具有生动形象的特点。3)纠错反馈策略。纠错反馈是指学习者错误使用第二语言进行口语或书面语产出时接收到他人提供的提示错误的反馈信息(徐锦芬,2015)。它是外语课堂中师生互动的一种重要形式。根据不同的分类标准,可分为口头纠错反馈和书面纠错反馈,也可分为隐性和显性纠错反馈。纠错反馈包括重复、打断、澄清请求等形式。教师使用纠错反馈策略应注意态度和时机,做到明示与暗示相结合。明示纠错时要注意选择恰当的、学生能接受的方式。4)实物反馈。教师可以用简笔画画出实物,时不时奖给学生,一个笑脸或一个哭脸、一个足球、一台电脑,甚至一辆车(自然是画在黑板上),既节约时间,又具幽默感,可以活跃课堂气氛。当然,如果条件允许,也可以以奖励实物进行肯定的反馈。

3. 英语课堂使用反馈语的建议

1)增加混合型反馈语的使用频率。教师普遍认识到反馈语在高中英语教学中的重要作用。教师应该增加课堂上混合型反馈语的使用频率。教师使用混合型反馈语的时候,从语音、语调、语法、词汇以及语境等方面对学生有的放矢地反馈,让学生更好地接收到教师传递的反馈信息。此外,教师还应该更加注重反馈的方式,改变教师主导的课堂,不再只是站在课堂前和学生互动,而是应该针对不同类型学生,充分挖掘课堂反馈的内涵,增加混合型反馈语的艺术性和科学性,促进不同层次的学生更愉悦地接受反馈语,更好地了解自己,认识到自己的不足与优点,从而更好地学习语言。

反馈语的分类及功能,帮助教师在运用反馈语的过程中更加细化,从而使教学手段更加丰富。教师使用混合型反馈语应贯穿于课堂演示、作业评比、视听演示、讲座演讲、学习报告、校外考察等等,将不同的教学形式运用得恰到好处。在课堂上使用不同的教学方法,使之相互交融,从而提高学生的兴奋点和求知欲,润物无声地使学生迅速掌握课内英语知识,提高英语水平。

2)对学生的反馈语要清晰,明确,尤其是集体出现错误时,老师应该明确地提出来,帮助学生纠错和改正。此外,当学生回答错误的时候,教师不应该以简单否定的反馈直接反驳学生,造成错误的引导。因为教师反馈语在高中英语课堂的作用不仅是完成对学生的答案的评判,更多的是起到引发师生之间的交流、讨论作用,具有总结和评价的特征。尤其是在某些场景中,对学生回答进行追问也可以帮助学生更好的打开思路,加深对知识领域的理解。特别是在口语教学的过程中,教师更应帮助学生养成良好的语言习惯。

3)反馈语应关注学生的心理需求。高中英语教学应树立以人为本,以学生为中心的教学理念。高中教学的目标是培养德智体美劳全面发展的人才。因此,教师应充分关注学生的心理需求。学生的心理诉求是衡量教师反馈效果和课堂效率的重要标准之一。由于高中生学习英语的需求不同,因此,教师需要根据他们的心理需求给予适当的反馈。

第三节　课堂教学与管理技能

课堂管理是指教师为了保证课堂教学的秩序和效益,提高课堂教学质量,达到预期的教学目标,通过有效的课堂管理而创造和保持的一个学生积极参与及相互学习和激励的良好的课堂环境。课堂管理可以分为课堂纪律管理和课堂时间管理。

1. 课堂纪律管理。所谓课堂纪律,主要是指对学生的课堂行为施加的外部控制与规范。课堂管理技能,就是教师维持良好课堂纪律,对违反课堂纪律的行为进行约束的技能。

对违反课堂纪律行为的管理。英语课堂管理技能很多,并且情况不同,采取的措施也应该有变化。通常来说,对违反课堂纪律的行为,可以采取以下几种措施:

1) 走到该生旁边。这是教师对不听课、开小差的同学的常用办法。教师边走边讲课,慢慢走到这位学生旁边,站在他(她)旁边,或轻轻敲击一下他(她)的课桌。这样做的优点是不影响教学进度和其他学生的注意力,又提醒了不听课的学生。

2) 突然提问。当教师发现有些学生在课堂上不注意听讲,或者和别人讲话、捣乱时,突然问他(她)一个问题,这个问题是老师刚刚讲过的,只要注意听一定就会答上来,但也要有一定的难度。这样做可引起不听讲的学生的重视,把注意力放在课堂内容上。

3) 把机会让给违纪的同学。这种情形多用于班级活动。教师请一部分学生到讲台前展示,但有时展示效果不一定理想,下面有的同学会跃跃欲试,想露一手,所以会故意搞出违纪的动静或行为,这时教师如果给予批评,

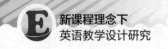
可能一下子会把班级活跃的气氛冷却下来,打击学生的积极性。不妨告诉捣乱的同学,接下来请他们来展示,看看是否比现在的同学做得好。这样,捣乱的同学就会立刻认真起来,投入到活动中。

4)停止讲课。在课堂上,若发现有的同学捣乱,教师可立即停课片刻,并注视着那位学生,这可引起全班同学的注意,更引起那位捣乱同学的注意。但要注意停课时间不可太长,否则会影响全班同学的学习,引起公愤,也不可瞪眼相视,那将会引起那位同学的反感。

很多教师认为,课堂管理,就是对课堂违纪行为的管理。其实,这种观点是不全面的。对课堂违纪行为的管理,是课堂管理最基本的管理,也是低层次的管理,仅仅是为了保证课堂活动得以顺利进行。高层次的管理,应该是激励性的课堂管理。这种管理,是为了进一步激发学生的学习积极性,启发学生的思维,营造和谐而又热烈的课堂氛围。学生的注意力高度集中,思维非常活跃,课堂生成频繁,课堂效率提高,课堂质量优化。

2. 课堂时间管理。课堂时间管理是教师的基本教学技能之一,教师需要考虑如何在课堂上的45分钟内合理安排和实施教学活动,以此提高学生的学习效率。

1)课堂时间的分类。皮连生(2000)把教学时间划分为四个层次:分配时间、教学时间、投入时间和学业学习时间。分配时间即课程作息时间,常指45分钟;教学时间指教师完成常规课堂组织管理及管理任务的时间;投入时间指的是学生把心思投入到学习上的时间;学业学习时间是学生以高度的成功率完成学业的时间。

2)课堂时间管理策略。为了解决存在于英语课堂教学时间管理上的问题,从而充分利用有限的课堂教学时间,英语教师需要采取一些有效的策略,进行合理科学地管理课堂教学时间。

首先,教师必须充分认识到课堂有限时间的宝贵,并注重提升课堂教学效率的意识,才能专注于对时间的管理,同时将其真正落实到课堂教学过程中。

第二,精心备课。备课是完成教学任务且保证教学质量必不可少的前提。教师在备课时除了要计划语言知识教学所用的时间外,还要考虑结合不同教学内容对学生的跨文化交际能力进行培养所花费的时间。同时,教师还要充分了解学生的认知水平和个体差异等多方面因素,据此安排每个课堂教学环节所要花费的时间以及采取的教学方法。只有在备课时对教材和学情了如指掌,实际教学过程才可能最大限度地与原计划相吻合,教师在课堂教学中即便遇见突发状况也能信心十足,有条不紊地开展教学活动。

第三,在课堂上,不经意利用计时工具进行课堂管理。教师可以利用墙上的挂钟,自己的手表或者闹铃等钟表类计时工具或电脑桌面的时间等来准确定位一堂课已用时间和剩余时间。据此,教师可以计算某个教学环节实际所用时间与计划所用时间之间的差距,根据差距以及当堂课剩余时间的多少,适当调整课堂教学计划,比如,加快不太重要的教学内容的进行速度,将时间节省到重点知识的讲解上。

第四、教师应结合学生的心理特征进行时间管理。在一堂课的 45 分钟里,学生的注意力和思维方式在不同的时间段有着不同的表现。在前 5 分钟内,教师要通过课堂有趣的导入将学生的注意力和兴趣吸引到与本节课相关学习内容上来;5—20 分钟这个时间段内,学生的注意力最集中,思维最活跃,因此教师应当在此时进行重点内容的解决,以便实现教学重点目标。20 多分钟后,学生思维开始倦怠,此时教师应安排能激发学生兴趣和主动性的活动。下课前的几分钟,学生注意力有所分散,此时教师应对该堂课教学内容进行总结,同时布置复习任务,加深学生印象。在每个不同时间段,采取适当的教学方法,充分利用最佳时域,从而有效完成教学任务。也正是基于此分析,我们对六步教学课堂时间分配做了细致的管理。

教学环节	时间分配
Step1 定任务	2—3 分钟
Step2 读材料	10—15 分钟
Step3 议问题	10 分钟左右
Step4 解困惑	5 分钟
Step5 讲规律	5 分钟
Step6 测所学	5—8 分钟

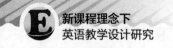

最后，在教学过程中，教师应当灵活调控课堂节奏。课堂教学是一个动态的过程，其中可能发生一些预料不到的突发状况，所以它不会按照教师提前备课时的计划丝毫不变地进行。这就要求教师具备丰富的课堂经验以及灵活多变的应对能力，努力将突发状况占用的时间降到最低，做到不浪费课堂时间，或者合理调整各环节所用时长，做到既不耽误教学进程又能顺利实现教学目标。

第四节　课堂活动开展与评价技能

1. 英语学习活动观

《普通高中英语课程标准》(2017年版)指出，英语课程内容是发展学生英语学科核心素养的基础，包含六个要素：主题语境、语篇类型、语言知识、文化意识、语言技能和学习策略，他们之间相互整合，形成了指向核心素养发展的英语学习活动观。

英语学习活动观，也叫整合式英语学习活动观，以学生为中心，以活动为中心，以经验为中心，重视对语篇的赏析、比较、探究，要求学生能在具体的主题语境中，基于不同的语篇而运用语言技能获取、梳理、整合语言知识和文化知识，进而理解其文化内涵，汲取其文化精华。

2. 英语学习活动观的内涵与意义

英语学习活动观是指学生在主题意义的引领下，通过学习理解、应用实践、迁移创新等一系列体现综合性、关联性和实践性等特点的英语学习活动，基于已有知识，依托不同类型的语篇，在分析问题和解决问题的过程中，促进自身语言知识学习、语言技能发展、文化内涵理解、多元思维发展、价值取向判断和学习策略运用。这一过程既是语言知识与语言技能整合发展的过程，又是文化意识不断增强、思维品质不断提升、学习能力不断提高的过程(教育部 2018)。英语学习活动观强调学科核心素养的发展，关注主题意义的引领和课程内容的整合性学习。课程标准将英语学习活动分成三类，即学习理解类活动、应用实践类活动和迁移创新类活动。这三类活动从基于文本的信息输入到深入文本的内化和初阶输出，最后到超越文本的高阶输出，以实现基于文本、聚焦文化、学习语言、发展思维的深度学习的目的，从而落实英语学科核心素养。

3. 核心素养指导下的英语学习活动观在教学中的实践

本案例以北师大版模块一 Unit3 Lesson1 Festivals 的 Reading 为例，阐述如何在阅读教学中体现核心素养指导下的英语学习活动观。

主题语境：人与自然——节日背后的文化

语篇类型：记叙文

语篇研读：本单元的主题是 Festival，主要介绍中国和其他国家的主要节日及节日的庆祝活动。学生通过学习，可以了解我国及西方的主要节日和活动，熟悉并掌握在谈论这些国家时需要的话题及词句，最后通过自主学习和合作学习用英语介绍或创建一个节日，这样就为后面几课语言学习和技能培养进行了铺垫。

教学目标：

1）能说出文章中节日的名称、日期、活动、食物、历史等。

2）能给每一篇文章加个题目，能画出每一篇文章的结构图。能够用所学语言知识介绍节日。

3）能创建并展示自己或小组的节日。

教学活动：

（1）学习理解类活动（Learning and understanding）。学生默读课文，然后回答下列问题：What is the name of the festival? What is the date of the festival? What are the typical activities of the festival? What are the foods eaten in the festival?

【设计说明】阅读的过程实际上就是在已有认知的基础上激发新的知识、优化认知结构的过程。学生通过阅读并思考有关课文的问题，可以概括、梳理和整合信息。

（2）应用实践类活动（Applying and practising）。在学生对课文阅读理解的基础上，教师引导学生讨论完成任务：Can you give a title to each passage? Can you draw the structure of each passage? Can you add some contents（内容）to each passage?

【设计说明】学生依据所梳理和提炼的结构化知识，采用交流合作的学习方式，实践和内化所获得的语言知识和文化知识。

（3）迁移创新类活动（Transfering and creating）。学生在前两类活动基础上，分组进行以下活动① create your own festivals.② describe your own festivals. ③According to what you have learn, evaluate your own description of your festival.

【设计说明】主题语境不仅制约着语言知识和文化知识的学习范围，还为语言学习提供意义语境，并有机渗透情感、态度和价值观。对主题语境活动的设置直接影响着学生的思维发展水平和语言学习成效。通过对主题语境的再创新，体现了活动设计的实践性原则。

4. 英语学习活动的设计应注意的问题

在设计英语学习活动时，教师应该注意一些问题。

1）引入或创设情景，要力求真实，力求贴近学生的生活经验和已有知识，力求短平快。

2）在情景创设中，教师要考虑地点、场合、交际对象、人物关系和交际目的等，有利于学生根据语境选择恰当的语言形式，得体地达到交际效果。

3）教师要善于利用多种工具和手段，可以采用传统的语言、简笔画等手段，更要开发利用多模态的信息化手段，把多媒体手段的辅助作用最大化。

4）学习活动设计的顺序应该遵循由易到难、由低阶向高阶的稳步发展，确保提出的问题由理解到应用，从分析到评价的层次性。

5）英语学习活动没有固定的模式，教师要根据所学主题内容、学习目标、学生经验和教师经验等，设计不同的英语学习活动。

5. 教学活动设计策略

1）要基于对语篇的解读。

2）应基于对学情的把握。

3）可以将不同的活动以不同的顺序串联或组合起来。

4) 也可以在学生获取语篇整体信息之后,将学生分成小组,请小组中的每位学生分角色去完成阅读任务。

5) 三类活动应依次体现基于语篇、深入语篇和超越语篇的特点。

6) 在每类活动中,都应该有机融入语言知识学习、语言技能运用、学习策略应用、思维品质发展和文化意识的培养。

7) 确保学生在探究主题意义的学习活动中,学会运用所学语言分析问题和解决问题,培养核心素养。

第五节 板书设计与简笔画运用

一 板书设计

1. 关于信息技术手段背景下板书设计的讨论

自从 PPT 课件进入课堂后,关于要不要板书设计的话题一直没有间断,尽管各类公开课和优质课明确要求必须要有板书设计,但实际的常规课堂中,由于使用 PPT 课件、PAD 等信息技术手段,教师没有板书的现象比比皆是。因此,我们有必要再次明确,课堂教学中教师必须要有板书,板书必须设计。

2. 板书的作用

关于板书的作用,在教师中流行的一种说法非常有益,那就是,当课堂结束后,教师学生收拾其所有教学材料,看一看板书,本节课的教学重要内容就一目了然了,这就是板书的作用。

3. 板书的类型

常见的有 1)提纲式板书,2)表格式板书,3)线索式板书,4)图画式板书,5)分析综合式板书。

4. 新手教师和老教师板书存在问题

新手教师板书时,常常存在四个问题,第一,不会布局,第二,没有行距,且上翘或下垂。第三,字体太大或太小,第四,板书内容重点不分,该板书内容没有板书,不该板书的内容却写得很多。老教师板书存在的常见问题是随意性太强,字体太草,没有布局。

5. 板书的技巧

1) 版面利用。一句话可以概括,那就是"上有天,下有地,两边要有自留地",板书从上到下,从左到右,都要留出一些空间。

2) 主副黑板。副黑板是用来写不重要的内容的,重要的内容应该写在主黑板上。通常,黑板右手边上部分为副黑板,其余为主黑板。

3) 字行的平行。黑板的第一行很重要,这一行常常决定后面的字行的美观程度。为了确保第一行的平直,书写时,应以黑板的上边线为平行线,让这一行与它保持平行,然后第二行与第一行平行,以此类推。

4) 使用关键字和关键词。板书的重点,也不能面面俱到,恰当使用关键词和关键字,会让板书内容容量大但简洁清晰。

5) 使用简笔画或思维导图,会让板书更形象、更美观、更有趣。

如下列 **Blackboard Design** 所示:

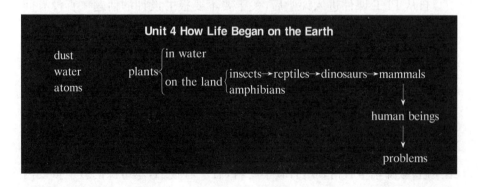

二 简笔画

1. 简笔画的概述

"简笔画"即"Stick Figures"或者"Blackboard Drawing",它是一个新的美术用词。它是用简单的样子表达作者意愿的绘画形式。至今,关于简笔画,还是没有确切的定义,现有的解释都是针对它绘画的特点而言的。综合已有的概念和解释,我们认为简笔画是以最快的速度,用最简单的绘画要素(如点、线、面),将事物最基本的特征进行图形化的绘画方式。

2. 巧用简笔画,辅助外语教学

1) 巧用简笔画,拉近师生之间的心理距离。

新接班级的第一节课或借班进行的公开课、比赛课,师生彼此陌生,教师借助简笔画介绍自己,既可以让学生了解自己,更能拉近师生之间的心理距离,并且有助于随之而来的课堂教学活动开展。

2) 巧用简笔画,可以为准备和组织课堂教学服务。

良好的开端是成功的一半。运用简笔画组织课堂教学,开始就能抓住学生的注意力,引起学生的兴趣,调动其学习积极性。

3) 巧用简笔画,可以进行旧课复习。

复习上节课讲的内容,有利于学生知识巩固。复习方式多种多样,可以背诵,可以默写,可以问答,复习经常带着检查的性质,而学生对检查常感紧张,唯恐表现不好,用简笔画则可以克服学生的紧张感,让学生轻松自如地复习旧课。

4) 用简笔画,可以使学生兴致盎然进入新课。

教师在组织上课,复习旧知后,就要引导学生进入新课环节。新课进入得自然、生动、新颖,学生就会感到轻松自如,容易产生参与兴趣,提高学习积极性。巧用简笔画,则会达到如此效果。例如,高三学生学习 Roots 一课时,教师就可以在黑板上画一棵树,从上到下依次问学生 What is it? 学生自然兴趣大增,积极回答,如 leaves, branches, trunk, roots 等,至此,教师抓住时机,问学生 Trees have trees, then do human beings have trees, too? 借此自然而然地导入新课……

5) 巧用简笔画,辅助词汇教学。

为了培养学生的英语语言思维,教师在课堂上应尽量少使用汉语。那么,如何少使用汉语?答案自然是用英语解释。然而限于学生词汇有限,英语解释难以进行时,简笔画的作用就会发挥得淋漓尽致。这种现象在英语教学中十分常见,不仅简单词汇如 desk, chair, ruler 等可以,就是一些高级词汇也可以,如 wrestling, minibus, fall in love, a surprised look, a deter-

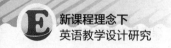
mined expression 等。

6) 巧用简笔画,可以帮助学生理解难点。

由于英语和汉语语言思维的差别,有些知识学生很难理解,有时甚至会出现教师越讲,学生越糊涂的现象。如果使用简笔画,学生则会"心有灵犀一点通",问题迎刃而解。如 a surprising look 和 a surprised look 二者的区别可为典型一例。A surprising look 意思是 a look which is surprising,而 a surprised look 的意思是 a look which shows that sb is surprised。但在教学实践中,即使这样的详细解释,学生还是不能理解。如果教师画上两个简笔画,学生则会哈哈一笑,心领神会。

7) 巧用简笔画,可以加深知识的理解和应用。

一堂课下来,往往内容很多,学生难免有些疲倦,利用简笔画,巩固当堂所学知识,既抓住中心,又保持了学生的兴趣。例如,学习完卓别林一课,教师随手在黑板上画出卓别林的简笔画,让学生用英语描述,或教师一边画简笔画,一边让学生用英语描述。再如,高二学生学完 At the tailor's shop 一课后,教师就可以布置任务:Tell the story to your partner in your own words, if you want you can use the stick figures given on the blackboard to help you.

8) 巧用简笔画,及时恰当地对学生进行表扬,活跃课堂气氛。

英语中有句话,Children are children。意思是,孩子就是孩子。换句话说,不管小学生、初中生还是高中生,谁都喜欢听到表扬,排斥批评,这也是人的本性。教师在课堂上除了用语言对学生进行表扬外,简笔画的作用也不可缺少。如教师奖给学生一个笑脸、一个足球、一台电脑,甚至一辆车(自然是画在黑板上),既节约时间,又具幽默感,还可以活跃课堂气氛。

9) 巧用简笔画,借题发挥,可以对学生进行思想教育。

外语教学的目的不仅在于发展学生技能,培养学生的能力,同时还要恰当地渗透思想教育。使用简笔画,则会使思想品德教育进行得自然、新颖而不空洞、抽象,容易发人深思。例如,学生学习完 Merchant of Venice 一课后,教师可以在黑板上画一个中间有方孔的古时铜钱,组织学生讨论或者辩论:Money is everything 或者 Money is not everything。引导学生认识到,

Money is indeed useful in our daily life，but it is not everything. It cannot buy love，friendship，health and so on. Sometimes it is even a knife which kills people.此时，教师在铜钱的方孔里画上一把尖刀，再在下面画上几滴血滴。这种简笔画不仅发人深省，还能给学生的心灵带来震颤，让学生受到思想上的洗礼。

第六节 教学语言与教态运用

一 教学语言

1. 教学语言的内涵

教学语言是教师教授知识、启迪智慧、塑造心灵的符号系统，作为信息传递的重要载体，它的表达方式在很大程度上影响学生对信息的吸收和理解。丰富的教学语言，也是教师最基本的教学技能。

2. 教学语言的特点

1）教学语言要具有准确性和科学性的特点，同时还应该具有语意连贯性、逻辑性的特点。

2）教学语言的语调应富有情感感染力。

3）教学语言既不能太快，也不能太慢，语速要适中。在学生理解的基础上，在单位时间内传递最大的信息量。

3. 英语教学语言策略

在我国英语课堂中，教师的语言是学生重要的目标语信息来源，因此，英语教师的语言应保证准确规范、清晰简明。

1）语音方面：要求发音清晰、停顿分明、语速适中。

2）词汇方面：以常用词为主，尽量避免俚语、习语及生僻词。

3）句法方面：多用短句、简单句，避免过多使用复杂句。

4）语篇方面：教师用熟读、熟记语篇，把语篇内容整合成自己的授课和交流内容,而不是单纯朗读语篇。

5)组织语言方面:英语课堂的语言内容分为语篇内容语言和组织课堂的语言两个方面。组织课堂的语言应注意地道性、得体性、多样性的特点。

6)课堂上应尽量用英语授课,以培养学生的英语思维。

7)英语课堂应适当使用汉语,汉语的使用应结合课堂内容和课型。使用汉语的目的是为了帮助学生更容易理解课堂内容。

二 体态语言的运用技能

1.体态语言的概念

体态语是指教师在课堂中通过表情、手势、姿态、动作等来传递教学信息的一种行为方式,通常用来辅助口头语言的表达,具有直观可视性。

2.体态语的分类

体态语一般分为外表言语、姿态言语和面部言语三大类。在外表言语方面,教师应注重自身外表,尤其是着装上的得体大方。在姿态言语方面,教师应重视手势语的运用,比如对学生的回答表示赞成或满意时,可以竖起大拇指以示肯定和鼓励。而在面部言语上,眼神活动和面部微笑是有效的传递信息手段。

3.体态语的运用策略

1)体态语可以拉近师生距离,增加师生感情。

在新学期的第一节课或借班级上公开课,师生之间不太熟悉,教师此时可以充分发挥体态语言的功能,指手画脚介绍自己,这样既吸引学生的注意力、介绍了自己,更向学生传递了"老师和蔼可亲、幽默风趣"的信号,无形之间拉近了师生之间的距离,增进了师生情感,使得随之而来的课堂活动轻松自如。

2)体态语可以帮助复习旧课。

旧课复习,形式各种各样,可以背诵、默写、提问、检测,也可以使用体态语言。例如,初中英语课堂复习"What's wrong with you?"句型时,教师或学生就可以捂着嘴,做出牙痛的姿态等让学生造句或问答,以此复习巩固该句型。

3）用体态语可以简洁、自然、新颖地导入新课。

课堂导入，如果构思新颖、巧妙，容易提高学生的积极性。巧用体态语言，就可以达到这个效果。例如，学习 Sports 的内容时，教师就可以先做一些运动的动作，边做边问学生，What am I doing? 学生就会饶有兴趣地回答，playing basketball，swimming，running，等等，这样就激活了学生的有关运动名称的英语知识，此时，教师随机总结，Yes，I am having sports. You know，sports are very important to all of us，so we should have a good knowlege of sports. Now let's learn Unit 10 sports.

4）体态语可以帮助学生学习新单词。

为了培养学生的英语语言思维，教师在课堂应尽量少使用汉语，如何少使用汉语？答案自然是用英语解释。然而限于学生词汇有限，英语解释难以进行时，体态语和简笔画一样，作用就会发挥得淋漓尽致。例如，学习 cry，smile，dance，cycle 等动词，excited，amazing，shocking 等形容词，以及学习 shadow，wrestling 等名词时，体态语都可以轻而易举让学生明白这些词语的意思。

5）体态语言可以帮助学生理解难点。

由于英语和汉语思维的差异，有些知识学生很难理解，有时甚至出现教师越讲学生越糊涂的现象。例如，wrap 和 cover，cut up 和 cut down 的区别。这个时候，教师不妨使用自己的体态语言，简单比划一下，学生就会心领神会。

6）体态语言可以及时恰当地对学生鼓励及暗示。

教师对学生课堂表现的鼓励，语言是不可替代的，但是体态语言也有语言所不能表达的妙用。比如，为表现好的学生竖起大拇指、拍起巴掌等，都能给学生以肯定、赞扬的鼓励。对做小动作的同学，教师不经意走过他/她身边，轻轻用手做以示意，有时效果远比大声训斥要好得多。

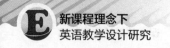

第七节　多媒体的应用

一　多媒体教学手段

1. 教学媒体的含义

媒体一词来源于拉丁语"Medium"，是指承载、加工和传递信息的介质或工具。当某一媒体被用于教学目的时，则被称为教学媒体。教学媒体是指在教学过程中承载和传递教学信息的工具或手段，它与一般媒体的区别在于它具有教学的功能，它是教学内容的载体，是教学内容的表现形式，是师生之间传递信息的工具，如实物、口头语言、图表、图像以及动画等。教学媒体往往要通过一定的物质手段实现，如书本、板书、投影仪、录像以及计算机等。

2. 媒体的分类

英国开放大学著名教育技术学者戴安娜·拉瑞劳德按媒体效能所提出的媒体分类观点，影响甚为深远。以下是她的分类：

表一　拉瑞劳德的教学媒体效能论分类观点

媒体类型	支持学习类型	实现技术
叙述媒体	授课	印刷品，电视，音频
交互媒体	调查	图书馆，网络
通讯媒体	讨论	讨论，讨论组，聊天室
可适应媒体	实验	实验室，仿真程序
著作媒体	著述	论文，产品，模型，建模

3. 教学媒体的特性

教学媒体有着多种特性，例如：呈现力、重现力、传送能力、可控性和参与性，下表是各种教学媒体特性一览表：

表二　教学媒体特性一览表

教学特性	媒体种类	教科书	板书	模型	无线电	录音	幻灯	电影	电视	录像	计算机
呈现力	空间特征			✓			✓	✓	✓	✓	
	时间特征		✓		✓	✓	✓	✓	✓		
	运动特征							✓	✓		✓
重现力	即时重现		✓			✓				✓	✓
	事后重现	✓		✓		✓		✓	✓	✓	✓
传送能力	无限接触	✓				✓			✓		
	有限接触		✓	✓			✓	✓		✓	✓
可控性	易控	✓	✓	✓		✓	✓			✓	✓
	难控				✓				✓		
参与性	感情参与					✓	✓		✓	✓	
	行为参与	✓	✓	✓			✓				✓

4. 英语教学课堂中教学媒体设计的原则

教学媒体是为教学服务的,教学媒体的选择必须要适合课堂的需要。为了满足课堂的需要,教学媒体的设计需要考虑以下原则:

1) 教学对象中心原则

教学对象的特征决定了教学媒体的有效性,不同阶段的教学对象心理特征是相异的,比如说小学阶段的学生思维简单,更适合形象化的教学,教学媒体多采用图片、音乐和动画之类的媒体;中学阶段甚至大学阶段,教学对象的心理逐渐变得成熟,形象化教学对他们而言显得过于幼稚,他们更倾向于抽象化的思维,教学媒体可选用一些符号或者文字等较抽象的语言。

2) 目标控制原则

教学目标是贯彻教学活动全过程的指导思想,指导学生对知识内容的选择和吸收,而且还要控制媒体类型和媒体内容的选择。例如,在英语阅读课上,教师要帮助学生完成培养阅读技巧的教学目标,需要的是文字讲解和练习,如果是要训练学生的听力能力,需要的则是录音或者动画。

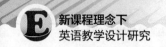

3）内容符合原则

对于英语而言,有新授课和复习课,不同的课型使用的教学媒体也是不同的。前者需要的教学媒体类型会更加丰富一些,比如音乐、动画、图片等视听媒体;而复习课需要的更多的则是板书或者印刷材料。教师要根据教学的需要选择合适的教学媒体。

4）最小代价原则

教学媒体的选择不仅要满足教学的需要,而且要考虑媒体使用时花费的时间和精力,力求做到代价最小,效能最大。

5）共同经验原则

选择的教学媒体,它所传递的信息必须是学生熟悉的已有的经验,若传递的信息不是媒体与学生共同的已有的经验,效果只会适得其反。

6）多重刺激原则

选择的教学媒体,应是从不同的角度、侧面,去表现事物的本质特征。所讲的对象,在不同的时间、地点、条件下多次重复出现;用不同的形式,表现同一内容,这种重复不应是机械的、无效的重复,而是不同形式的、有效的重复,每次重复,都应能提供一定的信息量,在学生的认识中添加一点新东西。

7）抽象层次原则

设计和选择的教学媒体,它所提供的信息的具体程度和抽象程度,要根据学生的实际状况(年龄、水平、智能情况)来决定,不同层次包含的具体成分和抽象成分的比例是不一样的。这两种成分的比例,应依学生的水平而有所改变。

教学媒体在英语教学过程中发挥了极大的作用,但是,任何事物都有两面性,教学媒体也有自身的弊端,教学媒体的过度使用不仅会使教师形成依赖心理,而且会让学生转移学习的注意力,达不到理想的教学效果。因此,在选用教学媒体时,要以上述原则为标准,选取最合适的教学媒体,帮助学生学习英语。

5. 英语教学课堂中设计教学媒体的建议

1）以教材为基础

教材是教授知识最基本的载体,无论是小学还是中学的英语教材,都包括了多种教学媒体,例如,文字,图片等。教师要认真研读教材,将教材中的知识与现实生活联系起来,创设真实的情境,激发学生的兴趣;此外,教师要将教材中的重难点知识通过简单易懂的方法讲授给学生,帮助学生增强记忆,巩固知识。

2)选择合适的教学媒体

随着多媒体的发展,一提到教学媒体,我们想到的更多的是幻灯片、投影仪等,其实不然,教学媒体的类型是多种多样的,教师要善于发现现实生活中的媒体,并将其有效地应用到英语教学过程中,使其发挥最大效用。同时,教学媒体的选择要根据教学内容来决定,不同的授课内容可以选择不同的教学媒体来呈现。在同一次课上也可选用多种形式的教学媒体来辅助教学。

3)合理利用有效资源

多媒体的出现为教学带来了极大的便利。通过多媒体,我们可以利用声音或者音乐设置情境,引起学生的兴趣;可以利用音频或者光盘,带领学生熟悉教材内容;可以利用网络,拓展学生思维。但是,任何事物都有两面性,多媒体在给教学带来便利的同时,也存在着一些隐患。比如,使用多媒体会使教师形成依赖心理,教师在上课时只展示课件,让学生不停地记笔记,不再板书,时间久了,学生会造成视觉疲劳。因此,在使用多媒体时,要摆正心态,时刻牢记:教学媒体在教学过程中发挥的只是辅助作用,我们应合理使用多媒体,进行有效教学。

二 多模态教学手段应用

英语课程标准要求,积极开发和合理利用课程资源是英语课程实施的重要组成部分。在英语教学中,除了合理有效地使用教科书外,教师还应该积极利用其他课程资源,特别是广播影视节目、录音、录像资料、直观教具和实物、多媒体光盘资料、各种形式的网络资源、报刊杂志等。

在此背景下,多模态话语理论逐渐引起中学英语教学研究者的重视。利用多模态辅助英语教学被认为是改变传统的教学方法,改变单一的课堂教学模式,适应多媒体信息技术发展趋势,优化学生学习方式,培养学生自主学习能力的有益探索。

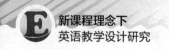
1. 多模态话语理论及其意义

多模态话语理论是国外学者于 20 世纪末期发起的一种新的分析理论，是指运用听觉、视觉、触觉等多种感觉，通过语言、图像、声音、动作等多种手段和符号资源进行交际的现象。Charwat(1992)认为，模态(modality)是一种经过三种渠道而实现的感知方式，分别为视觉模态(visual modality)、听觉模态(auditive modality)和触觉模态(tactile modality)，在信息传递过程中，通过单个感官进行的互动为单模态，通过两个感官进行的互动为双模态，而运用了三个或三个以上的感官的互动称之为多模态。Stein(2000)提出多模态教学法，他认为课堂上所有的交际活动都是多模态的。

毫无疑问，多模态教学能够充分调动学生的积极性，改变英语课堂教学的师生角色，体现新课程理念下的"学生主体，教师主导"；多模态教学将会改变传统的教学方式，形成多模态的新的课堂教学模式；课堂教学方式的改变也必将会带来学生学习方式的转变，学生由被动的知识吸收者转变为合作、探索、体验、交流活动中自主学习者。

2. 中学英语课堂教学中多模态教学手段

笔者认为，传统课堂教学也不乏多模态手段的，只不过常常被单模态手段所掩盖，例如教师的"讲"、黑板的"板书"、教材及阅读材料、录音与音乐、教学挂图和卡片、教学简笔画和课堂体态语。欲将这些单模态手段转化为丰富、有趣和有效的多模态手段，常常需要教师拥有先进的教学理念、丰富的教学经验、高度的教学热情和高超的教学技巧。例如，教师在教授 CHALIE CHAPLINE 一课时，可以用简笔画画出卓别林的形象、故事，再配上恰当的音乐，由学生讲述或表演。另外，这些传统多模态教学手段，往往受到教材内容等的影响，也时时面临网络环境下成长的学生的挑战。

现代教育信息化为英语课堂教学的多模态手段创造了条件。多媒体光盘、英语影视节目、英语录像资料、PPT 课件、网络平台的利用，都为多模态在教学中的使用提供了较为有利的条件。例如多模态课件的使用，越来越受到师生的欢迎和喜爱。教师根据自己的教学设计，通过视频、录像、文字、音乐、动画、图片、超链接等整合，在向学生传授知识的同时，极大地调动了学生的积极性，激发了学生的学习兴趣。在不远的将来，网络环境下的多模态教学将会展示更大的魅力。在多媒体和网络环境下,传统课堂的师生互动和生生互动模式将会得到突破,教师、学生、学习内容和资源、问题情景、网络环境等之间的互动将成为常态,网络将文本、图形、动画、静态影像、动态影像、声音媒体有机结合在一起,最终形成网络环境下的学生中心、教师主导的模式,充分体现学生的主体地位和学生之间互动的多维立体互动系统。

因此,中学英语课堂教学中的多模态手段既包括传统课堂教学的多模态手段,又包括现代教育信息技术下的多模态手段,还包括二者的有机整合。而主流应该是培养网络环境下多模态教学手段。

3. 中学英语教师实践多模态话语理论的建议

1) 真正树立新课标要求的先进教学理念。摆脱英语教学只是培养学生语言技能和语言知识的片面思想,树立外语教学是为了培养学生的综合语言运用能力和创新能力的先进理念。

2) 树立新的课程资源观念。教材不是课程资源的全部,只是英语教学的主要参考,教材的局限性必须通过与其他资源的整合,才能发挥其应有的作用。

3) 积极学习多模态话语理论,了解该话语理论产生的背景和实际意义,多关注该话语理论在英语教学研究方面的进展,了解其优势和不足。

4) 循序渐进,培养自己资源整合水平。例如可以从使用好简笔画、PPT课件开始,并将这些技能进一步熟练,并不断尝试微课和翻转课堂的教学实践,在实践中培养自己资源整合水平。为网络环境下的英语教学做好准备。

5) 开展行动研究,积极探索、不断积累。在自己的实际教学中,以多模态话语理论的应用开展行动研究,用多模态话语理论解决目前中学英语课堂教学中存在的问题。例如,由于"任务型教学"在我国中学英语教学中很难得以应用,能不能将"任务型教学"与多模态话语理论结合起来,发展任务型教学理论。

6) 积累行之有效的教学设计案例。"教学有法,教无定法",这句话也适用多模态教学。教师要按照课标要求,注意开发多层次和多类型的英语课程资源,满足不同层次的需要。不能脱离自己的教学实际、脱离自己的教

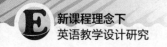
学内容,一味追求课程资源的多样性。

第八节　结课技能和作业设计技能

一　结课技能

1. 结课的概念

结课是指所有课堂教学活动结束后,教师组织学生对本节课的教学内容进行归纳总结,以便使学生所学的知识得以及时转化、升华、条理化和系统化,这个教学环节就叫做结课。

2. 结课的分类

结课并没有固定模式,结课往往会根据教学内容和形式以及教师的教学风格而变化。但梳理归纳起来,大致分为一下几类:

1) 归纳式分类。

归纳式结课是指教师在教学任务完成后用总结性的、简洁的语言,或用表格,或用图示梳理本一节课的知识结构体系。这种结课方式在中小学常规课中较为常见。

2) 活动式结课。

活动式结课是指教师采用过竞赛、表演、演示等形式进行结课的方法。活动第一要紧密联系前面的任务和内容,同时是对前面任务和内容的展示、总结和升华。

3) 情感提升式结课。

情感提升式结课是教师基于前面的教学内容,依照课程标准情感、态度、价值观及文化意识培养的要求,用生动的文字、音乐和富有感染力的视频等形式进行的结课。这是公开课常用的形式。

4) 伏笔式结课。

伏笔式结课,也叫悬念式结课,常被学生称为卖关子,是指教师借用传统评书的"且听下回分解"方法,通过设置疑问、留下思考问题以启发学生思考和课后探索的结课方法。这种结课方式常见于智慧型教师的课堂。

5)拓展式结课。

拓展式结课是指教师把前面的教学内容作进一步拓展、延伸的结课方法。

3.结课的基本要求

无论何种结课方式,都应该概括简练、针对性强、有质量和价值、有全面性。启发性、深刻性和教育性是对结课技能的更高要求。

二 作业布置技能

作业是对课堂教学的巩固和反馈,既有助于学生巩固知识和技能,也有助于教师在下节课教学过程中及时弥补和调整教学内容。但现实教学中,不顾学生的基础、时间等因素,大量布置作业的现象极其严重,不仅不能体现作业布置的真正目的,更成了加重学生课业负担的推手,因此,新课程理念下作业布置的技能更值得探索。

1.作业布置应正确处理质与量的关系

在作业布置中,题目要精,量要适当。这就要求教师布置作业前需要精选、需要先做,及早把握作业所用时间、对课堂知识的巩固程度等。

2.学生差异与作业梯度的关系

学生的学习能力有高有低,教师布置的作业往往针对大部分处于中等水平的学生,对于学有余力的学生,可以布置一些有难度的题目来启发学生的发散思维,提高学生解决难题的能力。对于基础薄弱的学生,则应多布置基础的、知识性的作业。

3.要有利于下节课反馈

不能一布置就是一张试卷,结果由于下节课的教学任务而不能处理试卷中的问题。

4.作业形式多样化

内容上可以朗读课文、记忆单词、预习语法,也可以写评论和感想,还可以制作 poster;要求上可以布置必做作业(required homework)和选做作(optional homework)。

本章参考文献：

[1] 李宝峰.教学技能理论与实践[M].北京：华文出版社，2008.

[2] 熊群红.英语专业师范生课堂教学技能培养研究——以九江某高校师范学院为例[D].江西农业大学，2016.

[3] 胥文玲.英语专业师范生教学技能的构成要素和培养路径[J].闽江学院学报，2011，32(6)：63—67.

[4] 张铁牛.教学技能研究的理论探讨[J].教育科学，1997(2)：28.

[5] 宋明江，胡守敏，杨正强.论教师教学能力发展的特征、支点与趋势[J].教育研究与实验，2015(2)：49—52.

[6] 徐洁.中学英语初任教师教学能力发展研究[D].西南大学，2015：28.

[7] 束定芳.外语教师与科研[J].外语教学理论与实践，2002(1)：1—5.

[8] 冯忠良.教育心理学[M].人民教育出版社，2010.

[9] 童菊英.小学英语课堂组织教学策略的探究[J].中国教育技术装备，2011，01：11.

[10] 鲁子问，王笃勤.新编英语教学论[M].上海：华东师范大学出版社，2006

[11] 施良方，崔允漷.教学理论——课堂教学的原理、策略与研究[M].华东师范大学出版社，1999.

[12] 李颖.课堂教学的信息传递模式及策略探讨[J].现代教育科学，2015(08)：150—152.

[13] 胡定荣.课堂反馈的学习理论视角与综合分类[J].上海教育科研，2013(03)：57—60.

[14] 康淑敏，王雪梅.从教学要素角度探究多媒体环境下的英语教学策略[J].外语界，2003(02)：34—40.

[15] 徐锦芬.纠正性反馈与外语教学[A].《第二语言学习研究》2015年第1期[C]，2015：14.

[16] 赵勇.优化教学信息传递过程的策略[J].四川警察学院学报，2008(06)：92—96.

[17] (美)艾默等著，王毅译.中学课堂管理[M].北京：中国轻工业出版社，2004：4.

[18] (美)布罗菲著，陶志琼译.透视课堂管理[M].北京：中国轻工业出版社，2010：2.

[19] 陈时见.课堂管理：意义与变革[J].教育科学研究，2003(6)：11.

[20] 刘家访.课堂管理理论研究述评[J].课程·教材·教法，2002(10)：26.

[21] 刘恩允，中小学课堂问题行为的成因分析几管理对策研究[J]，《山东教育》2002，29.

[22] 龙炳文.浅谈英语教师课堂纪律管理的艺术[J]教学与管理,2000,12.

[23] 王晓娟.中学英语课堂管理探究[J].大众文艺,2012(20).

[24] 袁鹏飞.初中课堂问题行为及其管理策略研究[D].南京:南京师范大学,2008.5.

[25] 张绍州.论中学交际英语课堂管理[D].四川:四川师范大学,2007,3.

[26] 张永耀.新课改下高中课堂管理现状的教育现象学研究[D].甘肃:西北师范大学,
2013.5.

[27] 陈时见.浅谈课堂中的时间管理[J].基础教育研究,1998(3):21—23.

[28] 孙孔懿.教育时间学[M].南京:江苏教育出版社,1998.

[29] 董晓波.谈外语教师的反思性学习与反思性教学[J].英语通(初中教研版),2007
(1):25—27.

[30] 高翔,王蔷.反思性教学:促进外语教师自身发展的有效途径[J].外语教学,2003,2.

[31] 卢真金.反思性实践是教师专业发展的重要举措[J].比较教育研究,2001(8):
92—94.

[32] 熊川武.反思性教学[M].上海:华东师范大学出版社,1999.

[33] 王天乾,彭湘萍.反思性教学与教师职业发展[J].北京航空航天大学学报(社会科学
版),2003(3):46—48.

[34] 郎雪.高中英语课堂形成性评价实施情况调查[D].东北师范大学,2006.

[35] 梁海群.基于学习档案袋的高中英语口语教学评价研究[D].重庆师范大学,2016.

[36] 杨凡.实施高中英语激励性评价的策略[J].语数外学习(高中版中旬),2017,12:77.

[37] 詹苏纳.新课标理念下的高中英语课堂教学评价[J].海外英语,2012,11:52—
53、64.

[38] 钟友泉.高中英语教学评价之工具性和人文性的和谐统一[J].新课程(下),2018,
01:212.

[39] 朱洪翠.高中英语教师课堂话语有效性评价指标体系研究[D].南京师范大学,2012.

[40] 网络资源.

下编

实践篇

Chapter 05

第五章 ● 课堂教学设计案例

第一节　小学课堂教学设计案例

案例一　译林版小学英语六年级下册 Unit 2 教学设计

一　指导思想及整体设计思路

1.《义务教育英语课程标准(2011 版)》要求:能听懂简单的配图小故事;能在老师的帮助和图片的提示下描述或讲述简单的小故事;能认读所学词语,并能借助图片读懂简单的故事或小短文,养成按意群阅读的习惯;能根据图片、词语或例句的提示,写出简短的语句。

2. 基于以学生为中心的基本理念,根据小学六年级学生的特点以及他们的知识情况,结合本单元教学内容 Good Habits(好习惯),我认真研读了本单元教学内容,通过图片和视频等形式设计出与习惯相关的听说教学活动。其中,一是让学生说出个人的读书、整理房间、起床等习惯,并且需要对这些习惯做出对比,辨别出哪些是好的习惯。二是通过图片将教学内容展示出来,让学生讨论:王兵和刘涛的好习惯体现在哪些方面,刘涛的坏习惯又表现在哪些方面,并让同学们总结出在生活中如何养成好的习惯。三是让同学们重述故事。从而达到训练学生知识、学会学习,提升学生健康生活等目标。

二 教材分析

本节课的教学内容源于译林出版社《英语 English》六年级(下册)Unit 2 的内容,为 Unit 2 的第一课时,是一节听说课,主要围绕"Good Habits(好习惯)"展开话题,涉及用一般现在时描述目前的习惯。以养成好习惯的轨迹展开知识,通过对比的方法展示出来。通过本节课的学习,学生能了解一般现在时的特点并用一般现在时描述个人习惯,为以后的学习打好基础。

三 学情分析

学生通过 Unit 1 已经基本掌握了用一般过去时描述过去的动作行为,并且学会了一些表示动作、时间的词汇和短语,能够为本节课"好习惯"话题的展开做好准备。六年级的学生思维活跃,英语学习积极性挺高,但不能用英语流利而且准确地表达自己。

四 教学目标分析

通过本节课的学习,学生能够达到以下目标:

1. 能正确理解、朗读短文并可以根据提示复述课文内容。

2. 能听懂、会读、会说单词和短语 brush, finish, habits, get up, in order, go to bed late 等。

3. 能尝试用所学的短语和句型来描述个人习惯。

4. 能初步根据提示写出好的习惯。

5. 能分清好坏习惯,并知道以好的习惯来要求自己,让自己拥有更多好习惯。

本节课的重点、难点

重点:1. 能正确理解、朗读课文并可以根据提示复述课文内容。

2. 能听懂、会读、会说单词 brush, finish, habits, tidy, messy, in order, get up 等。

难点:能尝试根据所学短语和句型来描述自己的习惯。

五 教学方法

结合本节课知识特点和学生实际情况,本节课将采用的教学方法:

1. 情景教学法　2. 任务型教学法

六 教学流程

Step 1:Warming up and Lead-in(mins 4)

T:Boys and girls, let's see some pictures. Then answer my questions.

T:Ok. Let's look at those pictures. The first one. The boy is late for school. Our class begins at 8 o'clock. Now this boy is late for class. Is it right or wrong for students?

S:Wrong.

T:Well done. Follow me:is late for ...

S:Is late for ...

T:The second one. The girl's room is very tidy. Like this room, it's tidy. Do you like her room?

S:Yes.

T:Good job. Follow me:tidy.

S:Tidy.

T:The third one. The boy is helping his mother to clean the room. So their room is clean and tidy. Is it right or wrong for students?

S:Right.

T:Very good. Follow me:clean and tidy.

S:Clean and tidy.

T:The last one. The girl is talking loudly with her friends in the reading room. Is it right or wrong for students?

S：Wrong.

T：Which students do you like best? Why?

S1：

S2：

T：We all like the students in the second and third pictures, because they have a good habit. We don't like the students in the first and last pictures, because they have a bad habit. So today, we are going to learn Unit 2 Good Habits.

【设计意图】学生观看图片，调动学生积极性，引入本课话题，用图片让学生感知生词和短语的意思。

Step 2：**Pre-reading**(mins 10)

T：Boys and girls. We need good habits, so do our good friends Wang Bing and Liu Tao. They also have good habits in their daily life. First, let's look at Wang Bing's habits. Please listen and tick.

T：How many did you tick? Please answer my questions one by one.

A：get up early in the morning. ( )

B：never go to bed late. ( )

C：brush his teeth in the morning and before bedtime. ( )

D：put his things in order. ( )

E：finish his homework before dinner. ( )

S1：

S2：

S3：

T：Ok. Very good. These are Wang Bing's habits. How about Liu Tao? Let' go on the video. Please listen and tick.

T：How many did you tick? Please answer my questions one by one.

A：listen to his teachers at school. ( )

B：keep his room clean and tidy. ( )

C：help his parents. （ ）

D：do his homework late at night and don't go to bed early. （ ）

S1：

S2：

S3：

设计意图 训练学生听力和语言表达能力,简单了解课文知识。

Step 3：while-reading(mins 10)

T：Let's read following new words：brush, finish, habits, get up, in order ...

S：...

T：Now open your books, please read the passage carefully. Then talk about the questions in your group. Now，I will divide you into six groups. Group 1，Group 2 ... Group 6. Two questions：What are good habits? What are bad habit? Ok, let's do it.

S：Talk about questions in groups, then answer the questions.

设计意图 小组合作谈论,寻求答案,理解短文。

Step 4：post-reading(mins 10)

T：Well done. We have finished the passage. Now，let's retell the story. You can talk about it in your group. Then choose one student to retell the story in your group, and we'll decide which group is the best. Please go on.

S1：...

S2：...

S3：...

S4：...

S5：...

S6：...

设计意图 小组合作,提高学生参与的积极性,训练学生复述短文的语言表达能力。

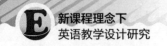
Step 5：Consolidation（mins 5）

1. Thinking and Talking.

T：Hello，boys and girls. We know Liu Tao has three good habits，and two bad habits. He wants to do better. Can you help him to change the bad habits?

（小组讨论，选择几个同学回答。）

2. Try to write.

You say a lot of things about good habits. Please write down some good habits you know. Then share them with us.

设计意图 引发学生思考：什么是好习惯？如何养成好习惯？同时，培养学生口头表达的能力。

Step 6：Homework（mins 1）

1. Review the story time and retell the story.

2. Copy some important phrases and sentences.

设计意图 巩固学到的知识。

Blackboard Design

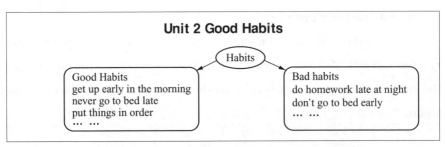

案例二　新版 PEP 小学英语五年级下册 Unit 1　My day Part C Story time 教学设计

1. 指导思想及整体设计思路

《义务教育小学英语新课程标准》倡导学生通过感知、体验、实践、参与合作等方式，实现任务目标，感受成功。因此，我们应该让更多的学生在学习过程中收获知识、体验快乐,真正做到在"以生为本"的教育理念的指引下,让学生的英语语言能力、思维品质、文化品格、学习能力得到更好地培养。

基于以上理念,本课时在设计时,师生一起复习与巩固有关人物一周活动安排的词汇和句型,而不是单纯机械地操练单词和句型。学生在完成任务后能够知道它们的含义以及在什么情景中去运用它们,达到与人交流的目的。

2. 教材分析

本课选自于新版 PEP 小学英语五年级下册 Unit 1 My day Part C Story time,这是一节阅读会话课,本单元的主题是学习日常生活以及周末活动安排的知识,该课时通过 Zoom 和 Zip 一周活动的情景,巩固和复习本单元的核心句型"What do you do on the weekend?"。

3. 学情分析

本课的教学对象是五年级的学生,求知欲和好奇心强,学习积极性很高,在课堂上善于表现自我。他们在前五课时里已经学习了描述日常生活的单词、短语和句型,具备了一定的相关英语知识基础。这些特点将有利于师生和生生在课堂上进行互动交流。

4. 教学目标(含重难点)

1)能在图片和教师的帮助下理解故事内容,复习与巩固有关人物一周活动安排的词汇和句型。

能按正确的语音、语调、意群朗读故事,并能表演故事。

渐渐养成合理安排时间的良好生活习惯,懂得分享的快乐。

2)教学重点:能够理解故事内容并讲解故事。

教学难点:理解新授词组 collect nuts 和 dry nuts 以及新授句型 He is always busy,并能分角色扮演完成对话。

5. 教学方法

采用任务型教学法、情景教学法、视听法。

6. 教学手段

交互式一体机,PPT 课件和动画视频。

7. 教学流程

Step 1:Warming up and leading in(热身互动,自然导入)

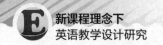

1) T：Let's sing a song together. (My weekend) Are you ready?

Ss：Yes.

设计意图 轻松愉快的歌曲，可以让学生复习之前学过的一周活动安排的词汇和句型，也可以很快形成学习英语的课堂氛围，激发学生学习兴趣。

2) T：How busy I am! Are you busy this week?

Ss：Yes.

T：I'm busy this week, because I have a lot of things to do, every day I must prepare my English and Chinese lessons, and after class I must check your homework, so I'm very busy this week. What about you?

Ss：We are also very busy. We have math lessons, English lessons, Chinese lessons, PE lessons and so on.

T：How many days are there in a week?

Ss：Seven days.

T：Yes. The first day is Monday in China, but in western countries Sunday is the first day. Let's continue, the second day is Tuesday, Wednesday, Thursday, Friday, Saturday and Sunday. We know Saturday and Sunday are weekend, we can do a lot of things to relax ourselves. (板书 busy, 星期一到星期日的缩写, 并完善思维导图)

设计意图 轻松愉快的谈话导入，让学生复习了周一到周日的英文表达，为后面的英语学习做了很好的铺垫。我给同学们介绍了东西方的文化差异，培养了学生的文化品格。

Step 2：Presentation(呈现新知)

1) T：Now let's enjoy our story time, first, Let's look at the picture, who are they? They are Zoom and Zip, and we are friends. This story happens between them. Now Let's listen and answer the question：What does Zip usually do on the weekend? Please listen carefully. And then I will ask：What do you usually do on your weekend? For me, I usually go shopping with my family. How about you?

Ss：play football, go for a walk, do sports and so on.

设计意图 巧设问题,培养学生的思维品质。阅读会话课让学生先从视听入手,整体感知整个故事,并让学生带着问题去听故事,孩子们的注意力会更集中,学习会更加专心。在回答完有关听力的问题之后,紧接着用本单元的核心句型 What do you usually do on your weekend? 再提问也让学生复习了之前学过的有关一周的活动的短语。

2) T:Now, Let's go on, what will they say? Zip says:It's Saturday. Now, I'm always very busy. Do you know what will Zoom say? Can you guess?

Ss:Zoom will say "why?"

T:Yes, Zoom says:Why? Follow me and read it, we should act like Zoom strongly and Zip gently.

设计意图 指导学生有感情并带动作朗读,读的时候一定要有 Zoom 强壮和 Zip 温柔的感觉,师生、生生和小组之间分角色朗读。

3) T:And why is Zip very busy? Do you want to know? I want to know. Let's continue and think:what does Zip usually do From Monday to Wednesday? Let's look and guess. Zip says:Let me see. From Monday to Wednesday, I usually collect nuts in the afternoon. Look at "collect", pay attention to the pronunciation and the meaning in Chinese, it's OK?

Ss:捡、拾。

T:Yes, you are right. This time, we do and say, ok?(板书 collect, nuts,并用自然拼读法强调 collect 的发音)

设计意图 本环节我采用 TPR 教学法,让学生带感情边做动作边说英语,让他们体会到学习英语的乐趣,也很容易记住新单词和句子。另外,我在教授单词 collect 的时候,使用了自然拼读法,让学生很快掌握了单词的发音规律。

4) Let's go on, what does Zip often do on Thursday? Zoom says:What else? Zip says:On Thursday, I often dry my nuts in the sun. Dry my nuts in the sun, do you know the meaning of "dry"? Yes, it's 晒干、晾干。We should read it like Zoom and Zip.(板书 dry my nuts 并带动作朗读句子)

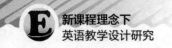

T：Let's see what happened then? Look，who are they?

Ss：They are Zip's friends，rabbit，hamster，dog and monkey. What does Zip usually do on Friday? On Friday，they eat nuts with their friends. They will be very happy，because sharing makes us happy，Yes? Now Let's read and act like Zoom and Zip happily.（板书 eat nuts）

设计意图 让学生深刻感受 Zip 和好朋友们分享东西的快乐心情,并让他们带着这种感情去朗读,课堂效果非常棒。

5）What do you usually do from Monday to Friday? Maybe you usually have many different classes，Chinese，English，Math class，and so on.

设计意图 以新知为切入点帮助学生复习旧知,通过图一、图二、图三和图四的学习,又引出本单元的核心句型 What do you usually do from Monday to Friday? 同时学生们又复习了有关一周活动的单词,短语和句型。

6）Zoom says：What do you usually do on the weekend? Zip says：I usually watch TV，but this weekend I have a show，I will play the *pipa*.（板书 watch TV 和 play the *pipa* 并指导朗读）

T：Is the story ending? Maybe "Yes"，maybe "No". Let's look at it together. Now，it's 11：30，Zoom says：When does your show begin? Zip says：Saturday，at 12 o'clock，Oh，no! What happens then? Can you guess?

Ss：Zip is late.

T：Anything else?

Ss：Zip is on time and she plays the *pipa*.

设计意图 开放式的故事结尾会让学生联想不断,我让他们大胆地猜测接下来会发生什么事情,猜猜他们会说些什么? 学生们对这个话题非常感兴趣,上课的热情不断高涨。

7）Look at the picture, why does Zoom look like having a big question? Because Zoom doesn't understand Zip，why does she run away? And how do you feel about this weekend?

Ss：It's very busy.

设计意图 本环节采用了讨论法,老师和学生共同讨论并猜想 Zoom 的疑惑并切身感受 Zip 的忙碌。

8) Now，let's look at the video，and follow it，OK？

设计意图 让学生整体观看 story time 的动画视频并跟读,学生们在理解故事大意的情况下,可以更快、更好的朗读并掌握 story time 的文本内容。

Step 3：Practising(巩固操练)

1) Let's review and fill in the blank. Please take out your paper, and write down your answers，then I'll check.

设计意图 学生在学完整个故事情节之后,根据表格的提示,可以很快地填出本课的关键短语。

2) Please put these pictures into right order.

设计意图 学生根据理解,回忆故事发生的情节,可以很轻松地给图片排出正确的顺序。

3) Make up a title of this story.

设计意图 为了训练学生归纳总结的能力,在他们学完了整个 story time 之后,我特别让他们给故事加个题目,学生们很容易就能想到许多不同的故事题目。

Step 4：Production(拓展运用)

Let's play in a role. Talk in your group. Several minutes for you. Have a show for us.

设计意图 古人云:"授人以鱼,不如授人以渔"。让学生们在具体的情景中正确的运用今天的短语和核心句型,培养了他们的语言能力和学习能力。

Step 5：Summary(归纳总结)

1) In our daily life, when we feel tired, we should relax and rest, then we will do a better job. And we also know "Sharing makes us happy." Because sharing together means being happy together.

设计意图 教育学生要养成合理安排时间的良好生活习惯,懂得劳逸结合。让学生们也要懂得分享的快乐。

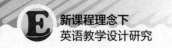
2) Who is today's winner? In my eyes, you are all winners, because you all did a good job, clap your hands.

设计意图 课堂最后及时适当的总结评价,可以让学生对英语保持很高的学习热情,也让他们很期待每一次的英语课堂。

Step 6:Homework(家庭作业)

1) Listen and read the story.

2) Write or draw an ending of the story.

3) Make up a new story about "My busy weekend".

设计意图 在这里我布置了三个作业,第一个和第二个作业是每个孩子都必须要完成的作业,第三个是选做作业。孩子们可以根据自己的实际情况来选择作业,这样的分层优化作业布置可以让学生课后的学习质量更高、效果更好。

8. 板书设计(Blackboard design)

Unit 1   My day

　　　　　　　　　　　—Part C   Story time

1. New Words

　Monday Tuesday Wednesday Thursday Friday Saturday

2. New phrases

　collect nuts   eat nuts

3. Important sentence

　What do you usually do on the weekend?

设计意图 简洁清晰的板书设计,黑板左边是重要的单词、短语、句型,可以让学生把握住本课的重点内容,右边是本课的思维导图,它可以帮助学生很轻松地复述出故事内容。

9. 教学评价及反思

评价是英语课堂的重要组成部分,适时有效的教学评价,可以大大鼓励孩子们学习英语的兴趣,也提高了学生的学习效率。所以在本节课我采用了以下的评价内容和方法:

1) 评价内容:评价学生单词的发音,如 collect, dry 等;评价学生分角色表演的情景剧。

2）评价方法：教师用激励的语言评价学生的表现：如 good，nice，perfect，excellent 和 good job 等。教师也可用激励性的手势表扬学生，与学生互动：如 give me five，give me ten 等。学生用激励性的手势评价同学的表现：拍手加鼓掌并说 good，good，very good。采用小组加分的竞争机制。

教学反思

优点：通过本节课的讲授，我觉得对话教学要由词到句，由机械性练习到真实的情景中去表演，把文本升华到另一个高度。在本节课的学习中，我针对学生的特点，使用了多种教学方法，适时适当地鼓励学生，学生们表现得很积极，精神状态饱满，课堂气氛活跃。

不足：由于课前准备的不充分，教授新知的时间有点太长。由于时间的关系，孩子们在分角色表演的时候，我给他们留的时间不是很充分，导致这部分完成的有点仓促。

再教改进措施：1.如果下次再上本课的话，课前我会做好充分的准备，使课堂的思路更清晰，把教授新知的时间再压缩一点。2.我会把课堂的时间分配得更合理一点，给学生留够充分的时间来表演对话。

案例三　新标准外研社版英语一年级 Module 4 Unit 2　These are your eyes 教学设计

一　教学理念

《义务教育小学英语新课程标准》指出，英语教学应该以学生为主体，首先要培养学生的学习兴趣、信心、策略和习惯；强调课程从学生的学习兴趣和认知水平出发，倡导体验、参与、合作与交流的学习方式，发展学生的综合语言运用能力。同时指出，教师在教学中初步渗透阅读策略，发展学生的自主学习能力。

二　文本分析

本课选自新标准外研社版英语一年级起点一年级下册 Module 4 Unit

2 These are your eyes。本单元是巩固练习,除了要用"this is my ..."来介绍自己的五官以外,还要用"these are your ..."的形式来介绍自己或他人的五官。通过创设课文情境:一只小蜘蛛向妈妈询问自己的身体部位,因为年龄很小,小蜘蛛不太清楚自己身体各部位的名称和功能,引导学生关注身体,掌握并运用身体部位的描述,初步了解复数名词、these 的用法。

三 学情分析

参与上课的是我校小学一年级的 38 名学生。学生年龄较小,绝大部分孩子刚开始接触英语,基础知识很少甚至没有。但是他们对英语有浓厚的学习兴趣,喜欢动手、动口,喜欢模仿、扮演角色,接受能力非常强,不过注意力还不稳定,容易分散。

学生已经基本知道"ear, mouth, eye, head"等等,也会用"this is my ..."来介绍自己的五官。这是学生初次接触英语中名词复数形式,要区分单数形式和复数形式有些困难。

四 教学目标

本节课结束时,学生将能够:

1. 听、说关于身体部位的名称,如:legs, hands, feet 等。

2. 理解并运用"these are my/your ..."来介绍自己的或者他人的五官。

3. 正确使用肢体语言和句型"What are these?""These are your/my ..."进行小组对话。

4. 提高学习英语的兴趣,能积极观察生活中遇到的动物或者人的器官及其数量,并能用英语进行描述。

教学重、难点

教学重点:

1. 能够听、说关于身体部位的名称,如:legs, hands, feet 等。

2. 理解并运用"these are my/your ..."来介绍自己的或者他人的五官。

3. 培养学习英语的兴趣,养成善于观察、使用英语的习惯。

教学难点:理解并掌握"these"和"this"的不同用法。

五　教学方法

情景教学法、全身反应法

六　教学手段

课本配套光盘、PPT、视频、单词卡片、头饰、黑板

七　教学过程

Step 1：Lead in

（1）Greetings：Good morning，boys and girls!

（2）Song：Ten little fingers.

（3）Reviewing：Point and ask：what's this? Then point and say：this is your ... Point to myself and ask：what's this?

【Design intention】

The lesson beginning with the song "Ten little fingers" can arouses the students' interest immediately and tells them that the topic of the lesson is body parts.

Step 2：Presentation

（1）Creating a context

Stick a spider on the blackboard and ask："what's this?" Then point to one leg of the spider and ask："what's this?" Teach the word "leg". Point to two legs and ask："what are these?" Ask students to answer with "these are ..." Ask the students to follow and read："These are legs."

（2）Watching a video about spider.

After watching, tell how many legs the spider has.

（3）Watching another video about mother spider and baby spider.

After watching, students answer two questions：

Which body parts did the baby spider ask?

How many eyes does the baby spider have?

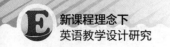
【Design intention】

Watching the video with questions can make the students more interested and the lesson more effective.

Step 3：Practice

① Open the textbook and turn to page 23. Listen, point and imitate.

② Work in pairs. One is the baby spider, the other one is the mother spider. Role play the conversation.

③ Show the conversation in the front of the classroom.

【Design intention】

Listening, pointing and imitating can lead the students to better learning habits. Meanwhile, it grasps their attention tightly on the conversation.

Step 4：Consolidation

(1) The teacher says … game

(2) I say, you do. Then one student say, the others do.

【Design intention】

By playing games, the teacher can evaluate the learning results of the students in a joyful and happy atmosphere.

Step 5：Summary

Spiders can use their bodies to do magic things. Our bodies can do many things, too. So protect them and keep them in health.

Homework

Introduce your body parts with "This is my …" or "These are my …" to your parents.

八　教学评价与反思

这节课中，学生的积极性很高，对身体部位的单词已经熟练掌握，大部分学生已经能够熟练运用中心句型"What are these?"和"These are my/your …"自由灵活地对身体部位进行问答对话。但是，仍有个别学生对名词复数形式把握不够,"these"与"this"区分不好,还需要继续加强练习。

在课堂上,我善于发现学生的闪光点,对于表现积极的学生,我会及时鼓励和表扬,同时进行了有针对性的评价。但是对极个别学生的关注可能还不够,需要多加关注。

九 板书设计

Module 4　Unit 2　These are your eyes.
leg
feet　　　　　　　　What are these?
hand　　　　　　　These are your eyes.

案例四　人教版小学英语三年级下册 Unit 5　Do you like pears? A let's spell 教学设计

1. Teaching ideology

The "Core competence theory", which emphases on "Fostering integrity and promoting the rounded development of people", has a profound impact on Chinese education. Based on this teaching philosophy as well as the National English Curriculum, this lesson focuses on cultivating students' all-round ability.

During this class, students will be the center. By leading students to participating in the meaningful activities, we aim at expanding their knowledge of language using, developing their language skills, forming their culture awareness and improving their thinking ability.

2. Analysis of the teaching Materials

The material is used for the second term in Grade 3. This class is concerned with the "Let's spell" parts in Unit 5 Do you like pears? The phonetic teaching is presented as "Let's spell" parts in this book, which introduces short vowels and the corresponding relationship between the vowels

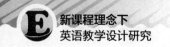

and the letters. This lesson is organized in the order of listen, chant and figure out the pronunciation of "u" in words fun, run, duck, under, etc. For consolidation, another material "It's fun to jump" is added.

3. Analysis of the students

The target students are from Grade 3 in a rural primary school. The class is very big and there are 53 students in it. Though having studied English for merely half a term, they have different levels. Besides those who are interested in English and willing to learn, some of them are weak in English and reluctant to talk or cooperate.

4. Teaching methods

In this lesson, I will adopt the Situational Language Teaching Method, and Total Physical Response Approach.

Teaching aids:

Electronic whiteboard

5. Teaching aims

1) Students will be able to understand, say, and read the following words: fun, run, under, duck. (语言能力:学习单词发音,尤其是字母 u 的发音)

2) Students will be able to infer that "u" sounds /ʌ/ among fun, run, under, duck, etc. (思维品质:归纳"u"在部分单词的发音。)

3) Students will be able to read and spell more words which contain "u" according to the rules of phonics. (思维品质:培养其推理、演绎能力。)

4) Students will be able to work with their partners and tell the story It's fun to jump. (学习能力:通过小组合作完成任务培养其协作能力。)

5) Students will know the meaning of fun run and learn to be warm-hearted and helpful. (文化意识:了解外国募捐长跑的传统,获得更多文化知识。)

6. Teaching important points

Students learn to read and spell more words according to what they have learned.

Teaching difficult points

Students may have difficulties in telling the story It's fun to jump.

7. Teaching procedure

Step 1: Warming up

Greetings.

The teacher introduces Peppa Pig and Daddy Pig to students.

Let's chant.

a. T: Look at Daddy Pig's big belly. What's in it? Let's chant together.

I eat apples.

...

A fruit bowl in my tummy!

b. Ask student to pay attention to yummy and tummy.

（借助动画人物创设情境，活跃课堂，帮助学生提前感知字母 u 在单词中的发音。）

Step 2: Presentation

Teach words "fun" and "run" by showing a piece of video in which Daddy Pig takes a part in a fun run.

T: Daddy Pig loves eating, but he is warm-hearted. He attends a fun run to raise money so that they can repair the school roof. He runs for love. So what's the meaning of "fun run"?

Ss: 募捐长跑。

The teacher invites students to spell the words, and write them on the blackboard. Then ask students to chant with him/her /f/-/ʌ/-/n/, fun./r/-/ʌ/-/n/, run.

（播放猪爸爸参加募捐长跑这一动画片段引入词汇 fun run，并对学生进行募捐长跑这一文化教育。）

Present a picture in which Peppa Pig is sleeping under the umbrella.

Peppa Pig is sleeping _____ the umbrella.

The teacher invites students to guess and spell the word "under", and write it on the blackboard. Then chant with the students /ʌ/-/n/-/d/-/ə(r)/, under.

Students guess word "duck" by playing a piece of music. The teacher writes it on the blackboard. Then chant ck, ck, /k/, /k/, /k/ together.

/d/-/ʌ/-/k/, duck.

（通过展示图画,播放声音并让学生猜测等手段,创设情境,唤醒学生关于 under, duck 的记忆。）

Dance with your fingers.（借助手指操复习拼读这四个单词。）

Can you say?

Show 4 pictures on P50. Invite students to guess the 4 words.（猜词活动,帮助学生记忆并提取词汇。）

Find the same letter u in the 4 words. U is pronounced/ʌ/.

（引导学生归纳这四个词的共同之处:都含有字母 u,且发音为/ʌ/。）

The teacher plays the listening material, and ask students to finish Read, listen and number on P50.

Read and tick or cross.

Step 3: Practice

Invite students to play a Treasure Hunt game, and finish 3 tasks.

Task 1: Have a try.（Round 1:辅音＋u）VS（Round 2: u+辅音）

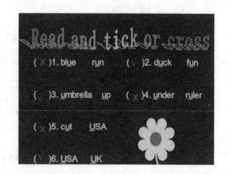

Task 2：Collecting coins on the blackboard!

Invites Ss to read and spell more words which contain "u" according to the rules of phonics.(男女生以竞争的方式拼读单词,发展演绎推理的能力。)

Task 3：Read aloud(Group work).

 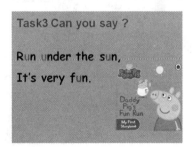

(展示动画小猪佩奇的一些场景,增加趣味性的同时,让学生接触、认读更多含字母 u 发/ʌ/音的词汇:bubble, muddy，puddle)

Step 4 Consolidation

1) Let's act out a story. It's fun to jump.(教师示范朗读及表演,学生模仿。)

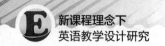
2) Work in groups of 6, read and act the story. Then present it in front of the class.

Step 5: Homework

Review the words learned and try to brainstorm more.

Tell the story It's fun to jump to your team leader.

Write 3 sentences with the word you learned in this class.

Eg. I like jumping in the muddle puddles.

8. Blackboard design:

> **Unit 5   Do you like pears**
> **A let's spell**
> fun /f/-/ʌ/-/n/, run   /r/-/ʌ/-/n/, run
> bubble, muddy, puddle
> ck, ck, /k/, /k/, /k/

案例五　人教版三年级英语下册 Unit 1　Welcome back to school 教学设计

1. 指导思想及整体设计思路

根据《义务教育小学英语新课程标准》,英语教学强调课程从学生的学习兴趣和认知水平出发,倡导体验、参与、合作与交流的学习方式,发展学生的综合语言运用能力。

基于以上理论和三年级下册 Unit 1　Welcome back to school 内容,以师生互动教学为指导,以学生为中心,以媒体融入、卡片、图片为教学手段来实现教学目标。学生通过相互介绍,从而了解大家来自哪一个国家,并且能够认识不同国家的国旗,和不同国家的同学做朋友,学生们能够用英语互相打招呼,从而提高他们的文化意识,以及自我介绍的能力。

2. 教材分析

本节课的教学内容源于人教版三年级英语下册 Unit 1　Welcome back to school 的内容,主要是通过学生自我介绍展开话题,包括一些句型 I'm from China，I'm from Canada 等,词汇 UK、Canada，USA,各个国家国旗等内容。例如 Amy 和 Wu Yifan 相互介绍,从而能够有一定的相互了解。通过本节课的学习能够提高学生的文化意识和语言运用的能力。本课时的学习为后面的学习降低了难度,也做了很好的铺垫。

3. 学情分析

知识基础:学生此前了解一些关于自我介绍的基本句型,国家的英语单词短语,能够为本节课的学习展开进行词汇的提取。

心理及技能特点:学生有英语学习的兴趣和热情,并且比较活泼,能够分组进行简单的自我介绍,根据图片能够认识各个国家的国旗。

学习需要:针对本单元的学习内容,学生需要学会自我介绍,掌握各个国家的国旗以及英语单词。

教学背景:通过分析理解学生掌握新知识的能力如何,分析学生的一般特征、学习风格和知识基础。据此设计教学任务的深度、难度和广度。教师

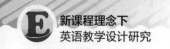

能够通过教学经验、课堂观察、提问等方式掌握学生的学习心理。

4. 教学目标分析

教学目标：

本节课结束时，学生将能够运用以下句子 I'm Amy, I'm from China, boys and girls, we have two new friends here 等进行简单自我介绍，如 I'm from China 等；能够匹配国家和相对应的图画；能够掌握各个国家的国旗，并且能简单的进行对话，熟练者遇见外国友人时能够进行简单对话。

教学重点：能够进行自我介绍，能够匹配国家和相对应的图画。能够运用 I'm from ..., I'm Amy 等句子。

教学难点：句型 I'm from ..., welcome 发音，而且学生遇见外国友人时能够用 I'm Amy, I'm from China 等进行简单对话。

5. 教学方法

本节课所使用的教学方法主要为任务型教学法。

6. 教学流程

Step 1(5 minutes)

Warming-up and Leading in：the teacher presents the picture of foreigners or places of interest，then ask students to answer it.

T：Ok，everyone，please pay attention to these pictures，think about who they are and guess where they are from? OK?

S：OK.

T：OK，look at this，who is he and where is he from?

S：He is Beckham，he comes from England.

T：OK，you are all right，everyone is good. Ok，next one ...

Step 2：pre-task(4 minutes)

T：Everyone is so good，can you guess what we are going to learn? Guess it.

S：Introduction and nation.

T：Wow，you are so excellent. Let's begin our class.

[Design intention] let students match the people or places with states, so that they can understand what we are going to learn.

While-task(18 minutes)

Show some pictures of nations with corresponding words, let students recognize the words and be familiar with national flags. And then start to learn the passage.

T: Ok, everyone, please pay attention to these pictures and these words in my hand, can you read them and match them?

S: UK, Canada, China, USA.

T: You are all so great. And then, let's do an introduction.

T: Nice to meet you.

S: Nice to meet you, too.

T: It seems that you all know this sentence, It's so easy, Right? Let's do it once again.

T: Ok, Very well. Firstly, let's listen to the tape carefully, I will ask some students to do a role play later.

T: Ok, boys and girls, we have two new friends today, please introduce yourselves.

S1: Hi, I'm Amy, I'm from the UK.

S2: Hi, I'm Zhang Peng, I'm from Shandong.

S: Welcome.

T: Ok, everyone. Follow me ...

T: Now, anyone volunteer? Ok, you please. And you please.

T: This time, let's look and say. Firstly, I will ask students to read it. Lily and Tom please.

S1: Hi, I'm Mike, I'm from Canada. What about you?

S2: Hi, I'm Sarah, I'm from the USA.

T: Good job. Now, I will give you 3 minutes to read it by yourself.

Post-task(4 minutes)

T: Are you done? This time, let's learn and you can imitate the following sentences.

For example, Hi, I'm Amy, I'm from the UK. I will ask 3 students to answer it.

S1: Hi, I'm Zhang Peng, I'm from China.

S2: Hi, I'm Sarah, I'm from the USA.

S3: Hi, I'm Mike, I'm from the Canada.

T: Well done. You have master it. And then, let's read the following sentence together. We are friends, ready go.

S: We are friends, we like to play ...

[Design intention] make students learn the new knowledge, so that they can introduce themselves fluently, and read the sentence by themselves. only in this way, students can improve their confidence.

Step 3: Summary and Homework(2 minutes)

T: Now, let's do a summary. Today, we learn introduction and flags. So after class, please recite the sentences in "Let's talk" "read and say". And what's more, you need to write the words about nation, try to familiar with nations and flags.

[Design intention]Students can understand the sentence, and get familiar with the sentence, so that they can use it conveniently.

Unit 1   Welcome back to school

Contents {
Introduction
Recognize nation flags
read and say
Role play and introduce
Recite the sentence
}

7. 教学评价及反思

表一：自我评价

Name_____   Date_____

The things I can do	5	4	3	2	1
I can match the nation and flags					
I can do a simple introduction					
I can understand the teacher said					
I can read the passage by myself					
I can have a simple conversation with foreigner					
Total					

表二：小组活动互评表

由组长或指定学生负责,组织小组反思填写

Criteria to be assessed	Excellent	Very good	good
Amount of cooperation work			
Creative ideas cooperation work			
Participate in group discussion			
Amount of questions raised			
Progress made in activity			

教学反思

学生是学习的主体,因此在教授过程中,以学生为中心,让学生充分发挥自己的作为,给学生提供机会让他们展示自己,让他们进行对话,角色扮演,这样可以增强学生的自信心,增加他们的成就感,每当他们回答或表演完之后我都会对他们进行鼓励夸赞,这样可以增强学生的自信心,增加他们的成就感。在教授单词方面,注意将图画和单词相结合,这样可以增强学生学习的积极主动性,不会像以往那样枯燥乏味。还有一个就是在教学过程中我把自己当成学生的同学,而不是老师,这样就能和他们拉近距离,让他

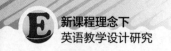
们感受我的亲切感。这个也是在后来才逐渐认识到的。有一个非常重要的问题就是有一些学生上课就比较害羞,常常不敢开口,这个就需要我回去好好研究一下该怎么解决这个问题。

8.教学过程结构流程图

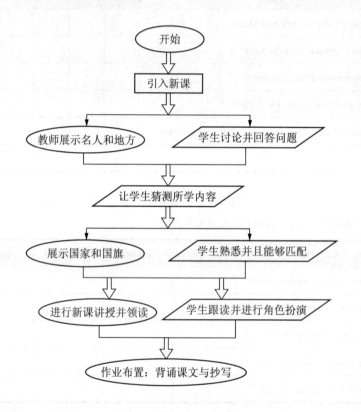

案例六　新人教版六年级英语上册
Unit 2　Ways to go to school 教学设计

一　指导思想

《义务教育课程标准(2011年版)》中首次明确了外语课程是"具有工具性和人文性双重性质"的理念,指出了"工具性和人文性统一的英语课程有利于为学生的终身发展奠定基础"。可见,英语这门学科要求的不仅是学生的学习能力提升,而且还对学生的思维能力、个性发展、情操素养等方面的提升做出了要求。它的总体目标就是培养学生的综合语言运用能力。

二 设计思路

基于这一基本理论,根据六年级学生的特点,结合 The ways to school 的教材内容,通过图片,视频,创设相关情景,主要包括三个活动:1.以前期语言情境为基础,继续补充完整的故事链,即 Mrs Smith 和她的学生们乘上公交车,公交车司机过红绿灯,以及最后她们下公交车,步行穿过十字路口的交通行为过程。2.采用角色表演的方法让学生体验生活中遵守交通规则的重要性。3.在对 Let's learn,Write and say 部分的单词记忆教学过程中,运用语音分类的方法,帮助学生巩固所学的语音规则,运用恰当的方法记忆单词;通过教给学生连读方法,便于学生形成良好的语音诣调。

三 教材分析

本课是人教版六年级上册 Unit 2 The ways to school,本课重点学习如何询问和回答人们日常出行的方式,这个话题与学生的日常生活紧密联系。其中 A 部分 Let's try,Let's talk,Let's learn,Write and say 四个环节主要学习日常出行方式,呈现基础知识。在学习单词过程中自然地将教学重点引到语言运用上来,学生通过学习能够灵活地询问和回答出人们日常出行的方式,能够体会到生活中遵守交通规则的重要性。

四 学情分析

六年级学生刚刚踏入初中校园,他们对学校充满了好奇和憧憬,他们活泼、好动、表现欲旺盛,且在以前已经学习过关于交通工具的单词,如 car,bike,bus 等,也在五年级下册接触过频率副词 usually,sometimes,often,所以能够在图片的帮助下分别理解频率副词和交通方式 by bike,by car,by bus 的用法;在教师的帮助下,理解词组和语篇。因此,教师在本课时的

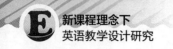

课堂教学将会利用语境 Mrs Smith，Mike and Amy are at school.让学生在针对主线人物讨论 How do they come to school？的话题,完成本节课核心句型的学习和运用。经过三年的英语学习,学生具备表演对话和运用核心语言做事的能力,可以为本课时中的表演活动和调查活动起到一定的支架作用。

五 教学目标

本节课结束时,学生将能够：

1. 听、说、读、写短语 on foot，by taxi，by bus，by train，by plane，by ship，by subway。

2. 运用句型 How do you come to ...? 询问别人出行时使用的交通工具;面对别人的询问能恰当地运用三个频度副词 usually，often，sometimes 做出回答。

3. 听懂,会说,会表演 Let's talk 的内容,并能够通过在真实场景中的交流和运用体会到遵守交通规则的重要性。

教学重难点

教学重点：

1. 学生能听、说、读、写短语"by train、by plane、by subway、by ship、by bike、on foot",并能在实际情景中灵活运用。

2. 学生能够运用句型 How do you come to ...? 询问别人出行时使用的交通工具;面对别人的询问能恰当地运用三个频度副词 usually，often，sometimes 做出回答。

教学难点：

1. 学生能够理解、区分并运用三个频度副词 usually，often，sometimes。

2. 学生能听、说、读、写词组 by bike，by car，by bus，on foot 等,并理解"步行"采用的是不同的介词。

六 教学方法

情景教学法,任务型教学法

七 教学流程

Step 1：Warming up(5 mins)

T：Hello，Children! How was your morning?

Ss：根据自己的情况与教师进行自由会话。

T：Oh，I felt bad this morning. My car didn't work，so I had to come to school on foot.（PPT 呈现，帮助学生理解 on foot 的意义。）How did you come to school this morning，on foot，by bike，or by bus?

Ss：根据自己的情况做出回答。

设计意图 通过师生间的自由会话，让学生在语境中理解 on foot 的含义，并在教师的提示下对交通方式做初步的了解，为主要内容的学习做好铺垫。

Step 2：Presentation(20 mins)

（1）对话学习的准备

教师使用 PPT 呈现 Mike 和 Amy 在学校的照片，提供 Mike and Amy are at school.的情景。然后教师播放录音，学生完成 Let's try 的内容，录音播放两遍。教师可向学生提供听力练习的相关技巧，如提示学生在第一遍听取录音时就对话的主旨进行判断，听取第二遍录音时详细了解对话内容，完成课本 14 页的判断题。

T：Look，Mike and Amy are at school now. Do you want to know how they come to school? I have a dialogue here. Listen carefully and answer this question：Are they talking about their ways to come to school?

（学生听录音）

T：So can you answer the questions：Are they talking about their ways to come to school? What's the answer?

Ss：No.

T：Yes，you're right. They are not talking about their ways to come to school. Then what are they talking about? Listen again and tick or cross.

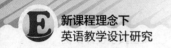

（学生再听录音，完成教材 14 页的练习。教师确认学生理解录音内容。）

设计意图 Let's try 是 Let's talk 的铺垫环节，学生对此部分内容的理解情况与交流将直接影响对 Let's talk 的学习效果，教师需明确学生对此部分的理解情况。

（2）了解大意

教师使用 PPT 呈现 Miss Smith、Mike 和 Amy 对话的情景图，再次提出问题 Are they talking about their ways to come to school? If yes, how do they come to school? 引导学生听对话，并依据对话内容自行设立问题如 How does Amy come to school? How does Mike come to school? How does Mrs Smith come to school?

T：Look! Who do Mike and Amy meet at school?

Ss：Mrs Smith.

（教师使用 PPT 出示 Mrs Smith 图片，并板书 Mrs Smith，引导学生注意 Mrs 的读音）

T：Guess what are they talking when they meet? Listen to the dialogue and answer this question：Are they talking about their ways to come to school?

（学生听录音）

T：Answer the question，please.

Ss：Yes, they are.

T：Then what do you want to know? （教师帮助学生提出以下问题，可先给学生做示范）For example, I want to know：What does Mrs Smith say to Mike and Amy?

S1：How does Mike come to school?

S2：How does Amy come to school?

S3：How does Mrs Smith come to school?

……

T：Good questions! Now let's listen again and find out the answers to your questions.

设计意图 Let's try 的呈现并没有解决导入环节中的提示性问题 How do they come to school？ Mrs Smith 的出现，为 Let's talk 呈现出完整的语言交流背景。在此语境下，教师带领学生对这个问题进行回顾，不仅有利于学生对文本内容与核心句型的关注，也培养学生学会提问的能力。

（3）文本分析

教师使用 PPT 呈现词组 on foot，by bus，by bike，by car，让学生预先了解出行方式，再带着问题再听对话，将上述词组与三个主要人物进行匹配。

T：Look at the screen and tell me：who comes to school on foot？

Ss：Amy and Mrs Smith.

T：How do you know Mrs Smith comes to school on foot？

Ss：She says "walk".

T：Yes，walk means on foot.

T：Who comes to school by bus？

Ss：Amy.

T：Who comes to school by bike？

Ss：Mike.

T：Does Mrs Smith always come to school on foot？

Ss：No. Sometimes by car.

设计意图 为了帮助学生在初次听取对话时顺利地了解大意，教师可利用 PPT 给学生呈现三个人物及一些出行方式，让学生在听完对话后进行连线匹配。这样的任务形式不仅降低了学习的难度，也有利于强化学生对 by bike，on foot，by car，by bus 词组的感知。

（4）副词 usually，often，sometimes 学习

教师再次播放录音，学生听对话，关注 Mike，Amy 和 Mrs Smith 的回答：

Amy：Usually，I come on foot. Sometimes I come by bus.

Mike：I often come by bike.

Mrs Smith：Sometimes, but I usually walk.

教师使用 PPT 呈现三个频度副词及示例图片，讲解这三个副词所代表的频率含义。学生能在教师的问题引导下用这三个频率副词进行造句练习。

T：Now listen to the dialogue again. Pay attention to these words：usually, sometimes and often.

（教师提示学生重点听取含有此三个单词的句子，也可多次播放）

T：Did you hear these words：usually, sometimes and often?

Ss：Yes.

（教师借助 PPT 比较三个单词，帮助学生进一步理解频率含义）

T：Can you find out some differences among usually, sometimes, and often?

Ss：根据图片的呈现，说出对这三个单词的理解（允许使用母语）。

（教师板书这三个单词，并教读）

T：Now, listen carefully and think. John gets up at six o'clock on Sunday, Tuesday, Wednesday, Thursday, and Friday every week. Wu Yifan gets up at six o'clock on Sunday, Tuesday, Thursday, and Friday every week. Zhang Peng gets up at six o'clock on Thursday every week. So who usually gets up at six o'clock? Who often gets up at six o'clock? Who sometimes gets up at six o'clock?

Ss：John usually gets up at six o'clock. Wu Yifan often gets up at six o'clock. Zhang Peng sometimes gets up at six o'clock.

T：Do you know who usually/often/sometimes gets up at six o'clock in our class? And do you know who usually/often/sometimes eats breakfast at seven o'clock in the morning?

Ss：根据教师提出的问题进行造句练习。

设计意图 日历的呈现更加形象地帮助学生将 usually, often, sometimes 进行比对，也有利于学生进行理解和掌握。教师围绕学生身边同学，引导学生进行造句练习，让学生的操练变得真实而有意义，也增加了教学趣味性。

（5）对话理解巩固

教师第三遍播放对话,要求学生在听后完整回答前面提出的三个问题：How does Amy come to school? How does Mike come to school? How does Mrs Smith come to school?

T：Now listen to the dialogue again and find out the answers to these questions.

（教师再次使用 PPT 展示本课时的三个重点问题：How does Amy/Mike/Mrs Smith come to school? 学生听录音,回答问题,跟读回答）

S1：Amy usually comes by bus. Sometimes she comes by bike.

S2：Mike often comes by bike.

S3：Mrs Smith usually walks, sometimes by car.

T：Good. Now let's listen to their answers again and repeat them.

（6）学生自读对话

学生自读课文,教师根据情况帮助学生在语境中理解 You're early. 的语义。

T：Read the dialogue by yourselves and see if you have some questions. If not, I have a question here. Why does Mrs Smith say you're early to Mike and Amy?

若学生说出句意,教师追问 How do you get it? 若学生不说、说不出或说不清,教师可带领学生再读对话前四句,给予下列提示 Who come to school first? Who do they meet then? 以帮助学生理解 You're early. 的意义。

设计意图 在学生对三个频度副词有了完整的理解之后,让学生带着问题再次听对话后直接回答问题的教学步骤,既突破了本课的一个重难点,即对三个人物上学所用交通方式的学习,也让学生对整个对话有了一个完整、准确的理解。同时,紧扣 Listen and match 环节中,教师给出提示性词组引导学生回答问题的教学方法,帮助学生加深对文本的理解和核心句型的体会、运用。

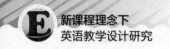

Step 3：Practice(5 mins)

（1）学生听录音，跟读对话。

（2）师生、生生分角色朗读对话。

（3）学生表演对话：先以小组为单位练习，再在全班进行示范表演。

设计意图 角色表演是受学生喜爱的学习任务。即使是六年级的学生，也愿意将自己置身于故事中，以自己的理解展现对话内容。更重要的是，表演的教学活动可以帮助学生更积极、主动地内化学习内容。

Step 4：Do a survey(10 mins)

教师使用 PPT 呈现一些交通方式，如 by bus，by bike，on foot，by taxi，by car，以 by bike 和自身出行情况作为示范，如 I usually go to school by bike.并在相应的表格内做记号。学生参照教师举例，调查其他同学到校的交通方式，在表格内做相应的标记。学生通过自己的调查情况，在表格下方写出调查的结果，如 Three students usually come to school by bike.并运用本课所学的三个频度副词在班内和其他同学进行交流。

T：Now let's do a survey about your classmates' ways to go to school. You can go around in classroom, ask your classmates：How do you come to school? Then mark in the table. During your survey, you may use the phrases to answer your classmates' questions. For example，I usually go to school by bike/by car/by bus … OK，let's do.

（学生做调查）

T：OK! Now do a summary about your survey and write them down：How many people you asked in your survey? How many people usually come to school by bike? How many people come to school often by bike? And how many people sometimes come to school by bike?

（学生整理调查情况）

T：Now tell us about your survey.

Ss：陈述自己的调查。

设计意图 交通方式词组的呈现为学生提供了语言支持。其中 subway 和 taxi 是生词，考虑到学生可能会用到，但单词教学又是下一节课的重点词汇,所以教师可进行简单的提示。调查活动让学生的语言学习从课本迁移到实际生活,调查后的总结汇报帮助学生对本课时的语言内容进一步运用和巩固,加深印象。

Step 5:Conclusion(3 mins)

教师请学生运用本课时的交通方式词组和频率副词来说一说自己喜欢的一些出行方式,陈述原因,引导学生选择健康、绿色的出行方式,实现在情感、态度价值观方面引导学生树立环保意识的教学目标。

设计意图 通过环保意识的教育,提倡学生多选择绿色出行方式,如步行、骑自行车、利用公共交通工具,减少对环境的污染。

Step 6:Homework(2 mins)

T:Today's homework is:Do a survey about other teachers' ways to go to school. Then make a report. We will talk about it next class.

设计意图 调查教师选择的到校交通方式,对学生来说是一个新鲜、意外、充满期待的作业,在这个过程中的语言运用是学生真正学会的、掌握的。

八 板书设计(Blackboard Design)

板书的主要内容共包括二块,左边是与对话内容相关的三个核心问题,右边是四种交通方式和三个频度副词,所有的内容随着教学进度的进展逐个粘贴,右边的箭头能帮助学生更加有效地区别三个频度副词。

Unit2　Ways to go to school

How does Mike come to school?　　　　On foot，by bike，by bus，by car
He usually comes on foot，sometimes by bus.

How does Amy come to school?　　　Usually　often　sometimes
She often comes by bike.　　　　　　⟶

How does Mrs Smith come to school?
She usually comes on foot，sometimes by car.

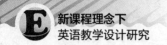

九 教学流程图

版式一：

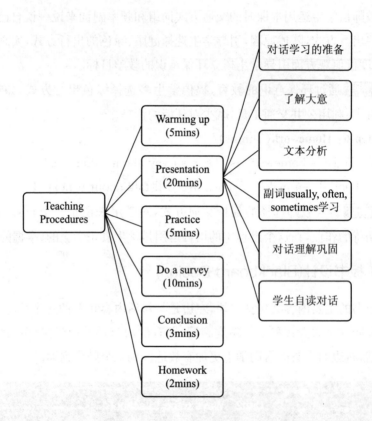

版式二：

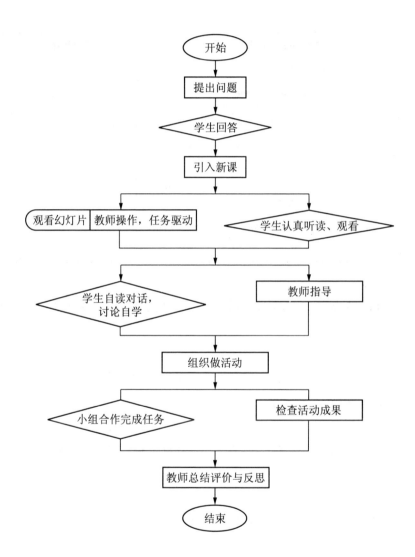

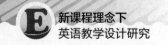
十 教学评价及反思

1. 评价:

The things I did	Evaluation
I played an active role in the class.	5 4 3 2 1
I expressed myself in English very well.	5 4 3 2 1
I followed my teacher well and took some necessary notes.	5 4 3 2 1
I worked together with my partners very well.	5 4 3 2 1
I have learned some phrases like: on foot, by taxi, by bus, by train, by plane, by ship, by subway.	5 4 3 2 1
I can use the sentence "How do you come to ...?"well.	5 4 3 2 1
Total	

2. 反思:

本节课结束以后,我认真进行了反思,也总结了一些自己的优点及缺点。

优点:

1) 导入比较新颖,容易激发学生的好奇心,探索新知。

2) 条理清晰,环节紧扣。

3) 以学生为主,把课堂交给学生,提高学生自学的能力。

4) 在课堂内容的基础上,能进行一定程度的拓展,提升主题。

5) 作业布置切合实际。

缺点:

1) 在教授新课的过程中,顾及到大部分学生,但是不能全面考虑一些学困生的问题。

2) 课堂评价语言比较单一,以后应加强这方面的学习。

再反思:

本节课的话题是交通工具,重点是学习如何询问和回答人们日常出行的方式,难点是学生能够熟练使用所学的语言询问并回答坐某种交通工具去某地。因此我觉得在课堂教学中,应该多创设情境,给学生提供综合运用语言的机会。注意与学生的日常生活联系,将目标语言运用于更多的真实情景之中,以加深学生对句型的理解。如 A Let's talk 的教学,就以学生熟悉的话题 How do you come to school? 为切入点,询问学生每周一是怎样上学的? 在教学过程中创设适当的情景,不仅为学生提供了运用语言的环境,也能提高学生运用语言的能力,活跃课堂气氛,学生比较喜欢,教学效果也不错。

六年级的学生对交通规则都比较熟悉,他们思维活跃,已经具有一定的英语听、说、读、写能力,在已有的学习经历中,学习成就感和自信心的体验让多数同学逐步形成了稳定的兴趣,但学生的个体差异也使两极分化现象逐步显现。本课我充分发挥教师为主导,学生为主体的作用,利用卡片,以训练为主线,努力培养学生听、说、读、写四项基本技能。兼顾后进生的学习状况,给他们以更多的关心与指导,使他们也能在新的学习中,树立自信。如教学交通方式之前先出示学生学过的交通工具,再引入到交通方式的学习,学生了解了交通方式的构成结构是 by 加交通工具后,就能自主运用,如by jeep, by car 等,这样新旧知识交融,也起到了温故而知新的作用。

课堂教学的精益求精是我在今后教学中应该追求的,任何时候都不应该满足于现状。要随时发现自己的不足之处,以便及时改正。比如,教学要面向全体学生,每上完一节课都要回顾一下,在这节课上是否仍存在着"死角"? 课堂上的发言面是否达到了 95% 以上? 学生们否能够主动地开口讲英语? 只有不断地反思,才能取得更大进步。

案例七　人教版小学英语四年级下册
Unit 2　What time is it? 教学设计

一 指导思想及整体设计思路

1.《义务教育英语课程标准(2011 年版)》倡导学生利用自己已有的知识和经验去实践,亲身参与和感受,发现和探究新的知识和经验,通过实践和体验,形成新的技能和能力,并充实丰富自己的经验。这样一来,就必然要求学生在真实而富有实际意义的任务活动中去学习、体验和运用语言知识而且要求学生学会与他人合作学习。

2. 基于这一基本理念,根据四年级学生的特点和有关时间观念的知识,结合四年级 What time is it? 教材内容,我在课堂的教学实践中,通过实物展示,观看视频等手段创设情境,设置听、说、演等活动,让学生说出在不同时间点做不同的活动,表演出某一时间段该做的事情,并根据自己的时间表做出一个日常计划安排,培养学生的语言能力、思维能力、文化意识等核心素养能力。

二 教材分析

本课选自人教版 PEP 小学英语四年级下册第二单元 What time is it? 话题围绕"时间"展开,主要分成两部分,Let's learn and let's do.第一部分,通过时钟展开对话关于 What time is it? It's time for ... .第二部分,让学生运用句型 It's time for ... let's ...边说边演。本课时的学习让学生掌握这一句型结构并学以致用,并为接下来的学习做了很好的铺垫。

三 学情分析

四年级学生已有了一定的知识储备,具备一定的听说读写能力;在课堂上他们善于表现自我,乐于思考,敢于发表自己的观点,有较强的求知欲和学习积极性,这些都有利于师生之间的课堂交流,但是,学生们缺乏自信,表达能力欠缺,缺乏一定的运用英语思维的能力。因此,本节课将以学生为中心,以活动为形式,运用多样化的教学方法,提高学生的语言表达能力,逐步培养学生的思维品质。

四 教学目标及分析(含重难点)

在本节课结束时,学生将能够:

1. 围绕不同时间点做不同的活动进行对话交流;

2. 给出建议关于某一时间段该做的事情;

3. 能根据自己的时间表做出一个日常计划安排并进行课堂展示;树立正确的时间观念,倡导健康的生活方式。

根据教材内容及学情分析,为了达成教学目标,本节课的教学重点:

掌握关于时间的基本词汇及句型表达;给出建议关于某一时间段该做的事情。

教学难点:

设计自己的时间表,做出日常计划安排并课堂展示;培养学生用外语思维的习惯,启发想象力和创造性思维。

五 教学方法

TPR,听说法,情境教学法

六 教学过程

Step 1:Warming up(5 mins)

Greeting

T:Good morning, boys and girls!

Ss:Good morning, teacher!

T:How are you today?

Ss:I'm very fine, thank you!

Sing the song about the numbers

T:Everybody, do you like singing songs?

Ss:Yes, very much.

T:OK, let's sing it together. "Ten little candles".

The material object- "clock"

T:Boys and girls! Attention please, what's this?

S1:It's a clock.

T:Wonderful! Then what time is it now?

S2:It's 9.

T:Yes, very good. We can also say it's 9 o'clock.

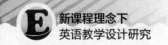
......

设计意图 通过打招呼,歌曲演唱活跃气氛,复习关于数字的知识,通过实物时钟展开关于时间的问答导入新课讲授,板书重点句型。

Step 2：Presentation(15 mins)

Learn the new words such as breakfast，lunch，dinner.

T：Everybody, now please listen carefully to find out what time it is and what John can do at the time.

S3：It's 7 o'clock. It's time for breakfast.

T：Well done. Pay attention to this pronounciation/br/，breakfast. What would you like for breakfast?

S4：I'd like bread，egg and milk.

T：Yeah, it's very healthy to drink some milk. Next，look at the clock，what time is it now?

S5：It's 12 o'clock.

T：What do you often do at 12 o'clock?

S6：It's time for lunch.

T：Cool! Please read the word "lunch" one by one.

Ss：lunch, lunch......

T：I'd like rice，fish，vegetables and soup for lunch. So，what about you?

S7：I'd like beef，chicken，rice and juice.

......

T：Oh，I'm hungry! What time is it?

S8：It's 6 o'clock. It's time for dinner.

T：Ok! Dinner, dinner. Let's eat some rice.

Learn the new words such as English class，music class，PE class.

T：Everybody，look at the time，it's 9 c'clock. What do you do at 9 o'clock?

S9：It's time for English class.

T：Great! Let's read and write，follow me，do the action.

T：As I know，you all like singing songs. So，do you know when the music class is?

S10：It's 2 o'clock.

T：Perfect! Now，let's sing and dance ...

T：Then，which class do you like best?

S11：I like PE class best.

S12：Me too.

T：Ok，let's jump and run ...

Play the games to consolidate the new words.

设计意图 通过形式多样的活动讲授并巩固新授单词,如,one by one,大小声,音节比较,Bomb game 等,注重教学形式与内容的结合,在玩中学,既活跃了课堂气氛,又使学生学有所得。

Step 3：Practice(5 mins)

Make conversations about the time using the clock.

S13：Hi, what time is it?

S14：It's 3 o'clock. It's time for PE class. Let's play football on the playground.

S13：Good idea! Let's go!

......

Let's do

T：Now, listen firstly, then, let's chant and do. Are you ready?

Ss：Yes, we are ready ...

设计意图 通过创设情境,编制对话,听,唱,演等 TPR 的教学方法巩固所学知识,学生兴趣浓厚,积极性高,教学效果显著!

Step 4：Consolidation(10 mins)

Make a plan for doing different kinds of things according to the time schedule and show it.

设计意图 让学生根据自己的时间表制定活动安排并课堂展示,达到迁移

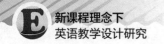
创新,培养学生语言能力、逻辑思维能力、学以致用的能力。

Step 5:Emotional Education(3 mins)

Watch the video about valuing time and let the students say what they can do to value time in daily life.

设计意图 观看视频,情感升华,引发学生共鸣,让学生意识到珍惜时间的重要性! Value time is valuing your life!

Step 6:Summary(1 min)

Guide the students to sum up the words and sentences learnt in this lesson with the help of the blackboard.

设计意图 让学生总结所学,培养学生知识总结能力。

Step 7:Homework(1 min)

Recite the key sentences.

Do a survey about what your classmates do at different time.

Blackbord Design

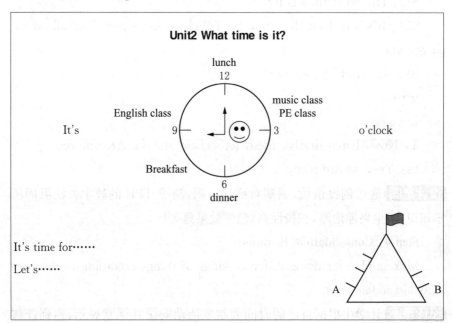

七 教学流程图

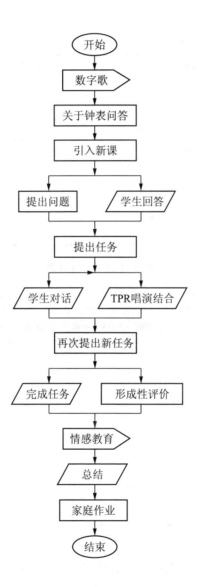

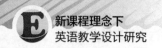

八 教学评价与反思

表 1：自我评价表

Name：_____   Date：_____

The things I can do	5	4	3	2	1
I can take part in the lesson actively.					
I can understand the conversation.					
I can understand the oral questions.					
I can answer the questions.					
I can make conversation about time.					
I can make a time and activity plan.					
I'v realized the importance of valuing time.					
Total					

表 2：小组活动互评表

由组长或指定学生负责，组织小组反思填写。Name：_____

Criteria to be assessed	Excellent	Very Good	Good	Adequate	Need Much Improvement
Amount of cooperation work					
Creative ideas brought in					
Participate in group discussion					
Number of questions raised					
Progress made in activity					

教学反思：

本节课是一节对话课，话题围绕"时间"进行展开，通过对话学习本节课重点词汇及句型，并进行 let's do 巩固所学，讲授重点词汇及句型时，我通过形式多样的教学活动进行巩固，比如，play games，借助实物时钟设置情景进行对话交流，TPR 形式，很好地激发了学生学习英语的积极性，提升了语言能力、思维能力,并让他们认识到珍惜时间的重要性,树立良好的时间观念。

但是我也认识到基于最近发展区的理论,根据学生的具体情况设计更富挑战性的内容也是急于改善的,以促使学生核心素养能力的不断提升!

案例八　人教版 PEP 六年级下册 Unit 6　Work quietly Read and write

一　指导思想及整体设计思路

1.《义务教育小学英语新课程标准》(2011 版)指出,英语教学应该以学生为主体,首先要培养学生的学习兴趣、信心、策略和习惯;强调课程从学生的学习兴趣和认知水平出发,倡导体验、参与、合作与交流的学习方式,发展学生的综合语言运用能力。同时指出,教师在教学中初步渗透阅读策略,发展学生的自主学习能力。

2. 基于这一理念,根据六年级学生的特点和发展要求,结合 Work quietly 这一课的教学内容,我在课堂上创设参观机器人展馆的情景,引导学生在情境中学习。我在课堂中创设以下几个活动,一在课堂上利用图片、视频导入本课所学句型"现在进行时态",引导学生描述;二小组合作完成表格内容;三角色扮演各个国家的对话,四小组讨论各国其他文化。通过活动的引导与呈现,激活学生已有的知识经验,培养学生的语言能力、创新思维和合作意识,培养学生爱国主义的情感。

二　教材分析

本节课的教学内容源于人教版 PEP 六年级下册 Unit 6 Work quietly,通过 Robin 参观机器人展馆和各国机器人的对话的场景让学生学习现在进行时态,用现在进行时态交流各国文化和特色。本课时的学习能让学生更好的把握现在进行时态的运用、表达,以及对不同国家的特色有一定的了解。

三　学情分析

六年级学生已经有一定的语言积累和知识储备,对语法时态有了一定

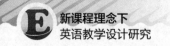
的了解。大部分学生对学习英语有很高涨的兴趣,课堂气氛好。但部分学生缺乏创造性思维,不能将所学内容举一反三,应当鼓励他们多思考、多实践,达到学以致用的目的。

四 教学目标(含重难点)分析

本节课结束时,学生将能:

1. 说出对话中国家的名称以及国家的特色、标志;

2. 用句型"be＋v-ing"熟练表达"正在做……"并能在实际交流中运用;

3. 合作完成表格,正确书写动词 ing 形式;

4. 了解外国相关文化,分享各国的特色、标志。

本节课的教学重难点如下:

1. 教学重点是学生能够掌握"现在进行时态"并能说出对话中出现的国家名称以及国家的特色;

2. 教学难点是学生能够在实际的口语交流中运用"现在进行时态",描述正在发生的事情。

五 教学方法

情景教学法

六 教学过程

Step 1(5 mins):**Warming up**

1. Greetings

2. Lead-in

T：Look at the screen. Last weekend, I went to the wild zoo. There are many animals. I took some photos. Let's have a look. What is the monkey doing?

S1：The monkey is eating bananas.

T：How about the elephant?

S2：The elephant is walking.

……

设计意图 通过设置动物园的场景,引导学生回答动物正在做什么,一方面可以激发学生的学习兴趣,另一方面能够激活学生已有的知识经验,为本节课所学新知做好准备。

Step 2：Pre-reading(2 mins)

T：Today we are going to visit the world robot exhibition with Robin. Do you know any other country besides China? Now let's have a brainstorm.

S1：Canada

S2：Australia

S3：USA

……

T：Let's make a world map in the blackboard. Look at the pictures. Can you guess which country's robot we can meet?

……

设计意图 通过头脑风暴说出已经知道的国家名称,并猜测我们跟随 Robin 能遇见哪几个国家的机器人,调动学生的学习兴趣,做好准备工作。

Step 3：While-reading(15 mins)

1. Skimming

T：Just now we guessed the countries' robot we will meet，now let's read the dialogue quickly and answer how many countries' robots we can meet.

S：Five countries.

T：You are so clever. So which country's robot can we visit?

S：……

2. Scanning

T：There are five countries' robots in the exhibition. What are they doing? Now read the dialogue carefully and talk about it.

S：……

3. The third reading

T：You did a good job！Read the dialogue carefully to find the culture of these countries and fill in the blanks.

S：······

设计意图 通过对文本的三次阅读使学生掌握材料内容，了解相关文本信息，把握"现在进行时态"的灵活运用。

Step 4：Post-reading(15 mins)

1. Role play the dialogue

T：Now it's your turn. Five students is a group and role-play the dialogue.

S：······

2. Pair work

T：Make a dialogue between you and any other countries' robot and demonstrate it in the class.

S：······

Step 5：Consolidation

Write a personal life schedule

T：OK. Boys and girls，I have a foreign friend Lily，she will send an E-mail to me to describe her life schedule in USA. Can you write down a personal schedule for her?

S：······

设计意图 通过角色扮演、小组合作、书写个人生活表三个活动让学生对对话进行练习，并进一步巩固学习"现在进行时态"。

Step 6：Homework

Gather some other countries' culture and share it in class.

Blackboard design

Unit 6 Work quietly		
The world robot exhibition		
The Canadian robot		drawing a picture.
The Japanese robot		making sushi.
The Spanish robot	is	playing music.
The Chinese robot		doing kung fu.
The American robot		talking with Robin.

七 教学流程图

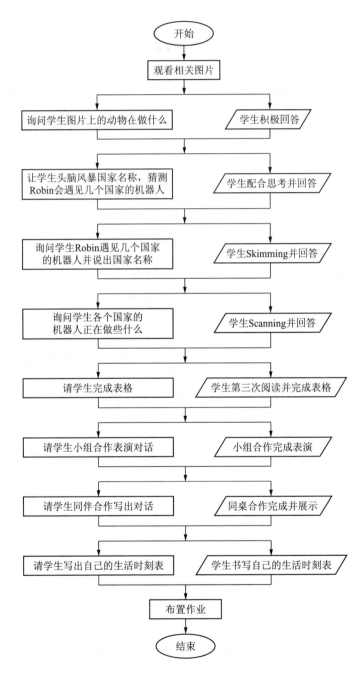

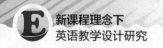
八 教学评价及反思

教学评价

表1：自我评价表

Name：_____   Date：_____

The things I can do	5	4	3	2	1
I can understand the reading dialogue					
I can take part in the lesson actively					
I can do activities with classmates					
I can know some countries' name					
I can write down my life schedule					
I can talk something by present continuous tense					
Total					

表2：小组活动互评表

由组长或指定学生负责，组织小组反思填写。Name：_____ Date：_____

Criteria to be assessed	Excellent	Very Good	Good	Adequate	Need Much Improvement
Amount of cooperation work					
Creative ideas brought in					
Participating in group discussion					
Amount of questions raised					
Progress made in the activity					

九 教学反思

本节课结束之后，我将会从以下几个方面进行反思：

1. 成功之处：本节课教学目标准确，教学环节清晰明了，学生的积极性很高，整体看来教学目标达成。

2. 不足之处：在阅读后环节，给学生布置了一项角色扮演的任务，在这一环节耽误过多时间，导致后面的环节进行地比较匆忙，时间没有把握好。

3. 学生表现：学生整体表现较好，能够跟随老师的思路进行阅读、思考、小组活动、角色扮演等各项活动都能积极参与，课堂活跃度很高。

4. 改进设计：教学设计应该更具合理性、科学性、实践性。在实际操作中要注意把握时间以及注重关注学生的参与度、配合度。

案例九　人教版新目标英语三年级 Unit 1　Hello!
第一课时教学设计

一　指导思想及整体设计思路

1. 课程标准倡导学生利用自己已有的知识和经验去实践，亲身参与和感受，发现和探究新的知识和经验，通过实践和体验，形成新的技能和能力，并充实丰富自己的经验。学生在英语的学习中要充分地参与、体验和运用语言知识，还要学会与他人合作学习。

2. 基于这一基本理念，根据三年级学生特点，结合 Unit 1 教材内容，我通过欣赏歌曲"hello"，让学生初步感知打招呼的用语并自然过渡到问候语的教学上来，通过向学生打招呼和介绍自己来呈现新语言；学生通过模仿、表演、游戏等形式来巩固操练所学内容。这最终培养了学生用英语解决问题和语言表达能力，培养学生养成良好的文明习惯，从而帮助学生完成知识目标，能力目标和情感目标的实现。

二　教材分析

本课是人教版新目标英语三年级 Unit 1 Hello! 本单元主要内容涉及英语日常用语，包括打招呼，介绍自己和日常用品等，是日常交往中最基本的内容。本课时是这个单元的第一课时，是一节听说课，主要话题是相互打

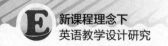
招呼和介绍自己,通过做游戏等形式,让学生能用英语打招呼和介绍自己,激发学生对英语学习的兴趣。

三 学情分析

三年级学生刚接触英语,他们有很强的求知欲和好奇心,在课堂上他们善于表现自我,乐于积极思考,敢于发言,这些都有利于师生在课堂上的互动。但部分学生新学习一门语言存在不自信、不能适应的情况。打招呼是日常生活的基本交际能力,学生对英语表达的兴趣和热情会促进他们对英语的学习。

四 教学目标(含重难点)

本节课结束时,学生将能够:1)能听懂、会说 Hello,I'm~. Hi,I'm~. What's your name? My name is~.等句子,并能够在实际情景中进行运用;2)能认识本课的几个主人公,并会说他们的名字;3)在游戏中熟练运用所学问候语及自我介绍用语,养成懂礼貌、讲文明的好习惯;4)乐于用英语交流,树立用英语解决问题的意识。

教学重点分析：能听懂，会说 Hello，I'm～. Hi，I'm～. What's your name? My name is～.等句子，并能够在实际情景中进行运用；能认识本课的几个主人公，并会说他们的名字。

教学难点分析：在游戏中熟练运用所学问候语及自我介绍用语，养成懂礼貌、讲文明的好习惯；乐于用英语交流，树立用英语解决问题的意识。

五 教学方法

情景教学法、直接教学法、游戏教学法

六 教学流程

Step 1：warming up(2 mins)

使用多媒体播放米老鼠、加菲猫等著名的英语卡通人物的图片，在播放时，教师使用 Hello! Hi! 向他们打招呼，让学生熟悉这两个打招呼用的句式。

Teacher：Hello，Mickey Mouse.（米老鼠）Hi，Donald Duck!（唐老鸭）Hello，Garfield.（加菲猫）Hello，Shaun the Sheep.（小羊肖恩）

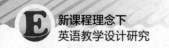
设计意图 使用学生特别熟悉的卡通人物来热身,激发学生浓厚的学习英语的兴趣,同时让他们熟悉如何使用英语来打招呼。

Step 2:leading in(3 mins)

使用多媒体课件,让动画人物向学生打招呼并做自我介绍。教师引导学生进行回应。

Mickey:Hello. I'm Mickey Mouse.

Teacher and students:Hi,Mickey Mouse.

Donald:Hi! I'm Donald Duck!

Teacher and students:Hello,Donald Duck!

...

设计意图 利用多媒体的辅助,让学生喜欢的动画人物向学生打招呼并介绍自己,能够极大地激发学生学习和交流的热情。在这样的情境中,学生能够极容易地理解新句式的含义,并在反复地倾听中熟悉重点句式的表达。

Step 3:Presentation(5 mins)

Activity 1.展示教材中人物的图片,教师和他们互相打招呼并自我介绍。

Teacher:Hello! I'm Miss ...

John:Hi, I'm John.

Sarah:Hello, I'm Sarah.

Miss White:Hi, I'm Miss White.

Wu Yifan:Hello, I'm Wu Yifan.

设计意图 沿用上一环节中的形式,引出本教材中的主人公,让学生在已经熟悉自我介绍句式结构的基础上,熟悉主人公的姓名。

Activity 2.播放课文内容,学生倾听。

Teacher:We know many new friends today. Let's listen to the tape now.

设计意图 让学生养成利用磁带等方式获取原声录音,通过倾听原汁原味的地道语言来培养自己的听力感受及倾听理解能力。

Step 4：Practice(23 mins)

Activity 1.展示主人公图片,学生向他们打招呼,能够正确地说出他们的名字。

Teacher：Boys and girls，say hello to our new friends，please. Hello，Wu Yifan. Hello，Sarah. Hello，Miss White. Hi，John. Hi，Chen Jie.

快速地变换主人公的头饰,随机请学生正确地说出其姓名并向其打招呼。

Teacher：Say hello，please.

设计意图 先按顺序出示主要人物的图片,让学生逐一熟悉地练习如何向他们打招呼。再以游戏的方式锻炼学生的反应能力,从而考查学生能否正确地说出主人公的名字,并以此鼓励学生大方、大胆地用英语进行交流。

Activity 2.再次播放课文录音。学生跟读课文。

Teacher：Boys and girls，let's read the dialogue after the tape. Please listen carefully，read carefully.

Activity 3.学生分角色朗读课文。

Teacher：Now，who wants to be the teacher? Who wants to be Sarah? Who wants to be Wu Yifan? Let's read the dialogue in roles.

Activity 4.请学生戴上头饰来扮演对话的角色,表演对话。

Teacher：Now we'll find the best actor or actress. Please come to the front and show the dialogue.

设计意图 通过以上三个活动,使学生能够充分理解课文内容,并且能够正确朗读课文。不同形式的读和表演活动,使学生逐步理解并掌握本课的重点句型,为其达到熟练表达奠定基础。

Activity 5.请学生戴着头饰,找到自己的朋友,去向他进行自我介绍并打招呼。

Teacher：Now，you are Sarah. Please find a friend and say hello to him. Introduce yourself to the friend. Say like this：Hello，I'm Sarah.

Teacher：It's time for John. Who wants to try?

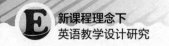

设计意图 在这个小游戏中,学生需要抛开自己的身份,使用头饰提供的新身份去进行交流。这能够提升学生参与的积极性。在这一活动中,学生从单纯地模仿开始到相对自由的表达,以及能更好地掌握新句型。

Step 5：Summary(5 mins)

再次呈现动画人物的图片,编制韵句,总结本课的重点内容。

Hello, hello, hi, hi, hi,

I'm Mickey, hi, hi, hi.

Hello, hello, hi, hi, hi,

I'm Donald, hi, hi, hi.

学生跟唱韵句,并加上自己的动作。

Teacher：Follow me, please. You can do some actions like these.

呈现动画人物及教材人物的图片,请学生自己选择人物名称编制韵句,并表演。

Teacher：Look at these pictures. You know their names. Please make a chant with them. Practice with your partner. Then show your chant.

设计意图 以韵句来总结,可以让学生在一课时的学习后,放松心情。同时,有节奏地吟唱能够帮助学生更好地巩固自己的记忆,增强学习效果。让学生自己编制韵句,可以达到替换单词操练句式的效果,使学生更加了解句式结构,从而进一步掌握重点句式。

Step 6：Homework(2 mins)

一、选择正确的名字,将其序号写在头像的下面。

A. Mike B. John C. Wu Yifan D. Miss White E. Chen Jie F. Sarah

_____ _____ _____ _____ _____ _____

二、判断下列句子是否与图片相符,相符的打√,不符的打×。

(　　)1. I'm Miss White.　　　　　(　　)2. I'm John.

(　　)3. I'm Wu Yifan.　　　　　(　　)4. I'm Sarah.

三、请你写下自己的名字,大声地读一读,向大家介绍一下自己:

Hello,I'm_____.

答案:

一、E,A,F,D,C,B

二、1.×　2.√　3.√　4.×

三、略

Step 7:Blackboard design

Unit One Hello!	
Hello!	Mike
Hi!	John
I'm ...	Wu Yifan
	Miss White
	Chen Jie
	Sarah

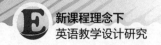
教学流程图：

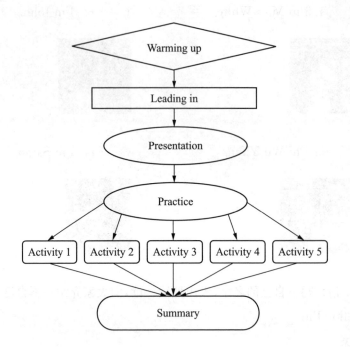

七 教学评价及反思

1. 学生自评

Name:_____   Date:_____

The things I can do.	★★★	★★	★
I can take part in the lesson actively.			
I can understand the oral questions.			
I can answer the questions.			
I can introduce myself.			

2. 小组互评

由组长或制定学生负责,组织小组反思填写。

Name：_____

Criteria to be assessed	★★★	★★	★
Amount of cooperation work			
Participating in group discussion			
Progress made in activity			

3. 教学反思

本节课结束后,我将从以下几个方面进行教学反思。

1) 教学设计:针对教学设计中的某一个或某几个环节进行反思,比如反思教学目标的设置是否得当,教学时间的安排是否合适,活动的安排是否合适。

2) 教学过程:主要针对教学过程是否流畅进行反思,是否突出了教学重难点。

3) 教学过程中存在的问题:课后我会对课堂教学中存在的问题进行回顾和思考,加强理论知识的学习,提高分析问题的水平及能力。

案例十　新版 PEP 小学英语五年级下册 Unit 1　My day Part C Story time 阅读会话课教学设计

一 指导思想及整体设计思路

《小学英语新课程标准》倡导学生通过感知、体验、实践、参与合作等方式,实现任务目标,感受成功。因此,我们应该让更多的学生在学习过程中收获知识、体验快乐,真正做到在"以生为本"的教育理念的指引下,让学生英语的语言能力、思维品质、文化品格、学习能力得到更好的培养。本课时我在设计时充分考虑词不离句,句不离景的教学理念及依据,复习与巩固有关人物一周活动安排的词汇和句型,而不是单纯机械地操练单词和句型。让学生在学完之后能够知道它们的含义以及在什么情景中去运用它们,达到与人交流的目的。

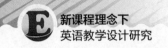
二 教材分析

我们选用的教材是人民教育出版社编写的小学英语教材。这套教材的学习内容和学生的实际生活紧密相连,形式活泼多样,其目的是激发学生学习英语的兴趣,培养他们学习英语的积极态度,培养一定的语感以及良好的学习习惯,初步形成用英语进行简单日常交流的能力。本课选自于新版PEP 小学英语五年级下册 Unit 1 My day Part C Story time,这是一节阅读会话课,本单元的主题是学习日常生活以及周末活动安排的知识,该课时通过 Zoom 和 Zip 一周活动的情景,巩固和复习本单元的核心句型"What do you do on the weekend?"。

三 学情分析

本课的教学对象是五年级的学生,他们在前五课时里已经学习了描述日常生活的单词、短语和句型,具备了一定的英语知识基础,而且学生们也有一定的求知欲和好奇心,学习积极性很高,在课堂上善于表现自我,这些个性和心理特点都有利于师生和生生在课堂上进行交流。

四 教学目标(含重难点)

知识目标:在图片和教师的帮助下理解故事内容,复习与巩固有关人物一周活动安排的词汇和句型。

能力目标:能按正确的语音、语调、意群朗读故事,并能表演故事。

情感目标:养成合理安排时间的良好生活习惯,懂得分享的快乐。

教学重点:能够理解故事内容并讲解故事。

教学难点:理解新授词组 collect nuts 和 dry nuts 以及新授句型 He is always busy.能分角色扮演完成对话。

五 教学方法

通过任务型教学法、情景教学法、视听法、交际法等教学方法,抓住关键词,掌握核心句型,并且尝试创编故事,从而提高学生的语言和学习能力。

现代教学手段:交互式一体机,PPT 课件和动画视频。

六 教学流程

Step 1:Warm up and lead in(热身互动,自然导入)

1. T:Let's sing a song together. (My weekend) Are you ready?

Ss:Yes.

设计意图 轻松愉快的歌曲,可以让学生复习之前学过的一周活动安排的词汇和句型,也可以很快把学习英语的课堂氛围里,激发学生学习兴趣。

2. T:How busy I am! Are you busy this week?

Ss:Yes.

T:I'm busy this week,because I have a lot of things to do,every day I must prepare my English and Chinese lessons,and after class I must check your homework,so I'm very busy this week. What about you?

Ss:We are also very busy. We have math lessons、English lessons、Chinese lessons、PE lessons and so on.

T:How many days are there in a week?

Ss:Seven days.

T:Yes. The first day is Monday in China,but in western countries Sunday is the first day. Let's continue,the second day is Tuesday、Wednesday、Thursday、Friday、Saturday and Sunday. We know Saturday and Sunday are weekend,we can do a lot of things to relax ourselves.(板书 busy、星期一到星期日的缩写,并完善思维导图)

设计意图 轻松愉快的谈话导入,让学生复习了周一到周日的英文表达,为后面的英语学习做了很好的铺垫。我给同学们介绍了东西方的文化差异,培养了学生的文化品格。

Step 2:Presentation(呈现新知)

1. T:Now let's enjoy our story time. First,let's look at the picture. Who are they? They are Zoom and Zip,and we are friends. This story happens between them. Now let's listen and answer the question:What

does Zip usually do on the weekend? Please listen carefully. And then I will ask: What do you usually do on your weekend? For me, I usually go shopping with my family. How about you?

Ss: play football、go for a walk、do sports and so on.

设计意图 巧设问题,培养学生的思维品质。阅读会话课让学生先从视听入手,整体感知整个故事,并让学生带着问题去听故事,孩子们的注意力会更集中,学习会更加专心。在回答完有关听力的问题之后,紧接着用本单元的核心句型 What do you usually do on your weekend? 再提问也让学生复习了之前学过的有关一周的活动的短语。

2. T: Now, Let's go on, what will they say? Zip says: It's Saturday. Now, I'm always very busy. Do you know what will Zoom say? Can you guess?

Ss: Zoom will say "why?" Yes, Zoom says: Why? Follow me and read it, we should act like Zoom strongly and Zip gently.

设计意图 指导学生有感情并带动作朗读,读的时候一定要有 Zoom 强壮和 Zip 温柔的感觉,师生、生生和小组之间分角色朗读。

3. T: And why is Zip very busy? Do you want to know? I want to know. Let's continue and think: what does Zip usually do From Monday to Wednesday? Let's look and guess. Zip says: Let me see. From Monday to Wednesday, I usually collect nuts in the afternoon. Look at "collect", pay attention to the pronunciation and the meaning, in Chinese, it's OK?

Ss:捡、拾。

T: Yes, you are right. This time, we do and say, OK? (板书 collect nuts、并用自然拼读法强调 collect 的发音)

设计意图 本环节我采用 TPR 教学法,让学生带感情边做动作边说英语,让他们体会到学习英语的乐趣,也很容易记住新单词和句子。另外,我在教授单词 collect 的时候,使用了自然拼读法,让学生很快掌握了单词的发音规律。

4. Let's go on. What does Zip often do on Thursday? Zoom says:

What else? Zip says：On Thursday, I often dry my nuts in the sun. Dry my nuts in the sun, do you know the meaning of "dry"? Yes，it's 晒干、晾干。We should read it like Zoom and Zip.（板书 dry my nuts 并带动作朗读句子）

5. T：Let's look at what happened then? Look，who are they?

Ss：They are Zip's friends，rabbit，hamster，dog and monkey. What does Zip usually do on Friday? On Friday，they eat nuts with their friends. They will be very happy，because sharing makes us happy，Yes? Now let's read and act like Zoom and Zip happily.（板书 eat nuts）

设计意图 让学生深刻感受 Zip 和好朋友们分享东西的快乐心情,并让他们带着这种感情去朗读,课堂效果非常棒。

6. What do you usually do from Monday to Friday? Maybe you usually have many different classes，Chinese，English，Math，and so on.

设计意图 以新知为切入点帮助学生复习旧知,通过图 1、图 2、图 3 和图 4 的学习,又引出本单元的核心句型 What do you usually do from Monday to Friday? 学生们又复习了有关一周活动的单词、短语和句型。

7. Zoom says：What do you usually do on the weekend? Zip says：I usually watch TV，but this weekend I have a show，I will play the *pipa*.（板书 watch TV 和 play the *pipa* 并指导朗读）

8. T：Is the story ending? Maybe "Yes"，maybe "No". Let's look at it together. Now，it's 11：30，Zoom says：When does your show begin? Zip says：Saturday，at 12 o'clock，Oh，no! What happens then? Can you guess?

Ss：Zip is late.

T：Anything else?

Ss：Zip is on time and she plays the *pipa*.

设计意图 开放式的故事结尾会让学生联想不断,我让他们大胆的猜测接下来会发生什么事情,猜猜他们会说些什么。学生们对这个话题非常感兴趣,上课的热情不断高涨。

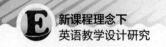

9. Look at the picture. Why does Zoom look like having a big question? Because Zoom doesn't understand Zip. Why does she run away? And how do you feel about this weekend?

Ss：It's very busy.

【设计意图】本环节我采用了讨论法，老师和学生共同讨论并猜想 Zoom 的疑惑并切身感受 Zip 的忙碌。

10. Now，let's look at the video，and follow it，OK?

【设计意图】让学生整体观看 story time 的动画视频并跟读，学生们在理解故事大意的情况下，可以更快、更好的朗读并掌握 story time 的文本内容。

Step 3：Practise(巩固操练)

1. Let's review and fill in the blank. Please take out your paper，and write down your answers，then I'll check.

【设计意图】学生在学完整个故事情节之后，根据表格的提示，可以很快地填出本课的关键短语。

2. Please put these pictures into right order.

【设计意图】学生根据理解，回忆故事发生的情节，可以很轻松的给图片排出正确的顺序。

3. Make up a title of this story.

【设计意图】为了训练学生归纳总结的能力，在他们学完了整个 story time 之后，我特别让他们给故事加个题目，学生们很容易地就能想到许多不同的故事题目。

Step 4：Production(拓展运用)

Let's play in a role. Talk about in your group. Several minutes for you. Have a show for us.

【设计意图】古人云：“授人以鱼，不如授人以渔”。让学生们在具体的情景中正确地运用今天的短语和核心句型，培养了他们的语言能力和学习能力。

Step 5：Summary(归纳总结)

1. In our daily life，when we feel tired，we should relax and rest，then

we will do a better job. And we also know "Sharing makes us happy", because sharing together means being happy together.

设计意图 教育学生要养成合理安排时间的良好生活习惯,懂得劳逸结合。让学生们也要懂得分享的快乐。

2. Who is today's winner? In my eyes, you are all winners, because you all did a good job. Clap your hands for your good work.

设计意图 课堂最后及时适当地总结评价,可以让学生对英语保持很高的学习热情,也让他们很期待每一次的英语课堂。

Step 6:Homework(家庭作业)

1. Listen and read the story.

2. Write or draw an ending of the story.

3. Make up a new story about "My busy weekend".

设计意图 在这里我布置了三个作业,第一个和第二个作业是每个孩子都必须要完成的作业,第三个是选做作业。孩子们可以根据自己的实际情况来选择作业,这样的分层优化作业布置可以让学生课后的学习质量更高、效果更好。

Step 7:Blackboard design(板书设计)

Unit 1 My day
——Part C Story time

1. New Words
   Monday Tuesday Wednesday Thursday Friday Saturday
2. New phrases
   collect nuts   eat nuts
3. Important sentence
   What do you usually do on the weekend?

设计意图 简洁清晰的板书设计,黑板左边是重要的单词,短语,句型,可以让学生把握住本课的重点内容,右边是本课的思维导图,它可以帮助学生很轻松地复述出故事内容。

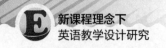
七 教学流程图

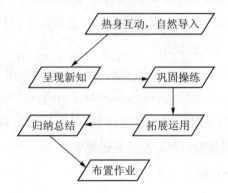

八 教学评价及反思

教学评价

评价是英语课堂的重要组成部分,适时有效的教学评价,可以大大鼓励孩子们学习英语的兴趣,也提高了学生的学习效率。所以在本节课我采用了以下的评价内容和方法:

1. 评价内容:评价学生单词的发音,如 collect、dry 等;评价学生分角色表演的情景剧。

2. 评价方法:教师用激励的语言评价学生的表现:如 good、nice、perfect、excellent 和 good job 等。教师也可用激励性的手势表扬学生,与学生互动,如 give me five、give me ten 等。学生用激励性的手势评价同学的表现,拍手加鼓掌并说 good, good, very good,采用小组加分的竞争机制。

教学反思

优点:1.通过本节课的讲授,我觉得对话教学要由词到句,由机械性练习到真实的情景中去表演,把文本升华到另一个高度。2.在本节课的学习中,我针对学生的特点,使用了多种教学方法,适时适当地鼓励学生,学生们表现得很积极,精神状态饱满,课堂气氛活跃。

不足:1.由于课前准备的不充分,教授新知的时间有点太长。2.由于时间的关系,孩子们在分角色表演的时候,我给他们留的时间不是很充分,导致这部分完成得有点仓促。

再教改进:1.如果下次再上本课的话,课前我会做好充分的准备,使课堂的思路更清晰,把教授新知的时间再压缩一点。2.我会把课堂的时间分配地更合理一点,给学生留够充分的时间来表演对话。

第二节　初中英语教学设计案例

案例十一　中职《英语 1》(基础模块) Unit 5　What's your hobby? Period 1 教学设计

设计主题:Unit 5 What's your hobby? Period 1:Listening and Speaking

一　指导思想及整体设计思路

1. 指导依据

《中等职业学校英语教学大纲》要求学生在九年义务教育基础上进一步提高个人的听、说、读、写等语言技能;通过亲身参与和感受,初步形成职场英语的应用能力;通过在不同情境中的小组合作来培养英语学习的兴趣,养成良好的学习习惯和思维品质;在已有知识的基础上积极创新,正确认识中西方文化差异,实现立德树人。

2. 整体教学设计思路

基于上述理念,根据中职学前教育专业新生的生理和心理特点,经过认真研读本课 What's your hobby? 的教材内容后,我在课堂教学实践中,通过图片、音频、视频和动画游戏等方式积极创设情境,开展了如下教学活动。首先,学生通过单词游戏和自由讨论,谈论个人兴趣爱好(学习理解层面);

接着,学生通过听说活动,提高用英语谈论个人兴趣爱好的表达能力(应用实践层面);然后,开展个人兴趣爱好的问卷调查以及分析总结同学兴趣爱好的数据(应用实践层面);最后,根据爱好进行分组合作,介绍一种和爱好相关的职业使同学们明白尊重他人的兴趣爱好、规划个人未来职业方向的重要性(迁移创新层面)。从而实现了学生语言能力、学习能力、思维品质和文化意识的提高。

二 教材分析

本课选自高等教育出版社《英语1》(基础模块)第五单元第一课时,是一节听说课,主要围绕谈论个人兴趣爱好展开,其语言结构为:—What's your hobby? —My hobby is ... —What do you like/love? —I like/love ...,旨在培养学生掌握表达个人兴趣爱好的常用词组和句型,为后面的阅读课和语法课做好知识建构。

鉴于教学和学情的需要,本课在教学内容上对教材进行了重组和改编:

● 课前发布自学任务,让学生运用百词斩 APP、制作生词卡来自学本节课的重要词汇,以便集中精力在本课时操练句型和对话;

● 将本课涉及的重要词汇制成 Flash 游戏,让学生在课上完成,方便教师检查学生的自学效果;

● 将 Activity 12 的内容略去,制成微课,在课前完成任务;

● 将本单元的 Unit Task:Make a survey about your classmates' hobbies to set up hobby groups in your class 提前到本课,目的是通过此项活动来巩固本节课所学知识。

三 学情分析

中职学前教育专业一年级的新生在初中已经学习了关于兴趣爱好的单词和短语,能够为本节课"兴趣爱好"话题的展开进行词汇的提取和运用。

学生的兴趣爱好广泛,能歌善舞,乐于尝试自己擅长的课堂活动。有学习英语的兴趣和需求,但是听说能力差,尤其缺乏科学的学习习惯和方法。自信心不足,害怕当众回答问题。

"兴趣爱好"的话题对于学前教育专业的学生来说是经常出现的。贴近学生生活实际,交际需要和学生知识储备缺乏的矛盾构成了本课的学习需要。

四 教学目标(含重难点分析)

通过本节课的学习,学生们将能够:

1. 听音看图说出与兴趣爱好有关的 8 个词汇:hobby, fly, collect, chess, stamp, favorite, enjoy, be crazy about;

2. 听录音,复述并在恰当情境下使用功能句谈论兴趣爱好:What's your hobby? / Do you like ...? / I love/ enjoy/ like V-ing .../ I'm crazy about ...;

3. 朗读并表演对话,描述个人的兴趣爱好;

4. 与人合作,并在教师的协助下完成一次问卷调查;

5. 与人分享自己对未来职业的理解,讨论该职业应具备的职业素养。

● 教学重点:

掌握表达个人兴趣爱好的重要词汇和功能句。

● 教学难点:

1. 学习在恰当情境下使用功能句谈论兴趣爱好;

2. 与人交流某种和自己爱好相关的职业应具备的职业素养。

五 教学方法和学习方法:

1. 教法:情景教学法、任务型教学法

2. 学法:小组合作法、角色扮演法

六 教学流程

● Before class:

1. Download the learning task on the Cloud platform:

课前"学习评价表"

姓名_____   学号_____

一、学习指南
1. 课题名称： 　　　**一年级英语(基础模块1) Unit 5 Period 1 Listening and Speaking**
2. 达成目标： (1) 掌握重点单词、词组和句型的用法； (2) 理解听力原文； (3) 朗读并表演文中的对话。

二、学习任务
1. 学唱英文儿歌"Head and Shoulders，Knees and Toes "。 https://v.qq.com/x/cover/h1cf41nhs2ez39j/q1400y02oah.html 2. 预习课本 P62—65 的内容，找出并识记有关描述个人兴趣爱好的新词汇，尝试用音、意、句结合的方式记忆生词。 　　E.g.　kite[kaɪt] n.风筝； 　　　　　fly a kite　放风筝 　　　　　I like flying a kite in spring.我喜欢在春天放风筝。 3. 听录音并模仿课本 P65 的表示兴趣爱好的动词短语，并上传音频至"云课堂"； 4. 阅读课本 P63—64 的英语会话，用下划线标出谈论兴趣爱好的语句。

三、预习评价
1. 通过预习，我找出了_____个生词,我共记住了_____个生词。 2. 通过自主学习，我理解的句子为_____；一知半解的句子为_____；无法理解的句子为_____。（可在文中标注） 3. 通过预习微课，我认为这篇听力原文的难度为： 　A. 难　　　　B. 较难　　　　C. 易　　　　D. 一般
4. 你需要老师解决什么问题? 需要老师做什么调整?

● In Class

Step 1：Lead-in(4 mins)

Activity 1：Watch and sing

T：1. Show the song "Head and Shoulders，Knees and Toes"，and invite all the students to stand up to do the gestures while singing.

2. Ask some students to answer questions.

S: 1. Sing the song loudly and do the instructions.

2. Practise the dialogues with the teacher.

Head and Shoulders, Knees and Toes

Head and shoulders,

Knees and toes, knees and toes.

Head and shoulders,

Knees and toes, knees and toes.

Eyes and ears and mouth and nose.

Head and shoulders,

Knees and toes, knees and toes.

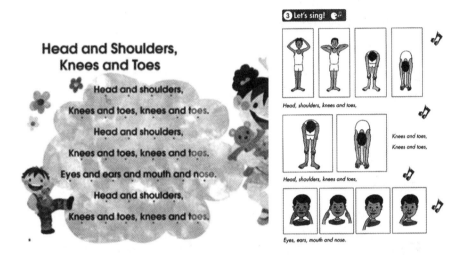

③ Let's sing!

Head, shoulders, knees and toes,

Knees and toes,
Knees and toes,

Head, shoulders, knees and toes,

Eyes, ears, mouth and nose.

(T: What can we do with the eyes?

S1: We can read books with our eyes.

T: Do you like reading books?

S1: Yes, I do. I like reading story books.

T: Good girl! Reading can widen our view, can make us clever, right? But don't read too long, it will make our eyes hurt.

T: What can we do with our ears?

S2: We can listen to music with our ears.

T: Good! Do you love listening to music?

S2: Yes, I do.

T: How often do you listen to music?

S2: Every day. Listening to music can make me happy.

T: Do you love listening to music? (to all students)

Ss: Yes, we do.

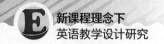
T：Very good. I like listening to music, too. Now, work in pairs and ask each other what he/ she likes doing? Ready? Go!）

设计意图 通过唱英语儿歌做动作来引入情境,活跃课堂气氛,激发学生的学习兴趣,为下面的词汇训练做铺垫。

Activity 2：Play and practise

T：1. Ask students to play the Youya game of the words.

2. Practice dialogues with some of the volunteers.

S：1. Play the Youya game of the words under the teacher's guidance.

2. Make short dialogues with the teacher and the partners.

（T：Do you like playing chess?

S1：Yes, I do. What about you?

T：No, I don't. I like swimming. Do you like swimming?

S1：Yes, I do. Swimming can make us strong.

T：I agree. What else? Volunteers?

S2：I like flying kites.

T：Really? Me, too. I love flying kites in spring.）

设计意图 通过在蓝墨云班课教学平台上监测学生"单词打地鼠"游戏的完成情况可以很好地了解学生的词汇能力水平,通过和学生反复操练功能句帮助学生实现"用中学",为下面的听力活动做准备。

Step 2：Listening(9 mins)

Activity 3：Read and tell

T：Show 3 pictures on the screen and ask students to describe them.

S：Watch the pictures and try to describe them.

Activity 4：Listen and tick.

T：Play the listening material once and ask students to choose the correct answers.

S：Listen to the tape and tick out the correct answers.

T：Oh，look！Here are three friends of mine，can you guess who is Li Xiaonian? Listen carefully and tick out the correct picture.

(1 min later)

T：Volunteers？Who can tell me which one is Mr. Li?

Ss：Picture B.

T：What does he like to do?

Ss：He likes playing computer games.

设计意图 通过首次播放课本听力，让学生完成课本听力练习 4 和 5，观察学生的课堂反应。如果学生完成不好，将准备预案活动 5。如果完成得好，就直接进入下一环节。

Activity 5：Watch and learn（预案）

T：Show the micro class，and ask students to take down the four steps of doing a listening drill.

S：Learn the micro class and do the listening exercises together.

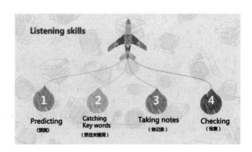

设计意图 通过播放微课的前半部分，对学生进行听力的学习策略的指导，在此基础上再一起进行其余听力练习。

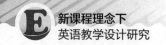
Step 3：**Speaking**(20 mins)

Activity 6：Listen and write.

T：1. Play a short dialogue twice and ask students to write down the two questions they hear.

2. Check their answers together.

S：1. Listen to the tape and take down the two questions；

2. Check their answers with the partners；

3. Practise the dialogue with each other.

设计意图 通过听录音写出两个问句,培养学生捕捉有效信息的能力；同桌之间相互核对答案并练习对话,可以培养学生的团结协作能力。

Activity 7：Underline and imitate.

T：1. Ask students to go through the dialogue first and underline the sentences for talking about hobbies.

2. Ask students to read out the useful sentences loudly.

3. Play the video for them and ask them to imitate.

4. Help the students to practise the dialogue in the whole class.

5. Invite some students to role play in front of the class.

S：1. Go through the dialogue quickly and underline the useful sentences.

2. Read them loudly.

3. Watch the video and imitate it.

4. Practise the dialogue together.

5. Role play.

设计意图 通过默读短文画出有用句型来检查学生是否已经掌握了本节课的功能句型；通过朗读、模仿视频对话并表演的方式来训练学生的语音语调，提高学生的语言能力。

Activity 8：Make a survey：What do you like to do？

T：Ask students to interview 3 classmates about their hobbies with the useful structures in class.

S：Make a survey of their classmates' hobbies in class.

Name	Like 😊	Don't like 😟

预案：Watch and learn.

T：Show students another micro class about hobbies.

S：Learn the micro class in class and after class.

设计意图 通过观看微课来帮助学生克服学习障碍，保护学生的学习积极性，既有利于顺利完成课堂活动，又培养了学生的语言能力和思维品质。

Step 4：Interview：What makes a good kindergarten teacher？（6 mins）

A man kindergarten teacher Chen Xuliang is going to visit our school. Luckily, you will be the interviewer. Work in group, and make a short interview according to the six pictures above. The theme is "What makes a good kindergarten teacher?"

(T: 1. Show the six pictures and let the students to discuss the qualities that a good kindergarten teacher should have.

2. Go among the students to join their discussion and offer some help if needed.

3. Choose one group to act out their interview and make some comments on their performance.

S: 1. Discuss the pictures with their team members and write down their conclusion.

2. Act out their interview in front of the class, and invite some students to comment on their performance.)

设计意图 通过创设情境让学生猜测 90 后男幼师陈徐良的爱好，以采访的形式帮助他们思考"作为一名好的幼儿园老师应该具备哪些品质？"培养他们的爱心和耐心，做到"学后用"。

Step 5：Homework(1 min)

1. Finish *the self-check and assessment* sheet；

2. Shoot another two interviews and upload to our E-class.

Blackboard Design：

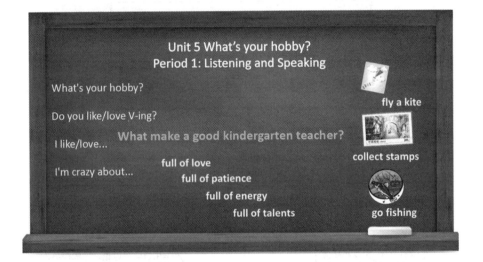

● After Class：

1. Watch the micro-class" How to express hobbies?" again to consolidate the expressions and sentence patterns of hobbies.

2. Learn something about hobbies on the MOOC-Xuetang online to imitate the dialogues.

http://www.xuetangx.com/courses/course-v1：TsinghuaX＋30640014X＋sp/about

3. Pick out your favorite video in our E-class and give a brief comment within 50 words.

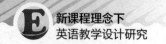

七 教学过程结构流程图

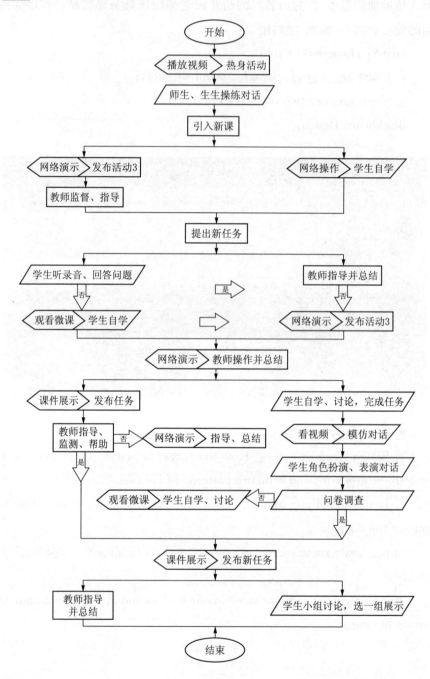

八 教学评价及反思

1. 教学评价表

Unit 5   Period 1 Listening and Speaking

Self-check and Assessment

Name_____   Student ID_____

By watching the micro class "How to express hobbies?"

I learned：

(   ) basketball   (   ) volleyball   (   ) badminton

(   ) tennis   (   ) yoga   (   ) chess

(   ) favourite   (   ) enjoy   (   ) fond

I can：

(   ) talk about hobbies in English.

(   ) ask and answer questions about one's likes and dislikes.

I know：

(   ) kinds of ways to express one's hobbies and interests.

A. 3   B. 4   C. 5   D. 6

评价方式

评价内容

基础知识

综合运用

课堂表现

进步(举例说明)

出错原因

(举例说明)

我想说

---

2. 教学反思

When I finish teaching this period, I am going to reflect on my teaching from the following three aspects：

● Teaching Effect

1. The students believe in "Every dog has his day" and become more confident than before.

2. They can think about the vocational skills needed in the kindergarten

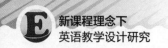

and know what to learn in our school.

3. The information-based teaching methods help deal with the teaching important and difficult points and improve the teaching effect.

● Highlights

1. It is convenient to learn many resources on the *Cloud platform*.

2. It is more vivid to watch the video of the dialog.

3. It is efficient to make dialogs in situational videos.

● Shortness

Although my class is exciting and happy, some tasks would be a little difficult for them to complete. So, maybe I should offer them easier home-work—finish the English fun dubbing of hobbies, which is the video of the dialog in this class I upload to the APP. It is more important to learn how to learn.

案例十二　译林版八年级英语第二单元 School life 第一课时教学设计

一 指导思想及整体设计思路

《义务教育初中英语课程标准(2017 年版)》倡导学生利用自己已有的知识经验去实践,形成新的技巧和能力。这要求学生在富有交际意义的任务活动中去学习、体验和运用语言知识并且让学生学会与他人合作学习。

基于这一理念,以及八年级学生的特点和发展需求,我认真研读译林版八年级英语第二单元 School life 第一课时 Comic strip & Welcome to the unit 教材内容,以学生为中心。我在课堂教学实践中通过图片、视频创设情境,采用情境交际法、任务型教学法让学生积极地参与教学活动,所以我设置三个活动,第一,让学生学习理解有关英美学校生活的基础知识并回答英美学校生活不同之处;第二,让学生带着问题阅读 Comic strip 与 Part B 对话;第三,通过知识迁移让学生感知英美文化差异性从而培养跨文化意识。

以此提高学生的语言能力、思维品质、文化意识等能力。

二 教材分析

本课是译林版八年级英语第二单元 School life 第一课时 Comic strip & Welcome to the unit 教材内容。本单元主要内容涉及相同概念在 British English 与 American English 的不同表达,What is … like? It's like …以及 There be 句型结构,学生了解英式英语与美式英语的区别。本课时是本单元第一课时,是一节听说课,本课时的学习为后面学习英美学校生活的差异性做了很好铺垫,自然地过渡到对英美文化的学习。

三 学情分析

八年级学生有了一定的语言积累和知识储备,有较强的自觉学习能力和积极性。在课堂上基本上能运用英语思维思考问题,并具有一定的英语表达能力。但部分学生仍存在不自信,羞于表现等顾虑;在活动设计中,我会充分考虑到学生顾虑,并鼓励他们勇于用英语表达自己的思想。同时,增强学生的团队合作精神。

四 教学目标(含重难点分析)

本节课结束的时候,学生能够

(1)了解不同英语单词在英美国家中表示同一事物;

(2)正确使用有关话题词汇,分析比较英美校园生活的不同;

(3)构建英美校园生活的词汇语义网,能归纳出 American English 和 British English 在读音和拼写方面的相同点与不同点;

(4)运用所学的词汇谈论自己的校园生活,并写一篇关于 My School life 60 词左右的英语作文;

(5)通过对比中外校园生活,学生能热爱自己的校园生活并能运用本课所学恰当表达。

教学重点难点分析

教学重点:

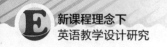

（1）掌握相关词组 go to school，be like，watch TV；句型 Why don't dogs go to school? What's school like? It's like watching TV，but there are fewer advertisements.等知识点

（2）说出并理解相关概念在 American 和 British 中的不同表达

教学难点：

（1）掌握及运用 There be 句型结构

（2）初步掌握英美单词差异并感知英美文化的区别

五 教学方法

任务型教学法、情境教学法

六 教学流程

Step 1：Warming-up(4 mins)

1. Greetings

2. Free talk about school.

T：Boys and girls，do you think school is fun? Is school like watching TV?

S：Yes，school is fun. But it isn't like watching TV.

设计意图 激发学生兴趣，消除学生紧张心理。

Step 2：Pre-task(6 mins)

1. Show a world map

T：What countries do you know? Which are English-speaking countries?

S：China，America …

T：What languages(语言) do they speak?

S：They speak Chinese，English …

2. Teach the students the new words：

T：As we all know，we can use different words to express the same thing. Can you list some words?

S：Rubber and eraser both mean 橡皮擦，橡皮……

设计意图 创设具体情境，用世界地图自然导入目标语言。学生能直观地接触到 British English 与 American English.

Step 3：While-task(20 mins)

1. T：Read the passage(5 mins)

T：Let's learn the new words together. Pay attention to the pronunciations and spelling.

BE＝British English　　　　AE＝American English

BE	autumn	lift	football	maths	rubber	post	ground floor	secondary school
AE	fall	elevator	soccer	math	eraser	mail	first floor	high school

S：……

2. T：Finish Part A on Page 23. I'll give you more words，such as sweets and candies，holiday and vocation，biscuit and cookie and so on.(5 mins)

S：……

T：I will show you some pictures and you can make a dialogue like this.

A：What is it in British English?

B：It's a football.

A：What is it in American English?

B：It is a soccer.

3. T：Write down both the British and American words，then finish Part B.

Different spellings(5 mins)

（1）T：There are also some differences in spelling between British English and American English. Try to find more words and make a table

227

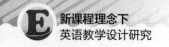

and write down some words.

Eg. favourite and favorite，centre and center.

4. Comic strip(5 mins)

T：Do you remember Hobo and Eddie? They are talking about school life.

Listen to the tape and answer：

What does Eddie think of the school life?

Listen again and read after it.

T：Pay attention to the language points：

Why don't you do sth.? ＝Why not do sth.?

be smarter than，be like doing sth.，there be，

few/a few 区别

Look at the pictures and practise the dialogue.

Act the dialogue in groups and pairs.

Work in pairs

Act out the dialogue

设计意图 逐步深入进行任务型教学，由易到难，既让学生保持适当的学习动机，也激发学生的学习乐趣与积极性。

Step 4：Post-task(5 mins)

Finish the exercise：Fill in the blankets in American English.

Discuss with your partner about your school life.

设计意图 适当练习不仅巩固新知，也让学生由文中学校生活过渡到自己的学校生活，为下文描写自己的学校生活做好知识储备。

Step 5：Homework(5 mins)

1. Try to find more different words which mean the same thing and different spellings after class.

2. Retell the story.

3. Write a passage about *My school life*(60 words).

七 教学评价及反思

T：This class，all of you did good job. What do we learn today?

S：It's about school life.

T：Our school life is meaningful and colorful. We should cherish our school life.

设计意图 总结本课时所学内容，并进行情感教育。

自我评价表

Name   Date

The things I can do	5	4	3	2	1
I can take an active part in the lesson activity					
I can understand the task and finish exercises					
I can answer questions					
I can work with classmates and act out the dialogue					
I can write my own school life					
Total					

教学反思

通过本课时，我将从以下几个方面进行反思

反 思 内 容	方法策略
时间的安排是否得当	
内容是否难易适中，层次清晰，重点突出	
是否调动学生积极性、主动性、创造性	
课堂设计是否科学、合理、新颖	
学生课堂自主学习、练习时间是否不少于三分之一	
教学目标达成度，课堂气氛，教学质量	

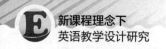
板书设计

Blackboard Design

Unit 2　School life

BRE：autumn, lift, football, ground floor, secondary school
AEE：fall, elevator, soccer, first floor, high school

案例十三　牛津八年级英语上册8A
Unit 3　A day out Task 教学设计

［教学理念］

按照新课标立德树人的根本任务,发展学生英语核心素养,实践英语学习活动观,着力提高学生学用能力。因此,本节作文课将以学生为中心,通过创设与学生相关的情境,培养学生的写作能力,并以此为契机,培养学生对家乡的热爱。

［教材分析］

Task处于每个单元的最后一项任务,考察学生的是综合运用本单元所学的词组句型,紧扣本单元中心,输出一篇作文。而Unit 3的中心话题就是旅游,范文是向朋友介绍北京旅游景点安排的一封信。在日常生活中,旅游话题是我们经常谈论的一个话题,也是学生非常感兴趣的,通过旅行我们可以增长见闻,培养学生欣赏美的能力。本课需要通过教师的引导,学生积极参与课堂活动,最终写一篇邀请朋友外出旅行的信。

［学情分析］

学生是初二上学期的学生,在以前的学习过程中,已经具备了关于旅游的部分知识,并且逐渐适应初二英语的学习,他们对学习有关英语的知识也是充满了兴趣,有极强的学习能力,但是也有着畏难的情绪。课堂上老师能够以学生感兴趣的话题开展写作教学,通过小组合作,积极创设情景,英语写作的表达能力和思维能力才能提高。

[教学目标]

到本课结束,学生可以

1. 掌握介绍旅行景点所需的重要词汇和句型;

2. 独立完成一篇介绍旅行景点的邀请信;

3. 学会作文进行自评和互评的方法;

4. 通过教师景点的介绍,对家乡产生自豪感。

[**重点、难点**] 重点:目标 2 难点:目标 3

[**教学方法**] 情景教学法 任务教学法

[**教学手段**] 多媒体 黑板

[**教学过程**]

Step 1: lead-in

1. Play a guessing game

T: Boys and girls, let's play a guessing game. I'll give you some clues. Can you guess these places of interest in Danyang?

2. Enjoy a video

T: Now let's watch a video about more places of interest in Danyang. I'm sure you'll know your hometown better after that.

After watching, T: Do you want to show your friends around these beautiful places in Danyang? (students say "yes") But you should know how to make a travel plan. Kitty and Daniel also want to make a plan of Beijing for their classmates Linda. Let's look at their plan.

设计意图 课堂初始,让学生看图猜家乡丹阳的景点名称,引起学生的兴趣。再进一步观看更多关于家乡的景点,自然导入今天所要教的话题旅游,这也为学生之后完成一篇旅游计划做准备,让他们能够有内容可写。

Step 2: A travel plan

Present the travel plan.

T: Look at Kitty and Daniel's travel plan. Work in pairs and talk about the following questions.

① How many places will they visit? What are they?

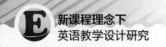
② How will they get to the Palace Museum from Tian'anmen Square?

③ How much time will they spend at Beihai Park? And what will they do there?

④ Where will they go after that? And what will they do?

T：So they are four parts of the plan. Think about it. They are when, where, what and how.

Learn the invitation letter

(1) complete the letter

T：Can you help Kitty and Daniel complete the invitation letter? You can use the information from the plan.

(2) learn the outline

T：there are seven parts of an invitation letter. What are they? (S：they are date, name of receiver, purpose of the letter, plan, instruction, closing and signatures.)

设计意图 让学生小组合作,学习旅游计划。同时提供相关问题,让他们在两人一组活动时更有目的性,最后老师提醒学生旅游计划的七个部分。接下来,学生根据旅行计划完成邀请函,并且分析邀请函的构成。

Step 3：Writing skills

Learn useful expressions for the purpose and instructions.

T：Look at the purpose and instructions of the letter. Can you use them in your letter? (S：Yes!) Of course, you also can write them in another way. For example, "It will be a great day", we also can say "The day will be wonderful". Now work in groups of four and write down as many sentences as possible.

Learn useful expressions for the plan

(1) Express the time

T：When you travel with your friends, you should tell them the time. Can you underline the sentences about time in the plan? (after underling) You all do good jobs. Would you like to share sentences with each other?

(2) Express places and transportation

T：Work in pairs and find out the sentences about places and transportation. Can you say them in another way? Write down the same sentences on your paper.

(3) Express the activity

T：We can do many things in different places of interest. Such as going shopping, rowing boats and so on. Try to say some one by one.

(4) Learn transition words

T：Transition word is an important part of the article. It can make the article rich and smooth. Let's find some in the plan. And I think you also can use them in your plan, right?

设计意图 通过小组合作、独立思考、接龙等各项活动,引导学生一步步学习有用的句型,怎么写开头和结尾,以及如何正确表达时间、地点和交通。更重要的是,通过学习过渡语,了解过渡语对文章的重要性,这些都是为他们之后自己写邀请信做了铺垫。

Step 4：A poster

Make a poster of travel plan

T：In the beginning of the lesson, we enjoy the beautiful sights in Danyang. It's your turn, boys and girls. Work in groups of four, make a poster of your travel plan about Danyang in five minutes. But remember, in the poster, you should have four parts of the plan.

Show the poster

T：Just now every group is very careful. And your posters are so great. Are you willing to show your poster to your classmates? We will choose the best poster in our class at last.

设计意图 四人一组设计一个旅行计划的海报,提高学生的团队合作意识,也能让学弱生在团队中得到帮助,不会出现有学生游离于课堂之外的现象。在此之后,每组展示小组海报,可以让学生了解各组海报的优缺点,有利于下阶段邀请函的写作。

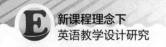

Step 5：An invitation letter

Write an invitation letter

T：Now you can write your invitation letter to your friends according to the poster. And don't forget to use the expressions we taught just now.

Examine the letter

T：You have finished your letter. Please examine the letter by yourselves.

Grade the letter

T：Now work in pairs. Exchange your invitation letter and grade the letter for your partner. You should circle the mistakes for your partner.

设计意图 利用海报写一篇邀请信，并且通过自评和互评，调动学生的积极性，增加学生的学习兴趣，也同时提高他们的写作和发现错误的能力。

Step 6：Finishing the letter

T：After class，remember to correct the mistakes and write the letter on your exercise books.

［教学评价与反思］

教师评价表

项目	序号	评　价　标　准	判断			
			A	B	C	D
教学态度	1	备课认真，情满课堂，责任心强，落实常规；关心学生，经常辅导，注重培养学科兴趣。				
	2	关注学生成长，寓教于乐，教书育人。				
教学内容与教学方法	3	依据课标，活用教材，开发资源；知识、概念、原理准确无误，突出重点；问题设计层次分明，思路清晰；学、讲、练结合，组织严密。				
	4	精心设计教学活动，体现学生主体；关注学习过程，教学手段多样，教法灵活；注意启发学生思维，善于调动学生学习的积极性，注意学生能力的生成。				
	5	课堂结构合理，展开有序；语言表达准确清晰，形象生动，深入浅出，逻辑性强；板书明晰，重点突出，布局有条理；重视必要的直观教学及演示实验，调动学生多种感官，增效课堂。				

续表

项目	序号	评 价 标 准	判断			
			A	B	C	D
教学效果	6	关注学生学习表现和情绪变化,及时实施教学评价,善于启发、激励和引导;能从学生的作业、测验、考查、考试成绩、调查和实验报告中,较好地把握学生学情,并及时调整教学策略。				
学习与提高	7	注意学习教育理论,注重吸取学科新知识;善于反思,教有心得;研究教法,常思改进。				
自我评价			汇总			

学生自评表

The things I did	Evaluation
I played an active role in this class	5　4　3　2　1
I expressed myself in English very well	5　4　3　2　1
I followed my teacher well and took some necessary notes	5　4　3　2　1
I worked together with my partners very well	5　4　3　2　1
I made some progress in this class	5　4　3　2　1
TOTAL SCORES	

20—25：Excellent；
15—19：Very good
10—14：Good
5—9：Just so so
1—4：Need to improve

[板书设计]

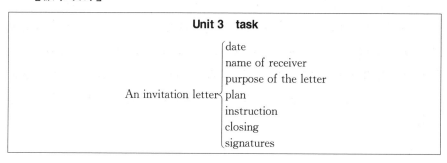

Unit 3　task

An invitation letter
- date
- name of receiver
- purpose of the letter
- plan
- instruction
- closing
- signatures

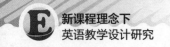
案例十四　牛津译林版七年级英语上册
Unit 5　Let's celebrate 教学设计

一　指导思想及整体设计思路

1. 根据《义务教育阶段英语课程标准》的要求,初一学生需要达到能听懂熟悉话题的语段和简短的故事并且可以和老师或者同学就熟悉话题交换信息。

2. 基于以上理论和初一新生的知识基础水平,结合本单元 Let's celebrate 的教材内容,通过展示图片以及视频让学生说出节日名称、日期等方式,学生能够对节日有初步的了解。接着通过创设节日情景(中西方典型节日对比)和设计活动,学生可以掌握特殊疑问句的概念及用法。最后,通过本单元对节日的学习,学生能够了解中西方文化的差异,提高学生的爱国意识。通过以上教学活动,学生能够在实际生活中熟练运用特殊疑问句交际并提高了文化意识。

二　教材分析

本节课的教学内容源于牛津译林版七年级英语上册 Unit 5 第一课时的内容,主要围绕"节日"展开话题。本单元主要内容涉及特殊疑问句来讨论关于节日的相关知识。特殊疑问句的构成和使用贯穿初中的整个英语学习,因此对于初一学生来说,是一个重要知识点。本课时是一节导入课,通过漫画中 Eddie 和 Hobo 的短对话引出本单元的节日主题。主要话题是:你最喜欢什么节日,学生根据话题分小组讨论自己喜欢的节日的基本情况。主要语言结构为 What's your favourite festival? How do you celebrate it? 学生通过本课时的学习,掌握以"what, how"开头的特殊疑问句。通过本课时的导入学习,学生了解特殊疑问句的基本用法,为后续学习做铺垫。

236

三 学情分析

七年级学生刚刚跨入初中,虽然单词量较少,但是学生此前已经掌握一些有关节日的词汇,能够满足本节课的词汇要求。并且他们也具有一定的认知能力。同时,他们对身边一切事物都充满着好奇心和求知欲,想要了解更多关于节日的信息。又有着丰富表达欲,想要与人交流,相互讨论自己喜欢的节日和起源。在课堂上,他们乐于思考,敢于说出自己的想法。少数内向的学生不善于发言,应鼓励他们敢于表达自己的观点。学生通过自身努力和老师指导能够完成一定难度的任务。七年级学生有着一定的学习能力和模仿能力,即便基础薄弱也能通过小组讨论迅速掌握"WHAT,HOW"特殊疑问句句型,但是需要教师从旁进行协助和点拨才能更快更好的完成交流讨论的任务。

四 教学目标分析(含重难点分析)

本节课结束时,学生将能够

1)用目标语言即英语说出自己喜欢的节日的名称、日期、喜欢原因和庆祝方式。

2)熟练运用 what、how 开头的特殊疑问句句型,并能够举一反三。

3)用目标语言即英语了解中西方的节日并能够进行评价。

4)能够写一篇以"My Favourite Festival"为题目的一篇英语小作文,字数 40 词左右。

重难点分析:目标 1)2)学生用英语说出节日的名称日期并熟练运用所学 When、What 句型为教学重点,是学生必须掌握的知识点。目标 3)4)用英语评价中西方节日并写一篇英语小作文为教学难点,是为学生拓展口语和写作能力所做的准备。

五 教学方法和学习方法

教学方法:本节课所使用的教学方法为任务型教学法。

学习方法:学生以小组合作的形式接受任务,讨论、完成自己喜欢的节日以及庆祝方式。

六　教学流程

Step 1：Warming-up（3 mins）

Greetings

The teacher shows pictures of moon cakes and asks students.

T：Do you like moon cakes?

S：Yes!

T：When do you eat moon cakes?

S1：At Mid-Autumn Festival!

T：Good! Sit down please.

T：Is Mid-Autumn Festival a Chinese festival or a western festival?

S2：Mid-Autumn Festival is a Chinese festival.

T：Great! Sit down please. Now I will play a video of festivals.

Teacher plays a video of western festivals.

[Design Intention] To attract students' interest in western festivals

Step 2：Pre-task（8 mins）

T：Now，tell me，is this festival a Chinese festival or a western festival?

S1：A western festival.

T：Good job!

Match and say and write

The teacher shows some pictures and let students say what festivals these are. And let students write on thee-board

[Design intention] To let students know some words about festivals

Step 3：While-task(25 mins)

The teacher shows PPT of questions and then play a video of the text

Q1：What is this festival's name?

Q2：How does Eddie celebrate it?

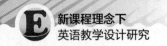

[Design intention] To let students know something about the text

The teacher plays the video again and shows the questions

Q1: Do Eddie and Hobo like Halloween?

[Design intention] Elicit the following task.

T: Do Eddie and Hobo like Halloween?

S: Yes!

T: Why?

S: Because Hobo says "let's celebrate it".

T: What does celebrate mean?

S: 庆祝

T: Can you describe it in English?

S: To show this day is important by doing something special.

T: (If students can't read the word) Now, read after me "celebrate".

[Design intention] To help learn new word

The teacher plays a video between Tommy and Millie. And asks students to try to find out what Tommy's favourite festival is and why he likes it, and how he celebrates it?

Millie:	What is your favourite festival, Tommy?
Tommy:	Christmas.
Millie:	Why do you like it?
Tommy:	Because we always get lots of nice presents at Christmas. What festival do you like, Millie?
Millie:	I like the Mid-Autumn Festival.
Tommy:	What do you usually do on that day?
Millie:	All my family get together and have a big dinner. Then we eat moon cakes and enjoy the full moon. It's great!

The teacher shows questions on the PPT

Q1：What's your favourite festival?

Q2：Why do you like it?

Q3：How do you celebrate it? / What do you usually do on that day?

T：We can change another way to ask. Like how do you celebrate it? Both of the sentences are right. You can use either of them.

Then the teacher divides students into six groups to discuss these three questions.

And let students make a dialogue with their partners.

[Design intention] Make sure students master the three question sentences and practice their oral English.

Step 4：Post-task(3 mins)

The teacher asks students "do you like Chinese festival or western festival?" Two or three students are accepted.

[Design intention] To let students evaluate Chinese festivals and western festivals and enhance their sense of patriotic.

Step 5：Summary(5 mins)

The teacher asks students to sum up and students write them on the blackboard.

Show some exercise about question words on the PPT.

Exercise(use why, what and how to fill the blanks)

1. _____are you—I'm a doctor

2. _____are you—I'm twelve years old

3. _____are you here—Because I want to play in this park

[Design intention] To consolidate what we learn in this class

Step 6：Homework(1 min)

1. Review festivals words

2. Write a composition about "My favourite festival"

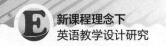

七 板书设计(Blackboard Design)

Unit 5　Let's celebrate

Festivals
- Chinese
  - Mid-Autumn Festival
  - Chinese New Year
  - Dragon Boat Festival
- Western
  - Halloween
  - Christmas
  - Thanksgiving Day

特殊疑问词

What 是什么

Why 为什么

How 怎么样

八 教学流程图

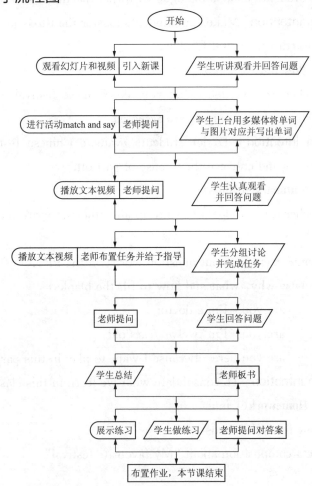

开始

观看幻灯片和视频｜引入新课　　学生听讲观看并回答问题

进行活动match and say｜老师提问　　学生上台用多媒体将单词与图片对应并写出单词

播放文本视频｜老师提问　　学生认真观看并回答问题

播放文本视频｜老师布置任务并给予指导　　学生分组讨论并完成任务

老师提问　　学生回答问题

学生总结　　老师板书

展示练习｜学生做练习｜老师提问对答案

布置作业，本节课结束

九 教学评价反思

1. 教学评价

1）学生评价

Name_____   Class_____

The things I can do	5	4	3	2	1
I can take part in the lesson					
I can discuss the questions in English					
I can understand the oral questions					
I can talk about Chinese festivals and western festivals					
I can use question words "what, why, how" to make sentences.					
I can write a composition about "My favourite festival"					
Total					

2）初中英语课堂教学评价表（教师用）

听课人：

课题		Unit 5 Let's celebrate	
评价项目		评价指标	项目得分
教师素质 15%	1	教态亲切大方，有感染力	
	2	用英语组织教学，话语流畅，表达准确、得体、清楚，有启发性和激励性	
	3	教学基本功扎实，教学技能娴熟，课堂调控能力强	
教学设计 20%	4	目标设置准确、具体，符合教学要求和学生实际	
	5	教材处理有创意，教学内容安排适度，重、难点把握得当	
	6	教学程序明晰，有层次；活动设计真实，体现语言运用	

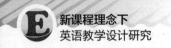
续表

评价项目			评价指标	项目得分
教学过程 45%	教师教学行为 25%	7	发挥教师指导作用,突出学生主体地位,面向全体学生,关注个体差异	
		8	给学生留有思维空间,体现自主、合作、探究式的学习,有利于学生学习方式的转变	
		9	教学实施符合语言教学规律、学生心理特征和认知水平	
		10	情景和语境创设真实,体现语言实际应用;师生之间、学生之间互动充分,注重语言运用能力培养	
		11	课堂结构严谨、有序,衔接自然;教学气氛民主、和谐	
		12	课件/板书设计科学、合理;辅助手段使用得当、有效,操作熟练	
	学生学习行为 20%	13	主动参与,勇于质疑,思维活跃	
		14	有足够的时间参与、体验和感知语言学习	
		15	100%的学生都能参与到各种形式的语言实践活动中	
教学效果 15%		16	完成教学任务,达到预期教学目标	
		17	大多数学生的知识和能力得到不同程度的提高	
		18	教学的时效性和实效性和谐统一	
教学特色 5%		19	教学的某一方面有独到之处	
主要优缺点分析				

3) 教学反思

这节课结束以后,我将从以下六个方面进行反思:

是否达到教学目标? 时间掌握是否准确? 是否恰当使用多媒体进行教学?

是否调动学生积极性? 教学手段是否适合学生? 处理突发状况发生时是否具有教学机制?

基于以上六点反思,我会在课后进行改进,让课堂教学更加有效。

案例十五　人教版七年级英语上册
Unit 3　This is my sister

1. 指导思想及整体设计思路

《义务教育英语课程标准》突出体现课程对国家发展和学生发展的意义,进一步明确英语课程的工具性和人文性的双重属性,在为学生英语学习打好基础的同时,提高语言应用能力,加强对学生综合素质的培养。课程标准坚持以学生为主体的教育思想,面向全体学生,关注个体差异。在学习方式上,重视语言学习的实践性和应用性特点,强调教师要创设有意义的语境,为学生学习、实践和运用英语创造条件。修订后的《标准》进一步反映了国际外语教育的发展趋势,外语教育从重视语言知识的传授转向对学生综合语言运用能力的培养,强调学习外语的过程不再是枯燥地背诵和记忆的经历,而是一个积极主动地学习过程,一个不断提高语言运用能力和人文素养的过程;修订稿仍然以描述学生"用英语做事"为主线,强调培养学生综合语言运用能力,在做事情的过程中发展语言能力,思维能力,以及交流和合作能力;修订稿在教学建议中,从八个方面为英语教师提出了既具有指导意义,又具有一定可操作性的建议,体现了以培养能力为导向的改革方向。

基于这一基本理念,根据初一年级学生的特点和发展需求,结合 Unit 3 This is my sister 的内容,创设了 3 个环节。环节一,Section A 1a 学生通过观察图片,能够将单词与图中人物配对并能用英语介绍他人;环节二,2d grammar focus,转换角色,练习对话;环节三,4 group work 带几张家人的照片到课上,每个小组将照片放在一起,轮流对照片进行问答。

通过这三个环节的循序渐进和层层相扣,逐步增强学生的语言运用意识,锻炼他们的语言运用能力,培养他们的语言思维品质等核心素养。本节课所设置的环节多以要与同学或者通过小组合作的形式来完成,这种模式可以提高学生学习的积极性和主动性,让学生在练习和合作时实现对知识的理解,语言的运用,资源的共享,让他们感受到学习英语的成就感和趣味性,把学生学习和运用有效地结合在一起,更有利于学生的学习和成长。

2. 教材分析

本节课的教学内容源于人教版七年级英语上册 Unit 3　This is my sister(Page 13),本课时是关于如何用英语介绍他人,确认人物,这一节课将会主要采用小组合作探究的形式开展,通过学习用英语单词正确的表达方法,并设置同伴合作和小组合作的方式练习运用语言和提高语言的应用能力,本课时的学习为学生后面的学习降低了难度,做了很好的铺垫。

3. 学情分析

初一年级学生对如何用英语表达他们所熟悉的内容具有很强的好奇心,比如这节课用英语介绍自己的亲人,他们对这一话题具有丰富的生活经验,因此他们对这一话题很感兴趣。根据初中生的发展特点,他们又比较喜欢合作交流,pair work 和 group work 活动能够调动学生参与课堂的积极性,培养他们学习的主动性和参与性,积极优秀的同学还能带动被动的学生参与学习。学生在小组活动中团结协作,取长补短,相互交流,自主探究合作,能够锻炼他们解决问题的能力。另外,不同的学生在学习方式上的差异,也会让他们在活动中取长补短,培养学生的发散性思维,在向其他成员交流的同时,不断改进自己的学习方式。

4. 教学目标分析(含重难点分析)

本节课结束后,学生将能够:

(1) 学会认知家庭成员,了解家庭关系。

(2) 学会介绍人,认识别人。

(3) 通过认知家庭成员及关系学会使用指示代词复数 these,those 的用法。包括一般疑问句和否定句式。

(4) 能写一封介绍别人的书信。

重点:

A. 掌握家庭成员的表达;学会指示代词、人称代词及 Yes/No 问句及简单回答;

B. 学会介绍自己的家人和朋友,并根据相关信息辨别人物。

难点:能够用写信的形式向朋友介绍自己的家庭。

5. 教学方法

情景交际法,任务型教学法,"3P"教学法。

6. 教学过程

A. 情景导入

Play an English song "I Love My Family". Let students review family members.

【设计意图】利用歌曲,引入家庭成员介绍问题,设置了家庭成员介绍情境,激发了学生的学习兴趣,通过从学生原有熟悉的知识经验中出发,激发了他们的求知欲,降低了理解后面内容的难度,更有利于他们的学习。

B. 知识新授

1) Do the exercise of page 11. Find the male and female first names in this unit and write them.

2) Play some pictures to practice the main sentence patterns.

3) Do the exercise of 2b. Read about Jenny's family and circle the names.

4) Do the exercise of 2c. Read the passage again and complete the sentences.

5) Listen to the passage and read after the tape.

C. 情景操练

1) Fill in the blanks.

2) According to the photo of Jenny, introduce the family members to others.

【设计意图】通过观察图片,知晓家庭成员,并用课堂所学知识,用英语向别人介绍,对知识进行学以致用,提高语言的运用能力和交际能力,通过学生之间的互相交流和强化,达到对知识融会贯通的目的。

3) Do the exercise of 3a. Complete the passage with the words in the box. Then talk about it with your partner.

【设计意图】做习题,是让学生对知识进行练习和巩固的一种手段,也是学生自主学习的一种有效方式,通过做习题,学生不仅巩固了课堂知识,也明确

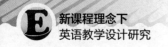

了自己哪里不足,更有针对性地去查漏补缺。

D. 情景回归

Revision part

设计意图 根据艾宾浩斯遗忘曲线,我们知道,遗忘是伴随知识的记忆同时发生的,因此需要对新授知识进行及时有效的复习,并合理分配复习时间,在第一轮学习结束后的5—10分钟进行第一轮的复习是科学合理的,避免因短时记忆造成的第一轮大规模遗忘,更加符合学生的学习规律和记忆规律。

7. 板书设计

Unit 2 This is my sister.

1) Here is a photo of _____.   Here are _____ photos of _____.

This is a/an _____.   These are _____.

That is a/an _____.   Those are _____.

2) grandpa   grandma   dad   mom   uncle   aunt   daughter son   sister
brother   cousin

---

8. 教学评价及反思

1) 教学评价:

After this class, I will let the students grade themselves:

Name: Date:

The things I can do	A	B	C
I can remember the new words			
I can identify the people			
I can introduce my family to others			
I can communicate with others in English			

教学过程结构流程图

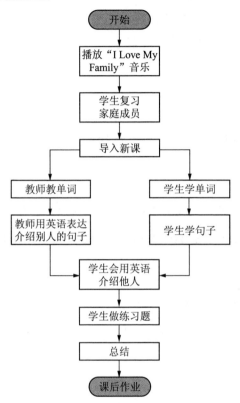

As for after-class，I will reflect from the following aspects：

	Yes/No	How to improve
Whether I have achieved my teaching goal		
Whether it is well organised		
Whether students take an active part in my class		
Whether the class is efficient		

2）教学反思：

优点：

1. 本堂课通过运用多媒体进行教学,利用与课文相关歌曲帮助学生回忆家庭成员,激发学生兴趣。

2. 通过插入学生感兴趣的图片来练习句型,达到了很好的教学效果。

3. 环节与环节之间环环相扣,过渡自然。

4. 以学生为主体,让学生多说多练。

不足:

1. 单词讲授不够。

2. 内容设置过多,缺乏总结。

3. 挖空单词时应围绕教学目标,选择重点词汇。学生做题前应明确阅读任务。

案例十六　人教版新目标英语七年级上册
Unit 4　Where's my school bag? Section B 教学设计

1. 指导思想及整体设计思路

课程标准倡导学生利用自己已有的知识和经验去实践,亲身参与和感受,发现和探究新的知识和经验,通过实践和体验,形成新的技能和能力,并充实丰富自己的经验。

基于这一理念,根据七年级学生的特点和发展需求,结合本单元内容,通过创设各种情景,直观地让学生辨别和判断方位介词的表达。结合合作与探究的学习途径,让学生通过小组活动积极地参与到教学活动中来,已达到熟练掌握方位介词的目的。然后,通过阅读短文学会思考并能在脑海中构想出房间中物品摆放的位置,结合实际判断出房间是否整齐。最后,创设一个活动,让学生自己设计一个房间并说明物品的摆放,既巩固了方位介词的使用,同时培养了学生的空间想象能力,并且间接指导他们如何保持房间整洁。这些都帮助了学生养成语言能力、学习能力、思维品质、文化意识。

2. 教材分析

本课是人教版新目标英语七年级上册 Unit 4　Where's my school bag? 本课时为 Section B 第二课时,主要内容是一篇小阅读,锻炼学生熟练使用句型 Where is …? /Where are …? 及回答语 It is/They are in/on/under/behind …,需要学生注意的是 be 动词的变化要跟随所描述物品的单复数情况而定。通过小组反复操练,学生能够熟练地运用句型进行对话,从而提高语言的输出能力。最后,设定任务,完成表格,培养学生提取信息的能力。

3. 学情分析

本单元主要内容为方位介词的学习和使用。方位介词的学习对七年级学生来说不难掌握,因为他们已经具备了一定的空间想象能力,可以进行简单的描述。而且,关于表方位的介词,学生在小学阶段已有涉猎。其次,文本中关于物品的生词,在本单元前三个课时过程中已初步掌握。但是,将方位介词和新词融入句型中,还需要反复操练加以强化。

4. 教学目标(含重难点分析)

本节课结束后,学生将能够完成以下目标:

1) 能够理解方位介词的内涵,并列举出所知道的方位介词。(学习理解)

2) 通过阅读全文能够快速收集关键信息,并完成表格。(实践应用)

3) 能够设计一间自己的房间,并说明物品摆放的位置。(迁移创新)

以上目标 1、2 为本节课重点内容,目标 3 为难点内容。

5. 教学方法

听说教学法、任务型教学法、情景教学法。

6. 教学流程

Step 1:Warming up[2′]

1) Daily greetings with students.

2) Revision.

T:Let's review some words we learned last class. Look at the screen. What's this?

S:This is a sofa.

…

T:Look at the picture. Is the dog on the chair?

S:Yes, it is.

T:Are the books in the bookcase?

S:No, they aren't.

…

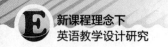
设计意图 通过复习前一课时的内容,帮助同学们回忆新词、句型。格外注意 be 的单复数形式,为本节课开展做好铺垫。

Step 2:Writing[5′]

T:Open your book at page 23. Please look at the picture in 2a,so what can you see in the picture?

S:I can see a chair, a desk, a CD, a schoolbag ...

T:Good,now you can write them on your book.

设计意图 让学生先找后说,然后再写。其中,在找的环节中学生会踊跃发言,看得更加仔细,既锻炼了观察能力,又尽可能多地复习旧词汇,为后面设计环节做准备。

Step 3:Pre-reading[10′]

T:Look at the photo, they're my friends Kate and Gina. Kate told me something about their rooms. But, Kate thinks Gina's is not tidy.

Now let's read the passage, and see who is the tidy girl.

1)New words teaching

T:First, while you are reading please circle the new words.

(give Ss 2 minutes to circle the words)

T:Can you find the new words?

Ss:Yes.

T:OK, let's write them on the blackboard one by one. First one, everywhere. E-V-E-R-Y-W-H-E-R-E, everywhere. Read and spell it together.

Ss:E-V-E-R-Y-W-H-E-R-E,everywhere.

T:Everywhere means here and there, for example, I put my toys here and there, I can also say "I put my toys everywhere".

...

(teach other words in the same way)

【设计意图】让学生先自己找出生词,培养探索发现的思维能力。教师——教授、领读新单词,为后面做阅读扫清障碍。

2）Guessing

T：Now let's make a guessing：who is the tidy girl?

S1：Kate

S2：Gina

【设计意图】导读,留下问题和悬念,激发学生阅读的兴趣。

Step 4：While-reading[12′]

1）Scanning

T：For the first time，you should read the passage quickly and try to answer the QUESTIONS：

a. Is Kate tidy?

Ss：Yes，she is.

b. Is Gina tidy?

Ss：No，she isn't.

2）Filling the chart

T：You did a good job! Now for the second time，let's read the passage carefully again，and try to fill the blanks in 2c. You should find the things Kate and Gina have，and where they are. Do you understand?

Ss：Yes!

T：So，here we go!

Kate		Gina	
Things	where	Things	where

（3 minutes latter）

T：Let's check the answers.

S1：...

253

S2：...

S3：...

3）Listening and reading

T：Now let's listen to the tape, and try to imitate the pronunciation.

(Play the tape player)

T：Now，I'll give you two minutes to read by yourself，and then I'll invite some students to read the whole passage for us，OK? Go ahead!

(invite 2~3 students to read)

设计意图 先让学生认真听一遍,然后尝试模仿语音语调,培养学生听和说的能力。

Step 5：Post-reading[10′]

T：Great! All of you have good pronunciation! And now we know that Kate is a tidy girl，she can put her things in right place，so do you want to be a tidy girl or boy too?

Ss：Yes!

T：Really? Suppose you have a beautiful bedroom，how can you make your room tidy? Can you make a design drawing(设计图)? give you 5 minutes to do it，then I'll ask some students to introduce your rooms to us.

(5 minutes latter)

T：Time is up! Who wants to share with us?

S1：This is my bedroom. My books are on the desk. My basketball is under my bed. Oh，where is my cat? She is sleeping in the box!...

S2：...

S3：...

设计意图 让学生充分发挥想象力,能够画出自己理想的房间,并能够运用本节课所学知识进行描述物品摆放的位置,达到会说会用的目标。

Step 6：Summary and homework[1′]

T：Today you have learned how to describe the positions of things by

using the position preposition. You can make a report about your parents'
room and your friends' rooms, and how they put things in their rooms. So
much for today, class is over.

Blackboard design

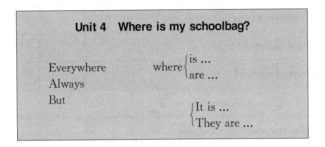

7. 教学流程图

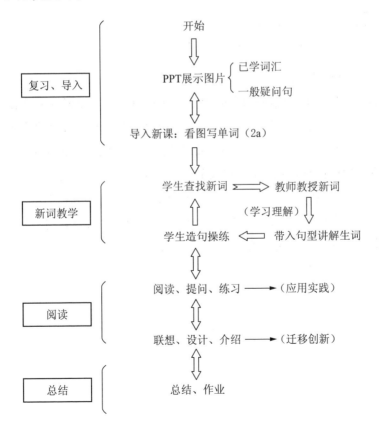

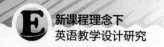
8. 教学评价及反思

1）学生自我评价

Name：_____   Date：_____

The things I can do	A	B	C	D
I can read the new words correctly				
I can read and understand the text				
I can understand the oral questions				
I can answer 3 more questions				
I can describe the positions of things				
I can design my room				
Total				

（备注：A＝10′ B＝5′ C＝2′ D＝1′）

2）教师自我评价

本节课为本单元最后一课时，重点是对本单元所学知识的汇总和巩固。在课堂实践中我做到了以学生为主体，鼓励学生积极地参与教学活动，并对学生的表现及时给出评价。但本节课仍然存在不足之处，我的讲解基本上还拘泥于教材信息，没有进行有效的取舍和拓展。此外，没有针对学生实际，对中考热点和难点缺少渗透，学生原有的知识没有得到适时地活化。在以后的教学设计中，还应做好充分的准备，做到备学生、备教材、备学案，让每一堂都计划有效率地完成。

案例十七　外研版中职国规英语教材基础模块第二册
Unit 8　Fighting Against Pollution

 单元整体解读及分析

Unit 8　Fighting Against Pollution

教学理念	中等职业学校学生与其他普通中学的学生有着非常大的差别,学生基础差,学习习惯不好,并且缺乏学习动力,这就要求英语老师必须改进传统填鸭式的教学方法,创新教学模式,多多利用实物、图片以及多媒体等有趣的教学方法,把班级不同层次的学生分成 A、B、C 三层,进行分层教学,提高课堂教学效率。
教材分析	外研社版中职英语教材基础模块中的话题能够紧跟时代步伐,语音和语法知识均有较好涉及,在听说读写四个语言技巧方面,教材设计的比较全面并且浅显易懂,学生非常容易掌握接受。本单元主要围绕环境污染和保护展开话题。听力、对话和课文三部分分别介绍了环境污染的危害性和环境保护的重要性,并提出了保护环境和节约能源的具体措施。
学生情况分析	1. 学生的认知情况 1) 知识方面 　　A 层次学生词汇储备为 1 000 个左右,B 层次为 600 个左右,C 层次仅为 100个左右。 2) 能力方面 　　A、B 两层次学生能够正确使用词汇,并完成简单对话;C 层次仅能说些简单的日常用语,如:What's your name?／How are you? 3) 心理方面 　　A、B 两层次学生能主动学习,喜欢被鼓励,渴望表现自己并期待获得他人的认可;C 层次缺少自主学习的意识,甚至厌学。 2. 学习中存在的问题 1) 学生的英语基础薄弱,尤其表现在词汇和语法方面。 2) 学生层次划分明显,C 层次学生缺乏学习兴趣。 3) 学生对于英语学习所投入的精力远远少于专业课。 3. 具体的解决对策 1) 采用游戏或竞赛的形式开展词汇教学,寓教于乐,激发学生学习英语的兴趣。

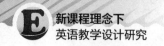

学生情况分析	2)"重口语,淡语法。"着重培养学生英语的口头表达能力,使学生能学有所用,真正实现英语作为一门语言的交际功能。而对于大纲所要求的语法内容尽量简化,不做过多深入的扩展,使学生能掌握基本的语法内容即可,降低学习难度,增强学习信心。 3)采用分层次教学等多种教学方法,尊重学生的个体差异,因材施教,使每名学生都能有所得。 ① C层次学生即学困生,表现为思维不够敏捷,但踏实认真或者既不敏捷也不踏实,对学习存在着一定的思想障碍。在教学中应以培养学习兴趣为主。通过表扬性评价,激发其学习的主动性。 ② B层次学生即中等生,表现为思维敏捷,但不够踏实认真,思考问题不够缜密,对知识理解不够全面。在教学中应以教授学习方法为主。通过激励性评价,增强其学习的积极性。 ③ A层次学生即学优生,表现为思维敏捷,学习踏实认真,听课效率高,接受能力强,能很快掌握每节课所学的内容。在教学中应以提高学习能力为主。通过竞争性评价,帮助其建立学习的自信心。
教学目标	知识目标:1.掌握与环境污染和环境保护相关的单词和语句。 2.掌握对话中的句型并能熟练运用。 3.熟悉单词表中 unit 8 的所有单词发音。 技能目标:1.不同层次的学生能够完成对话部分自己的相应目标。 2.能够谈论对环境保护的看法和措施。 3.根据提示简单的描述世界环境日。 情感目标:使学生明白环境污染的危害,引起对环境的关注。
教学重点	1.单词和句型的掌握。 2.对话部分的分层次学习。 3.表格的填写和交流。
教学难点	1.编写新的对话并情景表演。 2.根据提示简单的描述世界环境日。
教学方法	交际法
学习方法	讨论法
教学媒体	多媒体教学光盘、图片

教学过程

预设时间	教学环节	教师活动	学生活动	设计意图
32′	听说练习	让学生浏览完 Listening and Speaking 部分③中的四个陈述后,播放录音第二遍。听完后,检查学生问题的答案。 After-listening: 1) 教师讲解 Listening and Speaking 部分中②里重要的句子: It's so dusty. It is difficult to breathe. The traffic is moving so slowly. It may also cause traffic problems. We really have to do something to change this bad climate. 2) 教师按照提前将学生分好的三个层次,布置 Listening and Speaking 部分中②的相应的任务: A层:利用教师提供的污染图片与搭档编一个与原对话相似的新的对话,并能表演出来。 B层:与搭档分角色大致背诵对话。 C层:熟练朗读对话,能和搭档分角色朗读。 活动:每一个层次选出 2 或 3 组同学给大家展示对话的练习成果。表演的同学将得到加分奖励。 3) Listening and Speaking 部分中④里的填空练习: A. 教师讲解单词并举例:breathe, call on, drive, protect, use	带着问题合上课本再次听录音,并在纸上记录关键点,听完回答问题。 学生就重要句型做笔记。 替换练习:运用句型造句。学生根据教师给出的中文句子,使用句型翻译成对应的英语句子。 学生根据自己的层次情况与搭档合作完成相应的任务。学生分层次展示: A:两名同学作为搭档在全班表演编的新对话。 B:两名同学作为搭档在座位上大致背诵原对话。 C:两名同学作为搭档朗读原对话。 做笔记,掌握单词。	训练听力,了解对话的细节。 熟悉对话内容,培养朗读的能力。 掌握对话中的重要句型,培养学生造句的能力。 满足不同层次同学的学习目标。增加学习的积极性。 结合例句理解单词的使用。

预设时间	教学环节	教师活动	学生活动	设计意图
32′	听说练习	B. 要求学生利用所学四个单词的正确形式完成 Listening and Speaking 部分中④里的填空练习。	学生完成习题。	培养词汇运用能力。
		C. 教师给出正确答案并要求学生自己再次阅读 Listening and Speaking 部分中④里的文章。	五名学生回答出自己的答案，其他同学检查自己的习题正误。	获得文章中的信息。
		D. 教师给出短语提示，让学生根据提示简单地描述一下世界环境日： The United Nations in 1972 on 5 June every year call on protect the environment the theme of WED encourage people to do something	根据提示说一段介绍语。	培养学生综合运用语言能力。
		4) 教师将学生分成四人一个小组。要求学生在小组范围内完成 Listening and Speaking 部分中⑤里的表格。	每个小组的一名代表同学陈述总结后的结果。	培养团队合作精神和语句表达能力。
6′	单词	教师引导学生学习课本 159—160 页单元单词表中本单元的单词。 活动：学生尝试用音标依次读出单词，教师纠正学生读错的单词，并领读所有单词。	学生根据音标先读出每个单词。 学生跟随老师每个单词读两遍。	明确单词的发音，利于学生课下背诵。
1′	小结	教师用中文总结本次课学习的要点，告诉学生需要注意和复习的知识点。	配合教师的问答，回顾本课关键知识点。	强调知识并引起学生注意。
1′	作业	1. 抄写 Warming up 和 Listening and Speaking 中的新单词，让学生根据自己的情况决定每个单词写几遍。 2. 搜集身边发生的环境污染的图片，并练习用英语介绍。	课后完成在作业本。	加强新词汇的掌握。 提升口语能力。

板书 设计	Unit 8　Fighting Against Pollution Key sentences 　It's so dusty. 　It is difficult to breathe. 　The traffic is moving so slowly. 　It may also cause traffic problems. 　We really have to do something to change this bad climate.
教学 反思	1. 分层次教学,通过注重每名学生的个体发展,实现了真正意义上的因材施教, 　全面发展。分组竞赛和小组合作等,充分调动了学生的学习热情,增强了团 　队合作精神。 2. 能够了解新教材特点,掌握教学重点、难点,恰当的制定教学计划,合理安排 　教学内容,并熟练运用现代化的教学手段。在课堂教学过程中,不断创设机 　会,激励每名学生在原有的基础上努力获得成功。 3. 不足之处: 1) 课堂游戏的操作过程中,中文讲解过多,有待改进。 2) 课堂教学语言应言简意赅、生动形象、富有逻辑性,有待进一步加强。

案例十八　人教版八年级英语下册
Unit 1　Can you play the guitar? 教学设计

1. 教学理念

新课程标准强调要面向全体学生,以人为本,促进学生的全面发展,在实践中培养学生的核心素养,培养学生的语言学习和运用能力。所以在本节课中,要以学生为中心,仔细研究课本,创设与话题相关的情境,让学生从活动中理解主题,去解决问题,发展学生的语言技能,促进学生的文化意识,增强学生的学习策略,最终促进学生核心素养的目标的达成。

2. 教材分析

本节课教材分为三个部分,1a,1b,1c,围绕情态动词 can 的学习来展开。通过本课的学习,学生能运用情态动词 can 表达自己在某一方面所具有的才能,谈论自己的喜好与意愿,认识常见的乐器,能够自荐或参加各种课外俱乐部。该话题与学生的课余生活息息相关,可充分调动学生谈论该

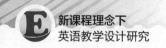
话题的积极性。通过学习,能鼓励学生积极参加各种课外活动,培养学生多
方面才能及团队精神。

3. 学情分析

该教材为人教版初一年级英语下册,初一年级学生经过上册一学期英
语的学习,已经有了一定的英语基础,学生们知道什么是情态动词,对情态
动词的用法有所了解,但并没有系统学习情态动词,对情态动词的句型转换
掌握不够熟练。并且对定冠词 the 的用法比较模糊,没有系统学习乐器类
的单词,不能熟练地表达自己能做某事,不能做某事。通过这一单元,系统
地学习情态动词,知道用情态动词怎样用于各种句型,能熟练地表达自己能

做某事以及参加某种俱乐部。

4. 教学目标

基于教学内容和学生情况的分析,本节课的教学目标设定为:学生能

1) 掌握重点单词 guitar,sing,swim,dance …,掌握重点短语 play chess,play the guitar,art club ….以及掌握重点句型—Can you …? —Yes,I can/No,I can't. —What club do you want to join? —I want to join … club.

2) 掌握情态动词的用法,能用情态动词can谈论自己的能力,能流利地表达自己的喜好和想加入的俱乐部的愿望。

3) 能提高用英语听,说的能力。

5. 教学方法

情境教学法,任务型教学法。

6. 教学手段

多媒体教学,PPT,录音机。

7. 教学过程

Step 1:Lead-in

Hello,everyone. Do you like Jay Chou? He is a very famous singer. He can sing,dance and he can also play the guitar. Can you sing? Can you dance? Can you play the guitar? Please tell us your talents.(由学生感兴趣的歌手周杰伦过渡到询问对方的才艺,让学生在轻松愉悦的氛围中接收到关于教学目标的信息。)

Step 2:Presentation

1) Present the new words with PPT

2) Sum up the phrases about "play" and complete the activity 1a.

3) Present new sentences:

    T:Everyone has his own ability. For example:

        I can speak English. Can you speak English?

    Ss:Yes,I/we can.

    T:Can you speak Japanese?

Ss：No，I/we can't.

Ask Ss to read the sentences.

（向学生传达语言目标，通过对话强化语言目标）

Step 3：Practice

1）Ask and answer.

T：Can you sing？

S：Yes，I can./No，I can't.

2）Pair work.

Make their own conversations in pairs，then ask students to show conversations.

3）Ask some students to talk about themselves.

（通过对话练习，让学生掌握 can 的重点句型，提高口头表达能力。）

Step 4：Listen and finish 1b

1）Ask students to read conversations first.

2）listen and number the conversations.

（听力练习，使学生熟悉目标语，提高听力能力。）

Step 5：Homework

Use Model verb "can" to write a short conversation.

（家庭作业是写一个小的对话，帮助学生巩固所学句型。）

8. 板书设计

Unit 1　Can you play the guitar？

—I want to join the ... club.

—Can you ...？

—Yes，I can./No，I can't.

9. 评价反思

要用英文组织课堂语言，多和学生互动，课堂多练习目标语，课堂上注意学生反馈。板书要设计合理。

案例十九　牛津英语九年级
Book 5 Unit 1 第二课时 reading 教学设计

1. 指导思想及整体设计思路

1)《义务教育英语课程标准》倡导学生利用已有的知识和经验去实践，亲身参与和感受，发现和探究新的知识和经验，通过实践和体验，形成新的技能和能力，并充实丰富自己的经验。这样一来，就必然要求学生在真实而富有意义的任务活动中去学习体验和运用语言知识而且要求学生学会与他人合作学习。

2) 基于这一基本理念，根据九年级学生的特点和发展需求，我认真研读第一单元第二课时 Reading 部分，通过图片、多媒体手段创设多种情境让学生积极地参与教学活动。我设计了两类活动：第一，根据图片说出不同人的工作及其特点（学习理解）；第二，讨论自己和同伴的性格及职业追求，然后与同伴分享（应用实践）。这些活动有助于学生语言能力、学习能力、思维品质目标的达成。

2. 教材分析

本课是牛津译林（2013 版）九年级上册第一单元第二课时阅读部分（Reading），介绍阳光镇里四位在不同领域取得杰出成就的人物。整个文本由四篇介绍艺术家、经理、工程师、医生的短记叙文组成，意在帮助学生探讨自己的性格特征，确立未来人生奋斗方向，进行合理的人生规划。

3. 学情分析

九年级学生有比较丰富的语言积累和知识储备，他们有较强的求知欲和好奇心，在课堂上，他们善于表现自我，乐于积极思考，敢于发表自己的观点，这些都有利于师生在课堂上积极交流。但部分学生由于基础不牢，可能会说错，应多多鼓励，积极引导他们与同伴合作完成任务。

4. 教学目标分析（含重难点分析）

本节课结束时，学生将能够：

1) 说出四位杰出人物的性格特征。

2）推断不同职业所需要的性格特征。

3）分析总结自己的性格特点并进行合理人生规划。

4）帮助同伴了解其性格特点并进行合理人生规划。

教学重点：

1）说出四位杰出人物的性格特征。

2）推断不同职业所需要的性格特征。

教学难点：

1）分析总结自己的性格特点并进行合理人生规划。

2）帮助同伴了解其性格特点并进行合理人生规划。

5. 教学方法

情境教学法、任务型教学法

6. 教学流程

Step 1：Warming up（3 minutes）

The teacher plays an English video about occupations.

T：What jobs can you find in the video?

S：Doctor，actor，lawyer …

设计意图 通过有趣的视频调动学生谈论关于个人性格特征、工作等话题的积极性，有利于接下来的教学活动顺利有效进行。

（Arouse the students' interest about the topic.）

Step 2：Pre-reading（5 minutes）

Match the new words with their correct meanings

设计意图 帮助学生认识课文中生词，以便更好地了解文章大意。

（Help the students know the meaning of the new words in order to understand the text.）

Step 3：While-reading（25 minutes）

Activity one：Fast reading：

Ask the students to find the main ideas of each short passage.

T：Please read the passage as quickly as possible and then find its main ideas of each short passage.

S1：Wu Wei is a born artist.

S2：Su Ning is a manager who likes challenges.

S3：

S4：

设计意图 帮助学生找到并总结归纳文章大意。

(Help the students know the main ideas of the text.)

Activity two：Careful reading：

Ask the students to finish the T or F questions.

T：Wu Wei's friend thinks that his work is not very good. True or false?

S1：False.

T：Su Ning changed her job five years ago. True or false?

S2：False.

T：Fang Yuan spends most of her time on her work. True or false?

S3：True.

设计意图 帮助学生对四个人物的具体描述进行更好了解。

(Help the students know the details of the four characters better.)

Activity Three：Further Reading：

Ask the students to fill in the blanks in the diagram.

Name	Job	Personalities
Wu Wei		
Su Ning		
Liu Haotian		
Fang Yuan		

设计意图 通过表格帮助学生对四个人物的描述进行总结归纳。

(Help the students summarize the details of the four characters better in the form of the diagram)

Step 4：Post-reading(8 minutes)

Ask the students to write a short description of their personalities and think about their future jobs.

设计意图 通过小型写作帮助学生了解自己性格特征并进行人生规划。

(Help the students to know themselves and think about their future jobs.)

Step 5：Summary and homework(4 minutes)

1) The teacher and the students summarize the content of the class.

2) The teacher asks the students to write a short description of their desk mate's personalities and help them to design their future jobs.

设计意图 通过写作帮助学生巩固关于职业的英语描述与表达，帮助学生树立合作意识。

(Help the students to master English expressions of jobs and form the awareness of cooperation)

7. Blackboard Design

Unit 1   Know yourself
The Second Period Reading

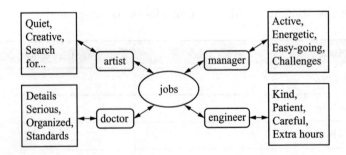

8. 教学评价及反思

1) 教学评价：

表1 自我评价表

Name:_____   Date:_____

The things I can do	5	4	3	2	1
I can take part in the lesson actively.					
I can understand the reading passage.					
I can answer the questions.					
I can write out the main ideas					
I can talk something about personalities and jobs					
Total					

表2 小组活动互评表

Group number:_____

Criteria to be assessed	Excellent	Very Good	Good	Adequate	Needs Much Improvement
Amount of cooperation work					
Creative ideas brought in					
Participating in group discussion					
Amount of questions raised					
Progress made in activity					

注:由组长负责,组织小组反思填写。

2) 教学反思:

本节课基本完成,学习目标基本达成。学生可以说出关于性格和工作的单词。学生可以根据自身性格特点对自己未来工作进行规划,并且能够帮助同伴了解自己。但仍然会有一些同学基础不牢,不太敢发言,应想办法调动其积极性。活动设置如果再加强学生合作对话与交流,可能会更好。

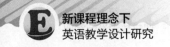

案例二十　外研版八年级上模块二 Unit 2　My home town and my country 第一课时阅读教学设计

1. 指导及整体设计思路

1)《义务教育英语课程标准》(2011 年版)倡导学生利用已有的知识和经验阅读,以学生为中心,在教师指导下与文本积极互动,通过合作探究并丰富自己知识和国际视野。

2) 基于这一理念,根据八年级学生特点及需求,结合本课教材内容,我通过图片、视频呈现与本节课内容相关的英语知识进行词汇教学,图片配对,完成表格,小组讨论,通过画思维导图复述课文,最后写一篇介绍自己家乡的短文并加深对自己家乡和祖国的热爱之情。

2. 教材分析

本课是外研版八年级上模块二 Unit 2 My home town and my country. 第一课时阅读。这是一篇说明文,作者采用对比的手法展示了两个城市和英国之间的关系和两座城市间的各自特点,进一步加深对这不同城市的地理方位、人口、著名景点的理解和认识,培养学生热爱他乡和故乡的情怀。

3. 学情分析

八年级的学生在经过第一单元学习后,对形容词比较级这个语法现象已有了一定认识和掌握。对异国背景文化求知欲比较强烈,而且思维具有对比分析归纳的能力,具有一定家国情怀。

4. 教学目标分析(含重难点分析)

在本节课结束的时候,学生能够:

1) 学习掌握本单元出现的新词汇:east, west, south, north, home town, be famous for, countryside 和重点短语句子 has a population of;学会并运用表示方位和位置的句型 Sth＋be/lie/stand＋in the ... of ...。

2) 学习并运用 predicting, skimming, scanning 等阅读技巧和阅读策略进行阅读训练,提高阅读水平;借助思维导图,分析作者写作方式并补充自己家乡的基本信息,向外国朋友介绍自己的家乡。

3) 对比、归纳城市之间的共性与个性。

4) 了解英格兰的地理风貌,开阔孩子的视野;通过向外宾介绍自己的家乡来培养跨文化交际的能力。通过本节课的学习,比较重庆和英格兰,培养热爱家乡,宣传家乡,热爱祖国的美好情感。East,west,home is the best.

教学重点:

学习掌握本单元出现的方位词汇来表示方位和位置。利用指南针和地图,先从单词到短语,再到句子逐步学习。

教学难点:

写一篇欢迎词:欢迎外宾到我校参观并向外宾介绍自己的家乡。以文本为参考,利用思维导图,帮助学生理清写作思路并提供家乡的基本信息,降低学生写作难度。

5. 教学方法

情境教学法和任务型教学法。

6. 教学流程

Step 1:Warming up and leading in(3′)

T:Ask students which country they'd like to visit? Then show a short video about Britain to lead in England. Show a map of England and ask students about the location of the places.

S:Learn to express the location with "in the east/west/south/north ... of England" by asking and answering in pairs.

设计意图 通过观看视频激发学生学习兴趣,在学生互动语境中教授新词汇,达到热身导入目的。

Step 2:Pre-reading(3′)

T:Ask students to read the title. Then guess what we'll learn from the passage.

S:Put down their ideas on the Blackboard to see if their predictions are right.

设计意图 指导学生使用阅读策略 predicting 来进行读前预测,激活头脑中已有背景知识。

Step 3：While-reading(20′)

1) Skimming for main ideas

T：Then the teacher shows the two pictures in the book and make the students read the whole passage quickly to do the match.

S：Students read the whole passage silently and do the match in their books.

设计意图 先迅速浏览全文,抓住文章大意并配对图片,对文章有个整体感知。

2) Scanning for details

T：Let Ss read Para 1 and Para 2 to complete the chart in Activity 3.

S：Students first look through the chart to make sure of the task and then read Para 1 and Para 2 to finish the chart.

T：Ask them to check the answers by working in pairs to ask and answer about the information of Cambridge and London. Then compare the two cities.

设计意图 通过表格形式借助 scanning 阅读技能让学生细读文本,找到关键点,培养学生精准阅读定位能力。

T：Make Ss read Para 3 and Para 4 to tell if the statements are true or false with the evidence in the passage.

S：Students read Para 3 and Para 4 to do the choice and discuss in groups.

设计意图 通过对错题练习再次对文本内容进行深化,提高学生合作交流和判断力,进一步加深对文本内容的理解。

3) Retelling the passage

T：Show how to make a mind map to retell the passage，give a part of the mind map and make Ss to complete it in groups and then retell the whole passage according to the mind map.

S：Students work in groups to complete the mind map and choose one member to retell the passage.

设计意图 通过思维导图的补充让学生合作、体验学习,重新梳理文本,复述环节不仅锻炼学生口语而且能提升学生思维品质,为接下来的写的环节打下语言和框架基础。

Step 4:Post-reading(17′)

1)T:Encourage Ss discuss if Tony likes his hometown and find the evidence in the passage.

S:Discuss in groups and find out the evidence in the passage.

设计意图 让学生跳出文本字面内容,启发鼓励学生思考作者的情感并找出证据,培养学生的阅读推理能力。

2)T:Ask the Ss about the most beautiful city in their mind to lead in the topic—hometown and teach them a famous saying "East,west,home is the best".

S: Talk about the most beautiful city and learn to love their hometown city.

设计意图 从文本过渡迁移到实际生活,引出家乡的概念,不仅为写作作了铺垫而且进行了情感教育,由人及己,由异国城市联想到自己家乡,加深对家乡的热爱之情。

3)Writing:write a speech to introduce your hometown to your foreign friends.

T:Make Ss answer the questions in the books and organize their words and sentences.

S:Answer the questions in books and make an outline or mind map for their speeches and then give their speeches in front of the whole class.

设计意图 以读促写,利用语篇中有用词汇和结构写一篇关于家乡的演讲稿,既巩固阅读知识又能拓展延伸加强写作能力。

Step 5:Sum up and homework(3′)

T:Sum up the language points and assign the homework.

1)Copy down the new words and phrases in your exercise books.

2)Try to retell the passage to your classmates.

3)Make a poster of the places you love in English.

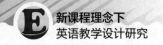

设计意图 梳理本节课重难点，分层次布置作业，满足不同层次学生。

7. Blackboard Design

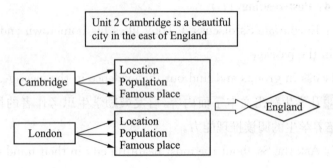

8. 教学过程结构流程图：

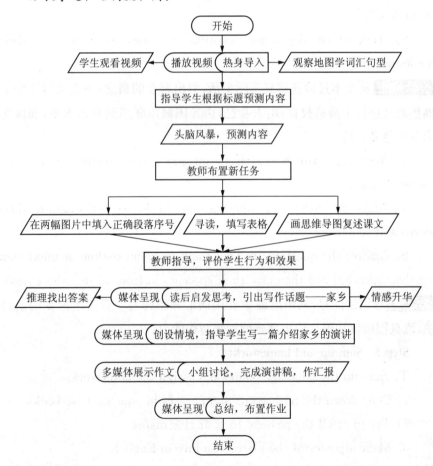

9. 教学评价与反思

表 1 自我评价

Name：_____   Date：_____

The things I can do	5	4	3	2	1
I can take part in the lesson activities actively					
I can understand the reading passage					
I can understand the oral questions					
I can answer the questions					
I can write out the main ideas					
I've known some background information of the text					
I can talk about something about Christmas					
Total					

表 2 小组活动互评表

Group number：_____

Criteria to be assessed	Excellent	Very good	Good	Adequate	Needs Much Improvement
Amount of cooperation work					
Creative ideas brought in					
Participating in group discussion					
Number of questions raised					
Progress made in activity					

注：由组长或指定学生负责，组织小组反思填写。

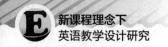

本节课教学反思：

优点：本节课的教学内容目标顺利达成。通过本节课的学习，学生能熟练掌握本单元出现的新词汇和重点短语句子并运用表方位和位置的句型正确表达位置关系；能运用比较级对两个城市——剑桥和伦敦以及自己家乡和英格兰进行比较；能精准理解课文并把握作者的写作意图。课堂上，学生积极活跃，课堂气氛较好。

不足的是：复述课文和写作的时间留得较少，导致学生们小组活动中个体间的衔接不很流畅，有些语言组织不到位。个别学生完不成写作任务，结尾稍显仓促。在今后的备课中，应注意时间的合理安排，把更多的时间留给学生。

第三节　高中英语教学设计案例

案例二十一　人教版高中英语必修三 Unit 4　How life began on the earth, speaking and listening

Teaching Plan for Unit 4 Book 3

Title：How Life Began to on the Earth

Period：the first period（speaking and listening）

Teaching Ideology
According to New Curriculum for English, English teaching should focus on comprehensive education instead of simply using English as knowledge or skills. So in teaching students speaking and listening, I will follow the students-centered discipline and act as a role of a helper, facilitator and guide.
Analysis of Teaching material
This unit comes from book 3, which mainly talks about astronomy, especially the origin of life. The lexical barrier is few and the structure of the text is clear. In order to train students' independent thinking, on the surface of the text is how life began on the earth, but the deep level is human beings' effects on the earth.

Analysis of Teaching condition

Grade: Senior 2   Number: 55

1. There are 90% students interested in English. 70% students can comprehend English class and 50% can express their ideas freely. But there are 30% weak in English, so they need more guide.

2. Students have a general idea of the origin of life, but they lack detailed information about how life began on the earth.

Teaching Objectives

By the end of the class, students will be able to

1. learn the meaning and pronunciation of some words which is related to different kinds of animals.

2. use listening skills to get how life began on the earth and cooperate with others.

3. conclude the process of the development of life on the earth.

4. have the awareness that protecting our earth is everyone's mission.

Key and Difficult points

Key points:

1. Learning the meaning and pronunciation of some words which is related to different kinds of animals.

2. Having the awareness that protecting our earth is everyone's mission.

Difficult points:

Concluding the process of the development of life on the earth.

Teaching methods

1. Situational teaching method
2. task-based language teaching
3. Interactive language teaching

Teaching Aids

multimedia device, PPT document, blackboard, books

Teaching Procedures

Teaching Steps	Teachers' Activities	Students' Activities	Teaching Intention
Step 1: Lead in (3 minutes)	1. Greeting 2. Ask students a question: What is the origin of life?	1. Greeting 2. Consider this question and answer it.	To arouse students' attention and interest in class.

续表

Teaching Steps	Teachers' Activities	Students' Activities	Teaching Intention
Step 2: Learning and understanding (20 minutes)	1. Ask students how to read the nouns of animals correctly. 2. Give students some time to go through the questions on the scrip. 3. Give Students some time to listen to the tape. 4. Ask students to conclude the process of life development.	1. Students will learn the meaning and how to read them. 2. Students will go through the questions on the scrip. 3. Students will be given some minutes to listen to the tape. 4. Students will conclude the process of life development.	To train students' reading ability and comprehensive ability.
Step 3: Applying and practicing (10 minutes)	Role play: An interview which is related to the process of life development.	Students will be divided into groups and some of them will play as an interviewer.	To help them understand the lesson and use the knowledge flexibly.
Step 4: Transferring and creating (8 minutes)	Discussion: What problems are caused by human beings?	Discuss in pairs and share their ideas in class.	To train their creative thinking and cooperative ability.
Step 5: Summary (3 minutes)	Educate students that protecting our earth is everyone's mission.	Write down their feelings in the note-books.	To make our knowledge clearly and help them have a correct emotional attitude.
Step 6: Homework (1 minute)	Compulsory Homework: Write a composition: How to protect our earth? (100—120 words) Optional Homework: Surf on the Internet and find more information about the process of life origin.	Review the text and ask some questions in the class.	To deepen their im-pression about our learning and give students more chances to improve themselves.

续表

Teaching Reflection
1. The teacher should give students more kinds of activities to attract their attention to class.
2. Some students are weak in finding information, so the teacher should give them more encouragement and help.

Blackboard Design:

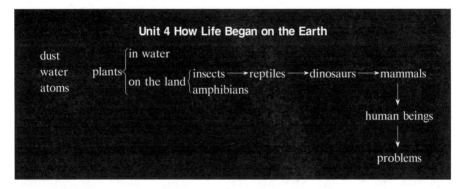

案例二十二　译林版高三英语上 Model 9 Unit 1　Other countries, other cultures 教学设计

Subject context: Human and society　Canada—land of maple trees

Type of discourse: Exposition

Length of one period: 45 mins

Teaching ideology:

National English Curriculum standard carries out the fundamental task of fostering integrity and promoting rounded development of people, develops the core competence English learning, puts into practice the activity viewpoint of English learning, and stresses the promoting of students learning and using abilities.

So in this reading class, following student-centered principle, I will

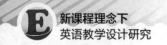
study and analyze the text, create the context closely related to the topic, lead the students to involve the activities of excavating the meaning of the theme, aim to solve problems, integrate the usage of learning knowledge of language, developing language skills, forming culture awareness and applying leaning strategies and finally achieve the goal of developing students' core competences.

Analysis materials:

This lesson's reading part is the focus of this unit. This part is mainly about students' reading ability, and it is also the central part of the whole unit in content. Other countries, Other cultures, and Other cultures are the main themes of this unit. The design of this lesson, in addition to cultivating students' reading ability of English, in two aspects, listening and speaking, depicts the content of this article, from the listening, reading, speaking and cultural knowledge penetration, to cultivate the ability of the students, to mobilize students' various senses, and stimulate their thinking and the ability of linguistic organization.

Analysis students:

Some of the target students are very poor in English. They have very bad reading habits. Some Ss don't often use English to express themselves and communicate with others. So they are not active in the class. The students in Senior Three have learned some of the reading skills but sometimes they can't use them properly. It is a good idea to try to help them use the skills in our daily teaching practice. It's also important to encourage them to communicate with each other so that they can express themselves more skillfully and It's also helpful to cultivate their spirit of teamwork.

Teaching objects

After the reading comprehension, the students will be able to develop their reading skills about this kind of text;

After the listening comprehension, the students will be able to develop their listening skills about this kind of material;

After learning the information about Canada, the students will be able to know more about the culture, major cities, tourist attractions and other things in Canada, thus developing their interest in foreign cultures;

After the discussion, the students will be able to develop their speaking skills, especially the ability to organize sentences.

Teaching important points:

1. How to make the students understand the passage better and to help the students finish all the exercises.

2. How to help the students develop their creative, comprehensive and consolidating abilities.

Teaching Difficult Points:

How to help students fully understand the cultural differences in this text and how to get students to fully participate in all activities.

Teaching approaches:

Task-based Language Teaching

Teaching aids:

The multimedia   The blackboard

Teaching procedures:

Step 1: Lead-in

Show a map of Canada to the students

What is this country?

Can you remember the information we mentioned about Canada yesterday?

The RCMP.　　Maple.　　Beaver

Do you have something more to add?

What is the capital city of Canada?　　　　　　　　　　　—Ottawa

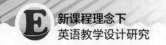

What is largest city of Canada?   —Toronto

What are the official languages that are used in Canada?

—English and French

Can you name some famous people from Canada?

—Shania Twain (a famous singer); Sir John A Macdonald ...

Purpose: introduce the topic of the passage and arouse the interest of students.

Step 2: Reading Comprehension

1. Pre-reading

Please go through the *Reading strategy*

(make sure students know how to read.)

Purpose: according to the reading strategy, let students know how to read this passage and what they should do.

2. While-readng

(1) Now let's go to the reading paragraph 1— 2— Canada—land of the maple tree.

Category	Description
Location	The Arctic is to the north, the USA is to the south, the Atlantic Ocean is to the east and the Pacific to the west.
Size	second largest country in the world;
Geography	frozen waste, vast mountain ranges; enormous open plains; countless rivers; endless forests;
Outdoor Activities	Walk, sail, cross-country ski;

(2) Read paragraph 3—7, compare the differences between the cities mentioned and fill in the following table.

Major cities	Toronto	the largest city in Canada, most multicultural, famous for the CN Tower;
	Montreal	second largest in Canada, second largest French-speaking city in the world, wonderful mix of Old World and New World architecture and culture;
	Vancouver	smaller in size but equally famous, has the biggest Chinese population in Canada; close to the ski resorts;
	Edmonton	a city in the province of Albert, home to the west Edmonton Mall, the largest pedestrian mall in the world;

(3) Let the students do part C2 on page 4

1) Montreal	2) Montreal	3) Toronto
4) Vancouver	5) Edmonton	6) Toronto

(4) Now, read the text again, and remember when you come across a new word, try to guess the meaning from the context. As you know, it is very important to read the sentences before and after the sentence which contains the unknown word. Finish Part D.

(5) Listening Comprehension

Listen to the tape for the information in paragraphs 8, 9, 10 and 11.

Answer the following questions.

How wide is the Niagara Falls?　　　　—670 meters wide.

What is Canada's national symbol?　　　—The maple leaf.

Purpose: going through the passage is to learn the detailed information about each paragraph.

3. Post-reading

Read the text again and choose the best answers according to the text:

(1) Which of the following statements is NOT true according to the passage?

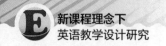
A. Canada is one of the largest countries in the world, second only to China.

B. Toronto is the largest city in Canada.

C. Maple syrup is Canada's most famous food.

D. Canada was named the best country in the world to live in by the UN in 1996.

(2) In which city is the tallest tower in the world located?

A. Montreal   B. Tornoto   C. Vancouver   D. Edmonton

(3) Why does Montreal has a wonderful mix of Old World and New World?

A. Because it's the largest French-speaking city in the world.

B. Because Quebec was once lost to the British.

C. Because it's a port and the second largest city in Canada.

D. Because Quebec was originally colonized by France and its population is still over 70 percent French.

(4) Which of the following facts about the Edmonton mall is wrong?

A. It is in the city of Edmonton.

B. It is said to be the largest pedestrian mall in the world.

C. It has an area of more than 20 football pitches.

D. It attracts over 55,000 customers every year.

(5) Which of the following words can not replace the word *name* in the last paragraph?

A. declared   B. called   C. considered   D. titled

Keys: ABDDC

Purpose: to conclude the comprehension of this passage.

Step 4: Consolidation

Read the text for a second time and finish Part E on Page 5 to consolidate what you have learned about Canada in the text.

1 settlement	2 hunters	3 westwards	4 malls
5 freezing	6 photographer	7 recreation	

Purpose: use new words to make deep applications to the context.

Step 5: Discussion

If you are to visit Canada, which city or place do you want to visit first, why?

Purpose: apply what have been learnt to communicating with friends.

For reference:

Canada in Brief

Landscape: Mountains, Prairies, Desert, Artic Tundra, Glaciers, Valleys, Foothills, Rivers, Lakes, 9,976,000 sq km^2(3.9 million sq m^2)

Population: 30 Million

Capital city: Ottawa, Ontario (pop: 1,010,500)

People: British descent (28%), French descent (23%), Italian descent (3%), aboriginal peoples (2%), plus significant minorities of German, Ukrainian, Dutch, Greek, Polish and Chinese

Languages: English, French and 53 native languages

Religion: Catholic (45%), Protestant (36%) and minorities from most of the world's major religions

Government: Parliamentary democracy

Prime Minister: Justin Trudeau

GDP: US$774 billion

GDP per head: US$25,000

Primary sectors: services 74%, manufacturing 15%, construction 5%, agriculture 3%, other 3%

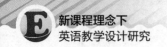
Annual growth：3%

Major products/industries：processed and unprocessed minerals，food products，wood and paper products，transportation equipment，chemicals，fish products，petroleum and natural gas

Major trading partners：USA，Japan，EU（UK，Germany，Netherlands），China and South Korea

Political Divisions：Key Attractions，Transportation，Wildlife

Assigning homework：

1. Work in pairs and share your opinions with each other.

2. Parts A1 and A2 on page 102 in Workbook.

Purpose：do exercise to use the knowledge to the application.

Teaching assessment and reflections：

Talk about the country Canada，trying to give as much information of Canada as you can. You may choose to focus on a specific subject about Canada，such as its history，its geography or cities. Prepare a presentation about the topic，based on the reading passage or any other resources you can find.

Blackboard design：

Unit 1 Other countries，other cultures

Canada—land of maple trees

Part 1 Para（1—2）Underground

Part 2 Para（3—7）Cities

Part 3 Para（8—11）Symbol

案例二十三　　新人教版高中英语必修第一册
Unit 5　languages around the world
Listening & Speaking 教学设计

【教学内容】

本节课为听说课,以"世界各地的语言"为中心话题,主要讨论了世界各国的语言尤其是英语的相关听说内容。通过本节课的学习,能够帮助学生对世界各国的语言尤其是对英语有更深层次的了解,培养学生的国际视野,激发学生对语言的兴趣。本节课就"Languages Around the World"综合训练学生的听说能力,通过音频、图片等教学手段,重点训练学生在听力中对关键信息的获取能力以及听力速记能力和准确性,并对口语中常见的省略句形式"Any advice?"进行对话练习,锻炼学生口语交际能力,排除听说障碍,为之后的读写课程做铺垫。

【教学对象】

高一的学生经过几年的英语学习,已经积积累了一定的词汇量,对基本的听力技巧也有了一定的掌握,初步形成了语感,但是,受语言环境的影响,学生的英语听说能力尤其是口语表达能力仍然不理想,学生也习惯了被动接受知识而不擅长表达。因此,着重培养学生的听说技能的训练十分重要。

【教材分析】

本教材将此单元设置为必修一的最后一个单元,可以使学生通过前几个单元的学习在语言上有所储备,通过之前听、说、读、写、看的训练使学生对语言有较为深层次的了解,能够有话可说,有感可发。本单元作为必修一的最后一个单元,让学生学习不同国家和地区的语言,能够加深学生对语言的了解,培养学生的国际视野,同时发现语言的魅力,降低学习英语的恐惧感,为今后的语言学习做铺垫,起到了承前启后的作用。

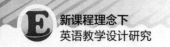

【教学目标】

1. 语言能力目标：

掌握本节课的词组：the number of ...（……的数量）、have a good knowledge of ...（精通……）等，并学会运用这些词组。

2. 学习能力目标：

① 能够对听力中的数字有较为敏感的反应，提高数字速记能力

② 能够提高在听力中关键信息的抓取能力、速记能力以及速记准确性

③ 学生能够说出英式英语和美式英语的不同之处

④ 学生能够通过同伴合作对如何学好英语进行熟练的口语表达并熟练运用询问建议的省略句句型："Any advice?"

3. 思维品质目标：

开拓学生的思维，对世界各国的文化产生创造性地认识，尊重并欣赏不同的语言思维表达。

4. 文化意识目标：

① 学生可以体会到英式英语和美式英语的区别，拓展国际视野，增加对不同国家语言文化的了解。

② 学会尊重并欣赏不同的语言文化，从而提高对语言的学习热情。

【教学重难点】

教学重点：

① 提高学生听力中关键信息的获取能力、速记能力以及速记准确性。

② 根据题型不同，使学生明确自己要听的主要内容集中精力抓住重点。

教学难点：

① 听力中涉及数字一直是学生听力的难点，要让他们对于数字比较敏感，听到之后能够快速反应并速记下来。

② 口语表达中，学生往往听得懂但表达时错误连连，要通过同伴合作进行纠错，使学生熟练运用本课句型进行建议的表达。

【教学方法】

交际法、情境教学法

【教学手段】

音频、视频、PPT、黑板

【教学步骤】

Step 1：Warming-up(7 minutes)

Listen to the following six song clips and match the country of the song to the country image. Then discuss which languages are spoken in these countries.

(Japan, America, France, South Korea, Thailand, Britain)

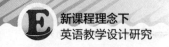

设计意图 通过歌曲、图片激发学生对语言的好奇心和热情，帮助学生开拓语言文化视野，从而导入本节课的主题。

Step 2：Listening(15 minutes)

Activity 1：(5 minutes)

Listen to a speech and tick the two languages with the most native speakers. Circle the official languages of the United Nations(UN). （教材P60）

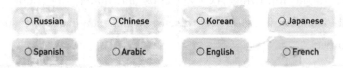

🎧 **2 Listen to a speech and tick the two languages with the most native speakers. Circle the official languages of the United Nations (UN).**

| ○ Russian | ○ Chinese | ○ Korean | ○ Japanese |
| ○ Spanish | ○ Arabic | ○ English | ○ French |

设计意图 第一次听之前要先明确问题，然后带着问题去听第一遍，找到关键词，提高学生对听力中关键信息的获取能力。

Activity 2：(10 minutes)

🎧 **3 Listen to the speech again and answer the questions.**

1 What is the main topic of this speech?

2 How many languages are there in the world?

3 How many **billion** people speak the UN's official languages as their **native** or second language?

4 What is the **attitude** of the speaker towards foreign language learning?

设计意图 第二次听主要锻炼学生对听力内容主旨内容、作者态度的把握以及对数字的快速反应和记录。

Step 3：Listening & Speaking(20 minutes)

Activity 1：Listening(5 minutes)

Fill in the blanks according to the recording.

English is a language spoken all around the world. 1. It's reported that English is used by almost a billion people in the world and 83％ of the world's emails 2. are written in English.

Now the number of people who learn English 3. <u>as a foreign language</u> is more than 750 million. Now，everywhere in the world children go to school to learn English. Most of them learn English for five or six years at school.

Lee is studying English because he wants to be a scientist and he knows that 4. <u>English is the international language</u> of science. Most scientists write in English. Wei Ling wants to work for an airline when she 5. <u>leaves school</u>. She needs to learn English because English is the international language used on airlines and all pilots speak English. Her teacher told her to go on an English course this summer 6. <u>to improve her English</u>.

I think with so many people 7. <u>communicating in English</u> every day，it will become more and more important to 8. <u>have a good knowledge of</u> English.

【重点词组】

1. the number of ... ……的数量

2. have a good knowledge of 精通……

设计意图 旨在提高学生听力中对空缺词的速记能力以及速记准确性。

Activity 2：Speaking（15 minutes）

Task 1. Watch a video clip about the differences between British English and American English，then discuss with your partner about *What have been learned about the differences between American English and British English?*（7 minutes）

For example：They are different in spelling and pronunciation.

British Betty   American Amy

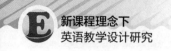
【设计意图】延伸听力中的话题进行讨论,激发学生学习英语动机;帮助学生区别英式发音和美式发音,注重语音、语调的模仿,提高发音准确性。

Task 2. With the world becoming a global village, it is a must for us to have a good knowledge of English. So discuss with your partner about "*Some suggestions on how to learn English well?*" *by using the following sentence patterns.*(8 minutes)

"Any advice?"是一个省略句,其完整形式是"Have you got any advice?"或"Do you have any advice?"。这是英语口语中的常用表达,用来询问建议。 例如:"I can never quite get the main idea. Any advice?"(我从来就没能完全搞懂过大意。有什么建议吗?)【教材附录P106 句型5】	
Student A:	I failed the final exam again. I really want to learn English well/practice my spoken English/improve my writing skills, <u>any advice</u>?
Student B:	Well, I'd like to suggest you ... Well, I think the most effective way to learn English is ...

【思考】除了"Sounds great!""How nice!""Any questions?"等表达以外,你知道口语中还有哪些省略形式的表达?

【设计意图】既能够对本节课所学内容进行巩固加深,又可以帮助学生通过同伴合作,针对本节课话题进行口语练习,掌握句型,提高口语交际能力,开拓学生的思维,增加对英语的学习兴趣。

Step 4:Sum up(2 minutes)

The teacher sums up what has been learned in this lesson, including listening skills, shorthand ability, oral expression and the use of sentence patterns.

【设计意图】总结本课时所学内容,并进行情感教育。

Step 5:Homework(1 minute)

Give an oral speaking about *my favorite country and why?*

【设计意图】帮助学会尊重并欣赏不同的语言文化,提高对语言的学习热情;练习口语,提高口语表达能力,增加学生的自信心。

【教学反思】

① 本节课运用音乐、图片等形式,学生积极性较高。

② 课程中,教师与学生互动较少。

③ 在进行同伴合作口语练习的时候,由于是同桌间的交流,学生间纠错能力有限,无法保证口语准确性。

【板书设计】

Unit 5 Languages Around the World

1. the number of ... ……的数量

2. have a good knowledge of 精通……

案例二十四　新人教版高中英语必修第一册
Unit 2　Travel Listening and Speaking 教学设计

教学理念

本节课教学设计严格贯彻《普通高中英语课程标准(2017 版)》提出的旨在发展学生的语言能力、学习能力、文化意识、思维品质的英语学科核心素养,落实立德树人的根本任务,在课堂中实践学习理解类、应用实践类和迁移创新类三种学习活动为一体的英语学习活动观,着力提高学生学用能力的基本理念。

教材分析

本单元主题为 Travel,其主要由六个部分构成:Listening and Speaking、Reading and Thinking、Discovering Useful Structures、Listening and Talking、Reading for Writing、Assessing Your Progress。在这其中,Listening and Speaking 作为本单元的开始部分。学习该部分将可以使学生了解到 Paul' and Meilin' travel plans,并学会用旅行相关短语和句型进行口语对话,谈论彼此的旅行计划。

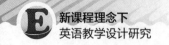
教学目标

本节课后,学生将会达到以下几方面的学习效果。在语言能力方面,学生将了解 Paul' and Meilin's travel plans,并掌握与旅行相关的词组与句型;在学习能力方面,学生将学习使用精听和泛听两种听力理解策略进行听力理解;在文化意识方面,学生将听到人们不同的旅行计划并体会到旅行计划背后的不同文化色彩;在思维品质方面,学生将学会利用所掌握的旅行相关词组和句型进行编撰对话,谈论自己的旅行计划。

教学过程

Step 1:Warming-up(3 minutes)

在课前导入环节,教师首先利用 PPT 向学生们展示相关著名景点照片(景点照片比例可按照国内 60%,国外 40%进行展示)并对学生进行提问:"What are these pictures about? What places in these pictures have you travelled to? Can you use some words to describe your trips?"等。学生对于教师的提问进行自由讨论后进行举手回答。教师在学生回答完毕后进行口头评价,之后引入本节课主题"Travelling Around"。

the Eiffel Tower,France

Lijiang,China

Neuschwanstein Castle,Germany

Tianshan,China

The West Lake，China

The Temple of Heaven，China

Seoul，Korea

Terracotta，China

Chiangmai，Thailand

May 4 square，China

设计意图 教师通过 PPT 向学生们展示相关著名景点照片,其中国内国外景点照片比例分别为 60% 和 40%。因为学生年龄偏小,且可能很多家庭经济条件尚不允许出国旅行,所以准备 6 张国内著名风景胜地照片和 4 张国外旅行经典照片,这在一定程度上不仅能够开拓学生的视野,而且还能培养学生旅行文化意识。

Step 2:Brainstorming(3 minutes)

2.1 教师将全班学生按照列的形式分成若干组别进行头脑风暴活动,通过老师的提问:"What do you need to do to prepare for a trip at home or abroad?",学生进行分组讨论之后举手抢答,答出一条得一分,在此过程中教师可以给予提示。

get a passport　　apply for a visa　　book tickets　　book a hotel room

rent a car　　buy a guidebook　　pack some clothes　　research the local weather

设计意图 通过"头脑风暴"这种活动,在一定程度上能扩大学生的词汇量,而且还能够为接下来学生理解听力材料内容扫除一些生词障碍。

Step 3: While-listening(16 minutes)

教师播放听力材料第一段并口头讲述泛听策略,即学生在听力过程中抓住文章关键词组进行理解,只需理解大意。学生听完听力材料第一段后完成如下单项选择题:

1) Circle the two places Meilin is going to for holiday.

A. Germany.　　　　B. England.　　　　C. Iceland.　　　　D. France

2) How is she going to get there?

A. By sea.　　　　B. By air.　　　　C. By train

3) How is she planning to get around after she arrives?

A. By car.　　　　B. By train　　　　C. On foot

设计意图 教师在学生开始听力之前向学生讲述泛听策略并要求学生实际运用,不仅在一定程度上更好地帮助学生理解听力材料内容,而且还使学生掌握了一种听力策略。

3.1　教师播放听力材料第二段并让学生继续使用泛听策略去理解第二段内容并根据所做笔记组织语言回答如下简答题:

1) Where is Paul's family going over the holiday?

2) Why are they going there?

回答完问题之后,教师让学生简要概括听力材料主旨内容。

设计意图 让学生进一步巩固泛听策略,在学生听完第二段听力材料内容后,教师让学生概括主旨大意,有利于学生从整体上把握听力材料。

3.2　教师播放整段听力材料并口头讲述精听策略,即学生在听力过程中试图抓住每一句话的具体意思,注意固定搭配。在此次听力过程中,教师让学生把下列横线填写完整:

Travel Preparations

Meilin

- Get her passport
- _____ for her visa
- _____ air tickets online
- _____ a car

Paul

- _____ a few light sweaters and a coat
- _____ a guidebook

〖设计意图〗让学生掌握另一种听力策略,除此之外,学生可利用头脑风暴环节中所学的词组填写表格并对其进行巩固记忆。

Step 4:Post-listening(20 minutes)

4.1 学生在听完整个听力对话并把横线填写完整后,教师让学生同伴之间试图根据信息进行对话角色扮演复述听力材料。在此过程中,教师对学生进行发音和意群上的纠正。

〖设计意图〗通过让学生进行角色扮演复述听力材料,这不仅能够加深学生对于听力材料内容的理解,而且还能够使学生记住相关旅行问答句型。

4.2 教师在PPT上展示如下图所示的两张照片,并在为学生提供图片相关信息后进行提问:

Where: Neuschwanstein Castle,Germany
Why famous: the model for the castle in Disneyland
Best time to visit:
September/October(autumn)

Where: Jiuzhaigou,China
Why famous: amazing waterfalls, colourful lakes,beautiful mountains
Best time to visit:
April/May or September/October

"If you have a chance to travel there, which place do you prefer to go? And try to make a dialogue with your partner according to the example given below". 之后让学生同桌之间上台展示。

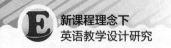

设计意图 学生自选假想旅行地点并根据书本中所给口语对话示例进行仿写和续写,最后进行对话练习。这不仅能锻炼学生的语言能力,还能够提升学生口语表达水平和培养学生合作意识。

Step 5：Summary(2 minutes)

教师在让学生进行完口语对话后对学生进行提问:"Who can summarize what we have learned today?"教师对其进行补充。

设计意图 以学生为中心,让学生总结所学内容,可以使学生更加清楚的回忆本节课所有内容。

Step 6：Homework(1 minute)

课堂小结之后,教师让每个同学自选旅行地点,并根据本节课所学内容仿照 Speaking 部分对话范例编撰两分钟口语对话,下次课进行随机展示。

设计意图 通过让学生课下仿写旅行对话,可以让学生将课堂所学充分运用到课下生活中,巩固所学知识。

Blackboard Design：

Travelling Around

1) Get ready for a trip(preparations).

2) Listening to the first paragraph、second paragraph and the whole passage.

3) Speaking practice.

案例二十五　新人教版高中英语必修第一册
Unit 4　Natural disasters Reading 教学设计

【教材简解】

本单元的话题是"自然灾害",通过一篇对唐山大地震发生前后环境变化的描写,使学生增加对自然灾害相关知识的了解。本单元的语用功能是能够从一篇新闻报道中迅速抓住关键信息,而且能够根据所给的关键信息将其延展为一篇完整的新闻报道,并能复述出大概内容。学生已经在初中和小学的英语课上学习了很多与生活、学习相关的日常知识,对于刚步入高中生活的学生而言,学会在有限的时间内从所给的材料中找到关键信息,并通过自己的记忆将事件复述出来尤为重要。编者在新版教材中将 Natural disasters 单独列为一个单元,着重训练学生从文章中获取关键信息的技能,用心良苦。

【目标预设】

1. 借助"U 校园"等学习软件,学生在课前预习后能够会听、说、读单词及短语:ruin,percent,brick,metal,shock,electricity,trap,bury,breathe,effort,wisdom,run out,thousands of 等。本课时教学完成后,学生能够会写、读、熟练运用上述单词及短语。

2. 在阅读课的学习中,学生能够逐步掌握"What happened at that time?"以及相应的回答,能够简单描述与自然灾害现象有关的现象。

3. 在教材的学习之后,学生能够在例句的示范下,根据与某次自然灾害相关的数据信息,合理组织自己的语言,将整个事件的大概叙述出来。

4. 通过教师的启发和自己的思考,学生能够树立尊重自然,保护自然的意识。

【重点、难点】

1. 在阅读课的学习中,学生能够逐步掌握"What happened at that time?"以及相应的回答,能够简单描述与自然灾害现象有关的现象。

2. 在教材的学习之后,学生能够在例句的示范下,根据与某次自然灾害相关的数据信息,合理组织自己的语言,将整个事件的大概叙述出来。

【设计理念】

学生在进行本节课的学习之前并非一点基础知识都没有,只是自己已熟练掌握的知识和即将学习的新知识需要建立起一定的纽带,通过"U 校园"之类的学习软件提前预习可以在无形中帮助学生回忆之前学过的单词、语法等基础知识,并且可以对即将学习的新内容有个大致的了解,方便教师

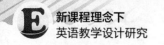

课上的教学。

课上,教师可以提供几张与"自然灾害"有关的图片,使用头脑风暴的方式引导学生进行一个小游戏。一方面,图片的形式更能直接地吸引学生的注意力,让学生快速进入上课的状态;另一方面,高中生不同于小学生,他们已经积累了一定的词汇量,看到图片提示肯定会有自己的感受理解,头脑风暴可以帮助学生从记忆中快速找到自己能想到的已经掌握了的词汇,这种方式能够迅速地建立起新旧知识的连接,有利于新课的进行。不仅锻炼了学生的口语,还能在较短的时间内通过学生争先恐后地表达自己观点的方式调动学生学习的主动性积极性,活跃课堂气氛。

【设计思路】

在课前预习阶段,要求学生利用"U校园"等学习 App 预习本单元内容;课上通过一小段汶川地震报道视频讨论 2008 年汶川地震来龙去脉引入本单元话题"自然灾害";给出几张与唐山大地震有关的图片进行头脑风暴,以这种方式帮助学生回忆起学过的与自然灾害有关的表达,然后小组讨论展示自己关于唐山大地震的信息或者报纸新闻中曾提到的异常现象;带着不确定的信息进行阅读文章的学习求证。活动难度层层递进,符合学生的认知规律,最后学生独立复述整篇文章的关键信息,并根据例句提示完成课后作业。通过整篇文章的学习,引导学生思考自然灾害和人类的关系,树立尊重自然、顺应自然、保护自然的生态观以及灾害发生后人们要团结互助的精神。

【教学过程】

Step 1:Warming-up(4 minutes)

1. Greetings

2. Free talk about Wenchuan Earthquake

T:(Show a short video of the news report) An unfortunate thing happened to our country in 2008. What do you know?

S1:Wenchuan Earthquake.

T:Do you know the exact time, Lucy?

S2：Yes，May 12th.

T：And do you know the number of casualties，Janson?

S3：Well，maybe 70,000 people died for this，and I don't know how many people were injured.

T：Yes，Wenchuan Earthquake is a very serious natural disaster，which brings destructive result to people. So today，let's learn something about natural disasters.（Write Unit 4 Natural disasters on the blackboard.）

3. Brain storm：（Show a few pictures about Tangshan Earthquake）

T：Say anything that you can get from these pictures.

S：Big earthquake，bad，dead，casualties，blood，cry …

T：Good job! Anything else? （Write down the students' answers on the left side of the blackboard，and add several new words on the right.）

Earthquake	Destroy
Bad	Disaster
Dead	Catastrophe
Casualties	Bury
Blood	Shocking
Cry	…
Ruin	

[设计意图] 展示与课文内容具有关联性的视频、图片，既能吸引学生的注意力，又能引起学生对于自然灾害相关信息的联想，同时头脑风暴的游戏能帮助学生回忆之前学过的与自然灾害有关的单词，帮助学生复习已掌握的知识，并且也能检验学生的预习效果，为下一步教学做好准备。

Step 2：Pre-reading（6 minutes）

1. Ask and answer（Work in pairs）

T：From these pictures we can see a very frightening scene which can be called a natural disaster. We all know that before a natural disaster such as a huge earthquake，there will appear a lot of unusual phenomenon. So what kind of phenomenon do you know? Let's discuss this in pairs. （3 mi-

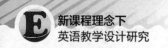
nutes) You can use the sentence pattern：What will happen before an earthquake?

......

(Show time)：

S1：Small animals' behavior will be abnormal.

T：For example?

S1：Dogs are wild, mouse run everywhere.

T：Yes, the dogs will be wild and the mice will run around, pretty good discovery! Any different answer?

S2：And the well will rise.

T：Yes! If you noticed the news report about earthquake, you will find this kind of description：the water in the village wells rose and fell ... About the details of Tangshan Earthquake, we can learn from the text on page 50.

【设计意图】同桌讨论后课上与教师沟通展示的形式有助于学生口语的练习,并且同桌之间可以角色互换问答,双方更加熟悉句型"What will happen at that time?"讨论得出的结论也与文章开头部分有关,进入课文细读时学生会更自如。

Step 3：While-reading(20 minutes)

1. Fast reading(7 minutes)

Before reading.

T：Read the text quickly and then match the main ideas with the correct paragraphs. Now, you will have 4 minutes to finish. Let's begin. (4 minutes)

......

Main idea	Paragraph
A. Destructions in the terrific earthquake.	1.
B. Efforts people made after the earthquake.	2.
C. Warning signs before the earthquake.	3.
D. The new face of Tangshan city today.	4.
E. Destroyed results after the earthquake.	5.

T：Okay，time is up. Now look at the blackboard，"A" matches which paragraph?

S（all）：2.

T：Very good！And "B"?

S（all）：4.

T：Correct！"C"?

S（all）：1.

T：Right！"D"?

S（all）：5.

T：Good！And the last one "E"?

S（all）：3.

T：Perfect！

Read and guess

T：Scan the text again and find the words below. Guess what they mean from the context.（3 minutes）

ruin	brick	trap	bury

T：Time is up，everyone！Have you gotten any idea? The first one "ruin"，what do you think the word means? What's your opinion，Lily?

S1：I think it's a dirty and destroyed place.

T：Good，so she thinks "ruin" means a kind of place which is dirty and destroyed，do you agree with her?

S（all）：Yes！

T：And in Chinese，"ruin" means "废墟". Then the next one "brick"，what's your idea? Any volunteer?

S2：I think it means a thing like a stone.

T：Nearly right. Usually we can see a lot of "bricks" among the ruins. So what exactly does it mean?

S2："砖块"?

T：Perfect! And "trap" means what? Who wants to share your opinion with us?

Silence ...

T：Well, I guess this word may be a little difficult for you to understand. "Trap" used as a verb means cover, catch, hold, capture or be in trouble. Here is a sentence, "Two people were trapped in ruins."

S (all)：埋?

T：Right, when "trap" was used as a verb, it means "捉住、使……陷于困境、埋"，which has the same meaning as "bury".

【设计意图】在快速阅读部分设置简单的段落匹配的小任务能够帮助学生更好地抓住文章每一段的大意，对文章段落有个清晰的认识，形成文本内容的整体框架，也在一定程度上锻炼了学生快速阅读抓中心思想的技能。猜单词意思的练习能够帮助学生联系上下文进行理解，增强其翻译逻辑能力，教师提问环节学生用英语回答也增加了口语表达的练习。

2. Detailed reading(11 minutes)

Read and fill.

T：Read the sentences on the screen describing what happened after a huge earthquake. Complete the sentences with the correct forms of the new words and phrases from the text.

The huge earthquake left nearly the whole city _____ .

Everyone was _____ , thinking the world must be coming to an end.

Millions of people were left without water, food, or _____ .

Soldiers and volunteers worked as hard as they could to pull away _____ and rocks, and rescue those who were _____ under the ruins.

Some were found alive, though they were suffering from terrible injuries, but others had already stopped _____ when they were discovered.

A few buildings were still standing, but people were afraid to use them as shelters, worrying they would be _____ if the buildings fell.

T：Time is up! Any volunteer wants to show your answer?

S1：First one, lie in ruins.

T：Could you read the whole sentence?

S1：The huge earthquake left nearly the whole city lie in ruins.

T：Excellent！Anyone else?

S2：Everyone was in shock，thinking the world must be coming to an end.

T：Is there anyone who disagrees with this answer?

S（all）：No.

T：OK，good answer，thank you. Next one?

S3：Millions of people were left without water，food，or money.

T：Do you have any different idea?

S（all）：electricity.

T：Actually these two words are grammatically right，however，the question asks us to get information from the content of the text，so I guess electricity is better，do you agree with me?

S3：Yes.

T：Then we will go on ...

设计意图 根据课文内容填空，锻炼学生找到重点细节的能力，还能够练习语法的正确使用，内化语言结构，同时也注重学生思维品质的培养。通过再一次阅读课文后填空能够帮助学生更加细致地了解文本，课上用英文回答也能适当锻炼学生的口语。

3. Listen and imitate（2 minutes）

Tip1：Pay attention to the pronunciation and intonation.

Tip2：Pay attention to the pauses in the long sentences.

设计意图 加强朗读的训练，注重重音、语调的模仿，并注意适当的停顿。

Step 4：Post-reading（7 minutes）

1. Question answering.（3 minutes）

T：

What does the writer mean by saying "Slowly，the city began to breathe again"?

What do you think helped in the revival of Tangshan City?

What lessons can we learn from these events? Work in groups.

……

T：OK，time is up. What's your opinion, Group 2?

S1：After our discussion, we think …

2. Retell(4 minutes)

T：Please try to retell the main idea of the text，and don't forget the important details.

S1：…

S2：…

T：Great!

设计意图 通过小组讨论的形式,进一步锻炼学生的口头表达能力,并且检测他们是否掌握了本节课的主要内容,以及是否具备较好地概括一篇新闻报道或故事的能力。

Step 5：Sum up(2 minutes)

T：What do we learn today?

S(all)：Tangshan Earthquake.

T：It's a report, right? So what do we need to express if we want to summarize a news story?

S：When and where, how many people, reason and result.

T：Also includes the influence, right?

S (all)：Yes!

T：So what do we know after studying this text?

S (all)：We should protect the nature.

T：Yes, we are supposed to respect nature, comply with nature and protect nature. And when natural disaster occurs, we should help each other and overcome it, right?

S (all)：Yes!

设计意图 总结本课所学内容,并进行情感教育。

Step 6：Homework(1 minute)

1. Finish the relative homework on "U 校园" App.

2. Form the following words into a news report with no less than 100 words.

novel coronavirus pneumonia(新冠肺炎)
virus(病毒)
wild animal
fever
cough
mask(口罩)
lockdown(一级防范)
online class

设计意图 借助"U校园"学习软件帮助检查学生作业完成情况,并将课堂所学适当延伸,根据所给单词组成一篇完整的新闻报道,一方面加强本节课语言知识的复习,另一方面培养学生的思维品质,并且训练学生会缩写也会扩写故事的能力。

板书设计:

Unit 4 Natural disasters

黑板一

Earthquake	Destroy
Bad	Disaster
Dead	Catastrophe
Casualties	Bury
Blood	Shocking
Cry	...
Ruin	

黑板二

Main idea		Paragraph
A. Destructions in the terrific earthquake.	1.	
B. Efforts people made after the earthquake.	2.	
C. Warning signs before the earthquake.	3.	
D. The new look of Tangshan city today.	4.	
E. Destroyed results after the earthquake.	5.	

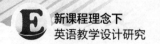
ruin	brick	trap	bury	

案例二十六　新人教版高中英语必修第一册
Unit 3　Sports and Fitness Reading and Thinking 教学设计

Ⅰ. Teaching Ideology

According to New Curriculum Standard for English (2017), English teaching focuses on students' comprehensive abilities, instead of just paying attention to language knowledge. So in this reading and thinking lesson, I will follow the students-centered principle, play the role of a planner, an organizer, an assessor, a prompter, a participant and a re-source-provider and help students study and understand this topic better.

Ⅱ. Analysis of Teaching Material and Students

This topic is from Unit 3 of Book 1, and the topic of this unit is about doing sports and keeping healthy, which is closely related to students' life, so they are familiar with and interested in it. The basic contents of this unit are the key vocabularies and phrases about athletes and sports events, and by studying, they can learn to write about health and fitness, and know more sports events and sportsmanship. What's more, they can realize the importance of doing sports and form healthy habits.

Ⅲ. Analysis of Teaching Condition

Grade: senior one　　Number: 60

Ⅳ. Teaching Objectives

By the end of this class, students will be able to:

1. Language Competence

(1) master and use the key words and phrases properly, such as "honour, captain, champion … lose heart, set a good example …".

2. Culture Awareness

(1) listen to and talk about sports events and sportsmanship.

(2) learn the knowledge about athletes at home and abroad and some sports events and games around the world.

3. Thinking Quality

(1) cultivate their logical, critical and creative abilities by reading and thinking.

(2) observe and understand the world from a cross-cultural perspective.

4. Learning Capacity

(1) improve their reading skills, such as skimming and scanning.

(2) cultivate their awareness of cooperating and communicating with others through some activities.

Ⅴ. Teaching Key and Difficult Points

1. Teaching Key Points

(1) Students can understand and master the new words, sentence patterns, the grammar, and know how to use them.

(2) Students can understand the meaning of some languages in the context of the text, such as "time seems to stand still ...".

2. Teaching Difficult Points

(1) Students can understand the legendary events of Lang Ping and Michael Jordan.

(2) Students can hear and talk about sports events and sportsmanship.

Ⅵ. Teaching Methods

The main teaching methods which will be used in this lesson include the Audio-lingual Method and the Situational teaching Approach.

Ⅶ. Teaching Aids

The teaching aids are Multimedia devices, PowerPoint document and blackboard.

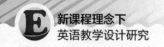
Ⅷ. Teaching Procedures

Teaching contents	Teacher's instruction	Students' activities	Design purposes
Step 1: **Pre-reading activities** Lead in and presentation (5 minutes)	1. Greeting. **2. Make predictions** Show some pictures about famous athletes at home and abroad and let students predict.	1. Welcoming. 2. Look at the pictures and think about the content before reading.	To attract students' attention and arouse their interest to learn about "living legends of sports".
Step 2: **While-reading Activities** *Learning and understanding* (20 minutes)	**1. Skimming** Let students read two stories and ask them the main idea of it. **2. Scanning** Give some questions and ask them to read in detail and answer questions. (p39, T3)	1. Read two stories quickly to get the general idea. 2. Read the text again and answer the questions.	To cultivate students' reading skills, and to gain more information about this topic.
Step 3: **Post-reading activities** *Applying and Practicing* (10 minutes)	**Discussion** 1. What reasons does the writer give for choosing Lang Ping and Michael Jordan? 2. What can we learn from successful athletes?	Work in groups and discuss the questions. Answer the questions based on the knowledge they have learned.	1. To help students master and apply what they have learned. 2. To develop students' ability of analyzing and concluding.
Transferring and Creating (8 minutes)	**Report** According to the characteristics of Lang Ping and Michael Jordan, can you choose another "living legend" and give your reasons.	Based on given information and what we have learned, write an outline and report in class.	1. To promote students' ability of transferring and creating. 2. To inspire their awareness of learning from the good features of those "living legends".
Step 4: Summary and Homework (2 minutes)	1. Summarize the features of "living legends of sports" we have learned today. 2. According to the outline of the report we wrote in class, write a complete composition.	1. Think about the sportsmanship we have learned. 2. Ask something if they have questions about homework	To help students enhance comprehension and consolidate what we have learned today.

Ⅸ. Teaching Reflection

1. The teacher should arrange different tasks for different levels of students.

2. This teaching design should be aimed at the development of thinking and the cultivation of cultural awareness.

Ⅹ. Blackboard Design

Unit 3 Sports and Fitness

"Living Legends of Sports"→Lang Ping ⟨honour captain champion
bring glory and honour

Michael Jordan ⟨strength failure graceful
lose heart graceful moves set a good example

案例二十七　人教版高中英语必修一

Unit 5　Nelson Mandela—a modern hero Reading 教学设计

Title: Elias' STORY

Teaching notion

New Curriculum Standard for English advocates quality-oriented education and all-around learning, so teachers should be the facilitator and helper of students, guiding them to read and interpret the text, deepen and transcend the text, and finally achieve the innovation of migration.

Analysis of the teaching material

This is Unit 5 Nelson Mandela—a modern hero of Book One, which mainly introduces Mandela's contribution to the equality of the black people. In the reading part, students will learn Elias' story, more exactly, the story between Elia and Mandela. The text uses time order to describe Elias' life before and after he met Mandela. Through reading, students can know the inequality of the black people and their struggle with the white, which will make students more concerned about the racial equality.

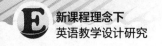
续表

Analysis of the teaching condition

Grade：Senior One   Size：44 students (22 boys and 20 girls)

Students' learning situation：

1. They all have great interest in English learning, but they need systematic training on language skills and learning strategies.
2. They are not familiar with Mandela, but they have known the unequal treatment of the black people.
3. Most of the students have a limited vocabulary, so they may meet some difficulties when expressing their opinions.

Teaching objectives

After class, students are expected to：

1. use words and phrases learned in class in their study and daily life.
2. describe Elias' story in the group.
3. write a brief news about Mandela to introduce his story.
4. realize that everyone is equal, and treat other people and races respectfully.

Teaching key and difficult points

Key points：

1. Enabling students to retell Elias' story
2. Making students understand that everyone is equal

Difficult points：

1. Guiding students to treat others respectly and equally
2. Developing students' reading ability by analyzing the text

Teaching methods

1. Task-based teaching
2. Top-down teaching
3. Situational teaching

Teaching aids

Multi-media devices、PPT document、Blackboard

Teaching procedures

Stages	Teacher's activities	Students' activities	Purpose
Lead in (3 mins)	Ask students about their heroes	Share the hero with the class	To encourage students to share in English

Stages	Teacher's activities	Students' activities	Purpose
Pre-reading (2 mins)	1. Give students a quotation of Mandela. 2. Ask students to guess the topic.	Guess the topic	To arouse students' interest in the topic and get them ready to read the text.
While-reading (20 mins)	**1. To be a clever reader** Ask students to guess the relationship between Mandela and Elias from the title **2. To be a faster reader** How did Mandela help Elias? **3. To be a careful reader** What did Mandela do to help black people?	1. Guess the relationship 2. Find the answers 3. Find Mandela's help to black people	1. To develop students' reading ability by fast reading and careful reading 2. To guide students to know Mandela's contribution to fight for the black people
Post-reading (15 mins)	**To be a critical reader** Group work: If you were a black people, what could you do to ask for equality?	1. Discuss with group members about the topic 2. Choose a representative to share the discussion	1. To develop students independent thinking 2. To improve students' cooperative spirits by group work
Summary (4 mins)	1. Ask one student to summarize the text 2. No one is ever born hitting one another, just because of the color of his skin, his background or his religion. We should respect everyone and treat them equally.	Summarize the text	1. To consolidate what students have learned today 2. To enable students to understand that everyone is equal and they should respect them and love them
Homework (1 min)		1. Finish the self-evaluation form 2. Write a composition: Introduce your hero in no less than 120 words	1. To check what students have learned today 2. To relate the topic with students' daily life and develop their writing ability

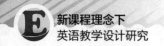

Blackboard design

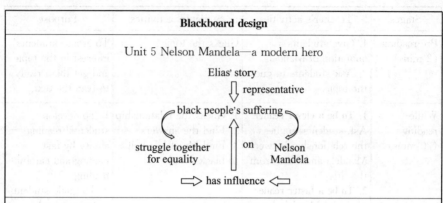

Unit 5 Nelson Mandela—a modern hero

Teaching reflection

1. Some students are too shy to express themselves in class, so the teacher should encourage them more.
2. The teacher should organize more activities based on the different levels of students to make all students be active in class.

案例二十八　人教版高中英语必修二
Unit 2　The Olympic Games Reading 教学设计

Teaching Design

Title of the text: An interview
Course type: Reading
Teaching grade: Senior Two

Teaching notion

New Curriculum Standard for English advocates quality-oriented education and all-round development, so the teacher should be students' facilitator and helper, guiding students to read and interpret the text, deepen and transcend the text, and finally achieve the innovation of migration.

Analysis of the teaching material

This is the reading part of Unit 2 The Olympic Games of Book 2. In this part, students will learn an interview between a Greek writer and a Chinese girl, and get more information about ancient Olympics and modern Olympics.

Analysis of the teaching situation

Grade: Senior Two

Size: 44 students (22 girls and 20 boys)

Learning condition:

1. Students all have the ability to read and analyze the text.

2. A third of the class are in a good command of English.

3. Students have experienced the 29th Olympic Games in 2008, so it will be easier for them to talk about the topic.

4. Most students have a limited vocabulary, so it will be a little difficult for them to express themselves freely.

Teaching objectives

After this period,

1. Linguistic competence

Students will be able to use the learnt words and expressions in their study and daily life.

2. Learning capacity

Students will be able to analyze the similarities and differences between ancient and modern Olympic Games.

3. Thinking quality

Students will be able to figure out the advantages and disadvantages on hosting Olympics.

4. Cultural awareness

Students will be able to know more Olympic events over the world.

Teaching key and difficult points

Key point

Enable students to master the similarities and differences between ancient and modern Olympic Games

Difficult points

1. Guide students to find the similarities and differences between ancient and modern Olympic Games.

2. To develop students' reading ability by fast reading and detailed reading.

Teaching aid

Multi-media、PPT document、Blackboard

Teaching method

Task-based teaching、Top-down teaching、Situational teaching

315

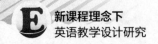
续表

Teaching procedures			
Stage	Teacher's activities	Students' activities	purpose
Pre-reading (5 mins)	1. Greet with students 2. Ask students about their experiences in the school sports meeting	1. Welcome the teacher 2. Share experiences in the class	To arouse students' interest in the topic and get them ready to read the text
While-reading (20 mins)	**1. To be a clever reader** What are the elements of an interview? **2. To be a faster reader** What does the passage mainly talk about? **3. To be a careful reader** What are the similarities and differences between ancient and modern Olympic Games?	1. Brainstorm the elements 2. Find the main idea of the text, and kick out the mentioned information 3. Pair work: find similarities and differences between ancient and modern Olympic Games	1. To develop students' reading ability by fast reading and detailed reading 2. To make students clear about the basic elements of an interview
Post-reading (15 mins)	**To be a critical reader** Group work: Why do some countries want to host the Olympic Games while others do not?	1. Discuss with group members about the topic. 2. Choose a representative to give a presentation	1. To encourage students to express their opinions freely 2. To develop students' cooperative spirits by group work
Summary (4 mins)	**Summarize the text** The ancient and modern Olympic Games have many similarities and differences.		To consolidate what students have learned today
Homework (1 min)		1. Finish the self-evaluation form 2. Write a composition to introduce one Olympic event, pay attention to the differences among different countries	1. To check out what students have learned today 2. To develop students' writing ability 3. To arouse students' cultural awareness through the introduction of an Olympic event

续表

Blackboard design		
Unit 2 The Olympic Games **An Interview**		
	Ancient Olympic Games	**Modern Olympic Games**
similarities		
differences		

Teaching reflection and evaluation
1. This teaching design proceeds from the elementary to the profound, points to the development of thinking and the cultivation of cultural awareness. 2. The teacher should arrange different tasks for different levels of students.

案例二十九　牛津译林版高一年级第四模块
Unit 3　Tomorrow's world 第一课时教学设计

1. 指导思想

《普通高中英语课程标准》(2017 版)指出课程内容与学生生活以及现代社会和科技发展的联系,关注学生的学习兴趣和经验,倡导学生主动参与,乐于探究,勤于动手,培养学生搜集和处理信息的能力,获取新知识的能力,分析和解决问题的能力以及交流与合作的能力。

2. 整体设计思路

基于《普通高中英语课程标准》(2017 版),根据高一学生的特点,结合本课 Not just watching a film 的教材内容,通过图片,视频,创设相关情景,主要设置三个活动:(1)描述一部你最喜爱的电影,(2)讨论文章相关细节回答问题,(3)通过想象,创设相关电影情境与最喜欢的人物对话,通过该活动培养学生的语言应用能力,思维品质,文化意识等核心素养,体现了以学生为中心的活动观。

3. 教材分析

本节课的教材内容来自牛津译林版高一年级第四模块第三单元的内

容,为该单元的第一课时,主要围绕"Tomorrow's world"展开话题,涉及词汇,句型和对话的学习。本节课的内容主要介绍了 RealCine 是什么,它和普通电影的不同,它如何运作的以及在其他领域的运用。文章是一篇 business presentation,介绍了一项新技术 RealCine,结构先总后分,全篇内容简单具体,有说服力,运用对比的手法突出 RealCine 的特点。这篇文章通过对 RealCine 的描述,给我们介绍了它的功能及用处,让学生感受科技发展给日常生活中带来的变化,享受科技的便利,激发学生的创新思维。

4. 学情分析

因为我校是太仓最好的高中,该班虽为普通班级,大部分学生的英语基础知识和基本技能还可以。但是,学生发音薄弱,加上部分孩子对英语学习没有太大的兴趣,因此在课堂上会出现不自信不敢张嘴的现象。其次,本课涉及很多科技词汇,对词汇量有限的学生是一挑战。

5. 教学目标分析(含重难点)

在本节课结束时:1.同学们应该会掌握相关的词汇,短语,句式。2.能够补全标题并会运用相关科技的词汇表达对 RealCine 的理解及在生活中的运用。3.通过对 RealCine 的理解及在生活中的运用,对科学产生进一步认识,激发自身的创新意识。本节课的重点为目标 1,2。本节课的难点为目标 3。

6. 教学方法

情境教学法,任务型教学法

7. 教学过程:

Step 1:Warm-up(2 mins)

T:Do you like watching films? What's your favorite film?

S:Yeah! I like watching films and my favorite film is …

T:Do you want to experience some plots like being your favorite character in that movie?

S:Yeah! Of course, I want to be …

T:The good news is that there exists a kind of technology called VR technology that can help you experience what you like in reality. Do you want it?

S：Yeah!

设计意图 引起学生注意力,激发学生兴趣,使学生快速进入课堂中来。

Step 2：Lead-in(2 mins)

T：Enjoy the movie clip please，and tell me what VR is?

S1：It's like a kind of experience ...

S2：It's a technology ...

设计意图 激起学生对文章内容的探索兴趣,为进一步阅读做准备。

Step 3：Reading(35 mins)

1. Pre-reading

T：You are excellent. Now，class，please look at the title "Not just watching a film ..." Is it a complete sentence? Give me your answer!

S：No ... I think it's not just about the film，but also about AR technology.

T：Can you give me a complete title with the help of this pattern?

Not just watching a film ... but also _____.

S：...

T：Now，let's explore more information about AR technology.

2. While-reading

Reading for information：

Structure

Questions：

T：Read para 1 and tell me the function of the para 1.

S：It serves as a "guide" to tell us how the passage is developed.

T：Which is the key sentence in para 1?

S：It's the first sentence "This presentation will give you some information about RealCine"：Why it is better than ordinary cinema，how it works，and how it can be used in other ways.

T：How many parts can this article be divided into? And what's the main idea of each para?

para	1	The introduction of RealCine
para	2	Why RealCine is better than a film
para	3	How RealCine works
para	4—7	How it can be used in other ways

Reading for details

Questions

T: Read para 2 and tell me why the RealCine is better than a film?

RealCine:	It puts you into action and connects with your senses
Film:	Passive audiences just watch and hear

Reading strategy

T: Are there any convincing examples in para 2?

S: Imagine that a VR user 'goes' sightseeing in the Himalayas. Not only will he or she feel every step of climbing Mount Qomolangma, but the user will also experience the cold, smells, sights and sounds of the surrounding environment; he or she will enjoy a feeling of happiness and a sense of achievement upon reaching the top.

T: Can you tell me what a good presentation should be like?

A business presentation should be:	clear and appealing
A good presentation usually includes:	specific information and convincing examples

Questions

T: Read the following paras and answer the questions.

1) How does RealCine work?

2) What did the teenager experience in RealCine?

3) Why do some people think that users will be disappointed by Real-Cine?

4) How could firefighters be trained with this new technology?

5) What fantastic technology does the RealCine provide for urban planning?

3. Post-reading

Reading for thinking

T：Use your imagination to try something new with the help of VR technology. It can be your favorite character in the film or the place you want to go to or the most interesting thing you want to experience.

Who/where/what	
why	

设计意图 使学生了解文章大意和文章结构,学会相关阅读策略,巩固学生阅读技能,通过活动激发学生的想象力及对 VR 技术产生兴趣,为后续采访做铺垫。

Step 4：Assignment(1 min)

Students collect the information about VR technology and then interview their classmates for more information.

设计意图 巩固所学知识,鼓励学生探索新知,同时逐渐培养学生合作学习,分析解决问题的能力。

板书设计：

Unit3 Not just watching a film

1. What is VR?
2. Not just watching a film ... but also _____.
   ◆ a feeling of happiness
   ◆ a high-tech exhibition
   ◆ a kind of wonderful experience
3. Assignment
   Students collect the information about VR technology and then interview your classmates for more information.

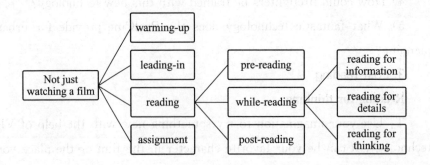

流程图：

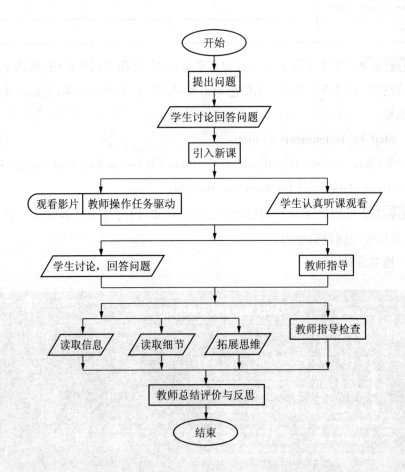

8. 教学评价及反思：

1) 评价：

Name：＿＿＿＿＿＿＿＿＿　　　　　　　　　　Date：＿＿＿＿＿＿＿

The things I can do	5	4	3	2	1
I can take part in the lesson actively.					
I can understand the structure of the reading text.					
I can understand the oral questions.					
I can answer detailed questions about the passage.					
I can talk something about VR technology.					
I can engage in the task freely with imagination.					
I am more interested in VR and want to explore more.					
Total					

2) 反思：

本节课结束后反思如下：

优点：思维品质、解决问题能力的提升——发散性思维

《普通高中英语课程标准(2017)》提出课程内容与学生生活以及现代社会和科技发展的联系，培养分析和解决问题的能力以及交流与合作的能力。英语学科的核心素养之一是思维品质。教师在进行教学设计时，需要关注提升学生的思维的逻辑性、批判性和创造性等方面表现的能力，提升学生分析和解决问题的能力。因此，目标达成方面，结合本课 Not just watching a film 的教材内容，通过图片，视频，创设相关情景，描述最喜爱的电影，通过想象，与最喜欢的人物对话等活动，培养了学生的语言应用能力，思维品质，文化意识等核心素养，体现了以学生为中心的活动观。同时也培养了在合作互助中围绕解决问题来提升学生的思维品质和解决问题的能力。

不足：在 reading for thinking 环节留给学生表达的机会不多，在讨论前应设定一些规则避免有些学生在讨论中使用汉语的情况。另外，讨论前可以通过多媒体提供学生更多的热门电影中人物、世界各地的名胜等信息。

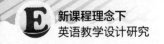

案例三十　人教版高中英语必修一
Unit 4　Earthquakes writing

一　教学设计

（一）教学目标

1. 学生会使用以下单词与词组：extreme，disaster，suffer，injure，bury，phenomenon，destroy，destructive，shock，frighten，frightening，consequence，trap，rescue，widespread，economical，advocate，electricity，circumstance，result in，in ruins，dig out，on the whole，on behalf of

2. 学生能掌握如何写好"如何应对地震灾害"的基本措施。

3. 学生认识到正确应对地震灾害的重要性。学会通过小组合作完成任务，并在课堂内敢于展示自己的学习成果。

4. 学生通过课前自学与预习，掌握有效的学习策略；通过小组合作讨论等形式，逐渐养成团结、合作的品质。

（二）教学内容

本单元以人类当今面临的地震问题为中心话题，主要讨论了地震的基本知识和在地震或突遇的灾难中如何自救、救人等。通过学习本单元，帮助学生树立"面对地震，如何自救"的自我保护意识。这节课就"An earthquake"综合训练学生的写作能力，使学生学习一些如何应对地震的基本措施。重点训练学生在学习写作导学案范例中获取写作的技巧，掌握与"An earthquake"相关的单词与词组，掌握应对地震的基本措施，并且会用英语正确表达。难点在于运用所学的知识能用英语准确表达，并且写一篇有关地震方面的短文。

（三）教学对象

高二的学生经过几年的英语学习，已经积累了一定的词汇量，对基本的语法也有了一定的掌握，初步形成了语感。但是，受山区学校条件的限制，课上的英语学习气氛不理想，学生也习惯了被动接受知识，用英语进行思考的能力较弱。但是,学生学习还是比较努力,有很强的好奇心与求知欲,对"An earthquake"这个话题也有一定的了解,因此,通过培养学生的听说读写技能的训练,从而提高其综合运用英语的能力,是十分必要的。

(四) 教学与学习方法

教学方法:任务型教学法

学生学习方法:自主学习,分组讨论,小组竞赛,突出以小组活动为主体的合作性学习。

(五) 教学流程

Steps	Teacher's activities	Students' activities	Aims
Step 1: Leading-in	Show a picture about earthquake	Look at the picture carefully and try to talk about it.	Arouse the students' interest and lead to today's topic.
Step 2: Correcting the mistakes	Show the students' mistakes of their self-learning paper guide.	Correct the mistakes.	Practise the students' writing skills and the ability to correct the mistakes.
Step 3: practice	Ask the students to write some right sentences, learning from the examples.	Write the right sentences and learn from the others' works.	Know better about the skills of writing sentences.
Step 4: Recitation	Ask students to recite some right sentences (attributive clause and appositive clause) in the self-learning paper guide.	Recite the sentences to consolidate their knowledge.	Help students write right attribute clause and appositive clause.
Step 5: Before-writing	Show the writing material and ask the students to divide it into five sentences.	Learn the structure and conjunctive words and phrases in the self-learning paper guide.	Learn how to organize the writing better before writing it.
Step 6: Writing	Ask the students to write a short passage about the earthquake in several minutes.	Finish the writing in the given time.	Practice the writing skills.

续表

Steps	Teacher's activities	Students' activities	Aims
Step 7: Presenting	Ask one of the group reporters to present the writing of their group on the screen.	Present the writing on the screen and show it to the other classmates.	Share the learning results with others. Practice their speaking skills.
Step 8: Discussing	Ask the students to discuss in groups and write down their opinions about what to do about earthquake.	Discuss in groups and write some opinions on what to do about the earthquake of the group members.	Know better about how to work in groups and learn from others.
Step 9: Conclusion	Enable the students to draw a conclusion of today's class and activities in the class.	Draw a conclusion of today's class and activities in the class.	Self-estimation
Step 10: Homework	Ask the students to hand in their writing works.	Finish the homework after class and hand it in.	Consolidate what have been learned in the class.

板书设计

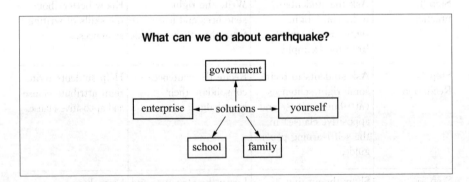

(六) 教学评价

1. 其他听课教师评价：

本节课能基本达到预定的教学目标，教学效果较好。课堂内学生思维活跃，信息交流畅通；学生会学，学习主动，课堂气氛好。学生应答面广、质量高。信息量适度，学生负担合理，学生的可持续发展得到了很好的衍生。

2. 学生学习行为评价：

Assessment criteria	Yes	No
Are you active in the class?		
Do you learn the sentence patterns by heart?		
Can you use the sentence patterns fluently?		
Do you organize your writing well?		

二 教学反思

1. 较为成功的地方：本节课教学步骤环环相扣，学习过程步步为营。学生一直处于一种积极向上的学习状态，在小组活动中能够聆听、讨论、分享，师生、生生充分互动。学生在讨论时产生了很好的学习资源，这些都是学生的学习成果。

2. 有待改善的地方：教学内容相对多了点，时间安排可以再松动一些。如在导学案中学生已经对范例学习有了较深的印象，可以适当地减少给予学生的朗诵时间，而直接进入有针对性的写作训练。这样可以有更多时间放在写作输出部分和展示学生的习作环节，也更直观地看到学生的学习效果。

三 教学再设计

1. 设置的练习比较有梯度，很好地体现层次教学，但是设计的内容相对较多。如果根据学生的不同层次设计出的练习相对精简，会使本案例的设计理念更趋完美。

2. 因为呈现了一些固定句型，这个步骤使得学生在表达自己观点和思想时有所限制，不利于成绩较好的同学的发展。时间上把握不是很好，可以在学生朗诵部分节省一些时间，为后面的 Post-writing 部分留下充足的时间，让学生进行一个语言输出的过程，展示学生的习作，以便更好地检测学生的学习成果。

图书在版编目(CIP)数据

新课程理念下英语教学设计研究/徐修安著.—上
海:上海三联书店,2021.4
ISBN 978 - 7 - 5426 - 7229 - 2

Ⅰ.①新…　Ⅱ.①徐…　Ⅲ.①英语课-教学设计-中
学　Ⅳ.①G633.412

中国版本图书馆 CIP 数据核字(2020)第 195578 号

新课程理念下英语教学设计研究

著　　者 / 徐修安

责任编辑 / 殷亚平
装帧设计 / 一本好书
监　　制 / 姚　军
责任校对 / 张大伟　王凌霄

出版发行 / 上海三联书店

　　　　(200030)中国上海市漕溪北路 331 号 A 座 6 楼
邮购电话 / 021 - 22895540
印　　刷 / 上海惠敦印务科技有限公司

版　　次 / 2021 年 4 月第 1 版
印　　次 / 2021 年 4 月第 1 次印刷
开　　本 / 640×960　1/16
字　　数 / 300 千字
印　　张 / 21.25
书　　号 / ISBN 978 - 7 - 5426 - 7229 - 2/G·1579
定　　价 / 88.00 元

敬启读者,如发现本书有印装质量问题,请与印刷厂联系 021 - 63779028